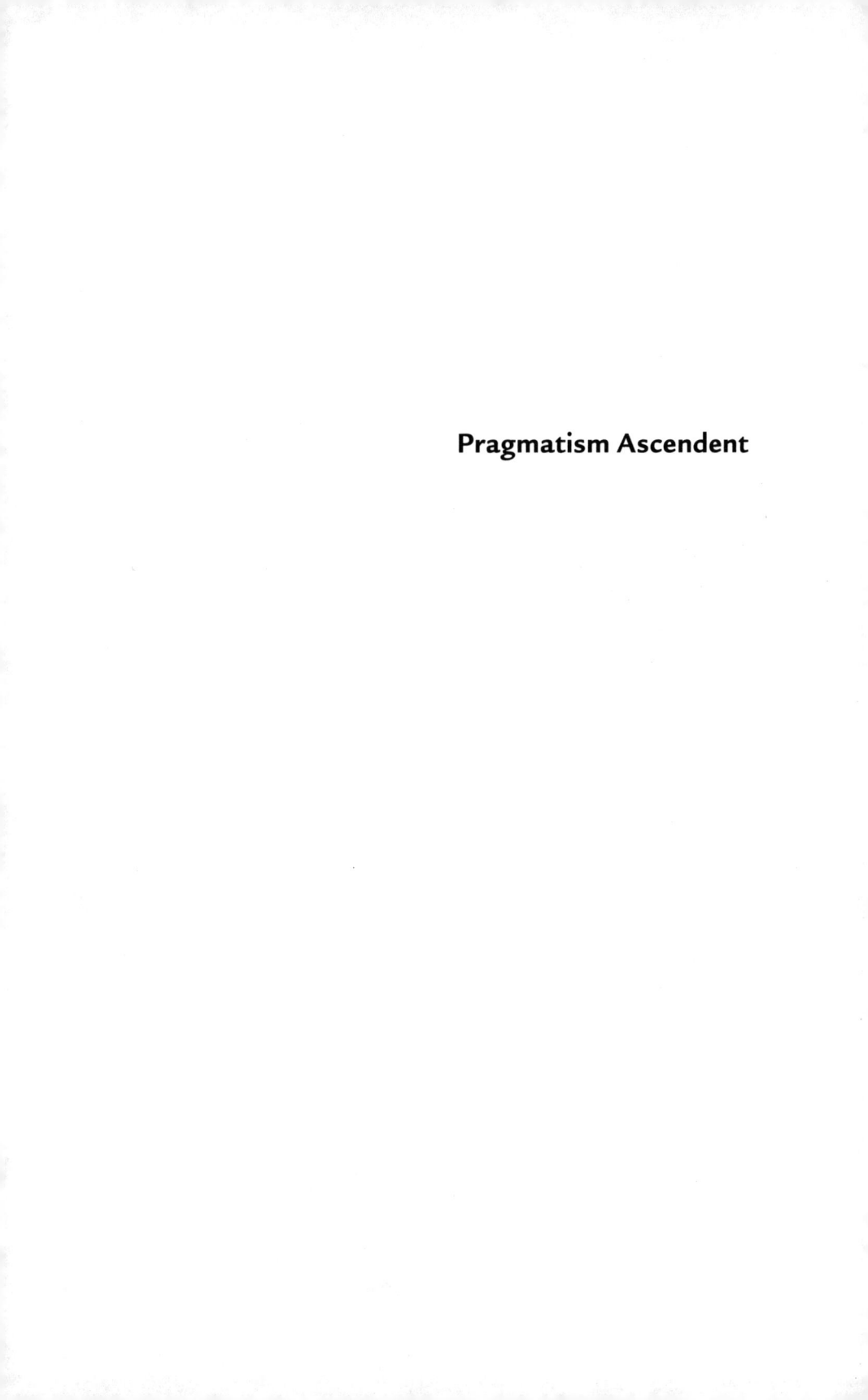

Pragmatism Ascendent

Pragmatism Ascendent
A Yard of Narrative, A Touch of Prophecy

Joseph Margolis

Stanford University Press

Stanford, California

LIBRARY OF
CONGRESS
WITHDRAWN
ADDITIONAL
SERVICE COPY

Stanford University Press
Stanford, California

© 2012 by the Board of Trustees of the Leland Stanford Junior University.
All rights reserved.

No part of this book may be reproduced or transmitted in any form or by any means, electronic or mechanical, including photocopying and recording, or in any information storage or retrieval system without the prior written permission of Stanford University Press.

Printed in the United States of America on acid-free, archival-quality paper

Library of Congress Cataloging-in-Publication Data

Margolis, Joseph, 1924– author.
  Pragmatism ascendent : a yard of narrative, a touch of prophecy / Joseph Margolis.
      pages cm
  Includes bibliographical references and index.
  ISBN 978-0-8047-8227-2 (cloth : alk. paper) — ISBN 978-0-8047-8228-9 (pbk. : alk. paper)
  1. Pragmatism—History. 2. Philosophy, American. 3. Philosophy, European. 4. Analysis (Philosophy) 5. Continental philosophy. I. Title.
  B832.M196 2013
  144'.3—dc23
                                2012014038

Typeset by Bruce Lundquist in 11/15.5 Adobe Garamond

the global is never the universal

Contents

Preface ix

Prologue 1

1 The Point of Hegel's Dissatisfaction with Kant 7

2 Rethinking Peirce's Fallibilism 51

3 Pragmatism's Future: A Touch of Prophecy 111

Notes 157
Index 183

Preface

ONE MUST BE CAREFUL what one says in print, but not so careful as to withdraw from convictions that have needed a lifetime to take form. I'm persuaded, for instance, that ours is a time for changing cosmologies, political systems, religious allegiances, the touchstones of art and sensibility, and perhaps, at a level of lesser presumption, the orientation of the philosophical canon, if there is a canon to confront. A risky time. My own competence, such as it is, is pretty well confined to speaking about this last matter. It's already a commonplace to say that our world is a global world: take care! We must remember that we surely knew the change was nigh for some time, though we've largely ignored the call to think carefully about what that might require of us. The disorders of our very young millennium have already shown us the unwisdom of our insouciance. We find ourselves bewildered by the seeming, sudden inadequacies of our form of life. I'll mention only two bits of evidence: one, a public secret; the other, a truth confirmed by the vehemence of its denial. Thus: the great monotheisms stand before us plainly exhausted, their creative powers spent now almost entirely in the noisy (often violent, even murderous) service of reversing their greatest teachings. In the same spirit, our largest conceptions of war and peace have hardly any relevance any longer for the least conflicts of our every day. Perhaps it was always so, though I more than doubt it. These disorders are much too deep to be merely local.

I won't spell out the relatively minor analogy that may be drawn from a review of contemporary philosophy. I've made the argument elsewhere, and I'm bent on building on it here. Quite simply, I'm committed to laying a proper ground for a very unlikely, very unfashionable surge of speculative enthusiasm restored, however lightly, to philosophy's most essential reflexive question: the analysis of what it is to be a human self. I hope to avoid anything that might risk trading rigor for short-lived advantage. Nevertheless, an answer suited to our time cannot but recover something of philosophy's embeddedness among the fundamental occupations of the race—indeed, something of its genuine grandeur. We have no other inquiry but whatever is informed by our understanding of what it is to live as a human being. I confess I take that seriously: seriously enough to believe we are at a crossroads now, at which the question might well support a radical reorientation. Not an altogether unfamiliar conceptual start, of course. That would be unlikely. But a new perspective and a new formulation nevertheless, something capable of yielding a new sense of the unity of all our purposes within the limits of natural life within the limits of the natural world. A philosophically responsible offering, that is: hence, one modest enough regarding the practical or executive redirection of our lives. As you'll see soon enough, it will have taken me an entire book's worth to voice no more than the first sentences of a turn in thought brave enough to close the lid on undertakings begun a good many years ago and to open others that have already escaped the controls of the first.

Philosophy has no point (for me) if it has no convictions about the right orientation of human life; but it has no resources of its own by which to validate any such change directly—except by subtraction. So it plays its part under extraordinary constraints.

Notoriously, in our time, this has been taken to signify that philosophy, as standardly practiced, has already come to an end. In fact, this last doctrine may be the single most arresting thesis to have surfaced in American philosophy in the past thirty-plus years. No doubt there's a paradox there that must be met. But the doctrine itself I regard as the spoiled, self-congratulatory expression of considerable but barely earned material comfort, the persuasion of whiggish minds turned against the perpetually incipient chaos of the world. Philosophy ought to provide an indictment of such cold comfort; but if it should, then it has forgotten to reclaim its proper function. That cannot now be recovered in any cognitivist way. But it can, I'm persuaded, be reclaimed, contingently, diversely, historically, responsibly, perspicuously—in medium-sized practical terms. The challenge remains the same in every large movement of Western philosophy. Which,

I would like to believe, invites and supports risks of the sort I find myself happily entangled in.

I must thank Doug Anderson, who permitted Stanford University Press to disclose his having authored a very careful and helpful reading of the original manuscript: no question that it has benefited from his remarks. Also, a word of thanks to Phillip Honenberger, who kept an eye out for infelicities of style and substance as he put the manuscript in final order and who shared his very perceptive research regarding the interface between philosophy and biology, with special emphasis on the work of the near-contemporary German "philosophical anthropologists."

J. M.
Philadelphia, 2011

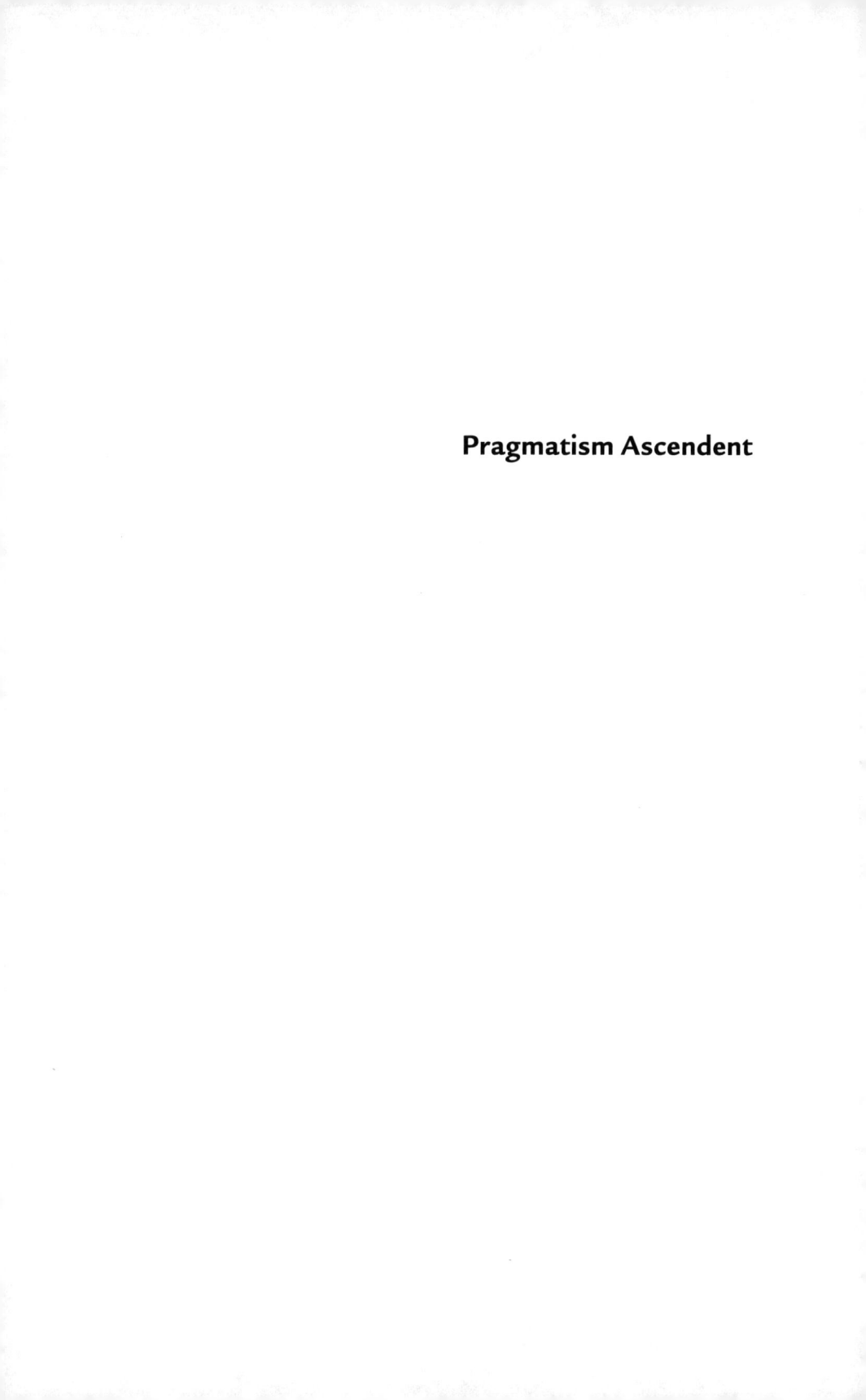

Pragmatism Ascendent

Prologue

THIS IS THE FOURTH of a trio of books I planned as an overview of pragmatism and American philosophy in the second half of the twentieth century. It sounds a little odd to say, but it's true enough. Its topics became too insistent in the process of writing the earlier trio to be turned away now. This book violates my original constraints in two agreeable ways: for one, it reaches back to the middle of the eighteenth and the beginning of the nineteenth centuries, to the entirely new speculative direction afforded by Immanuel Kant and Georg Wilhelm Friedrich Hegel, in order to provide a sense of how pragmatism took form as an unusual variant of the radical turn in European philosophy due to Kant's and Hegel's innovations; and, for the other, it ventures to guess at the future of pragmatism and the whole of Eurocentric philosophy—by which I mean "modern" modern philosophy focused by Kant and Hegel on what we now understand to be acceptable transforms of transcendental questions and the demands of historicity. That is to say: it guesses, now, at the best of philosophy's future from the vantage of a correct guess at philosophy's future at the turn into the nineteenth century. If we add an appreciation of the influence of Charles Darwin's discoveries as well, which first appear in 1859, the year of John Dewey's birth, we have in hand the largest sources of the scatter and continuity of the entire trajectory of American philosophy from a period beginning shortly after the American Civil War and coursing down to the present—legible enough to venture a prophecy for the whole of Western philosophy. The sheer prospect of such a vision proved too much of a temptation to resist. The result is the book before you now.

The extraordinary thing is this: the same themes that were influential but distinctly scanted in the earliest phase of pragmatism have surfaced once again, in some respects rather little altered, from the 1970s and 1980s to the end of the first decade of our new century. These themes, largely led by the strong presence of W. V. Quine's careful selection of the still-viable undertakings of somewhat more than the previous half-century's collection of analytic philosophy's most daring initiatives, became increasingly distant (nearly invisible) with the sudden rise to prominence of the American wing of analytic philosophy in the 1950s.

About 150 years have passed since Charles Peirce published his first papers in 1868, toward the end of his twenties. Some readers find the abiding thread of the spectacular, still rather little-known huge heap of papers already shaped in those first few pieces. Peirce, who entered into the debates of post-Kantian Europe in a commanding way that we are still not entirely able to assess correctly, was surely the first of the new voices of American philosophy to have survived in force down to our own day. But the need for some such account has grown more insistent with pragmatism's quite sudden, unanticipated revival toward the end of the twentieth century, against the scattered failure of analytic and so-called continental philosophies to match its challenge. Western philosophy has been in disarray, I believe, since at least World War II and its aftermath, despite its admittedly brilliant figures, nearly all of whom seem to have been infected with an essentially nostalgic weakness for the most privileged enthusiasms of the first half of the twentieth century, which they knew in their hearts could never be successfully revived, though they nonetheless were willing to commit themselves to living out the reprise of one or another important first failure—or to spending their best energies in exposing the practice in others. The first tendency is perfectly illustrated by the hegemony of analytic scientism in America following the collapse of the strong programs of the logical positivists and the unity of science movement; the second is perhaps best illustrated by the enormous industry of what has come to be known as French poststructuralism.

My thought is that pragmatism recovered its standing, almost unscathed, by way of its relatively inexplicit adherence to what in the leanest way it was able to respect and preserve from its Kantian/Hegelian influences—in its explicit adherence to the flux of experience, to various forms of naturalism without foundations or privilege, to its Darwinian lessons, to its sense of the primacy of practical and societal life, to historicity (however inchoate or weakly developed), and to its political application. It's been given a free pass for a second (or a third) beginning.

I think the whole of Western philosophy, spent by the false (recycled, diminished) starts of the late twentieth century, is curious to learn what pragmatism will make of its unearned invitation to begin once again. But now, pragmatism is no longer a merely American territory. Its revival is manifest almost everywhere in Europe: in Poland and Slovakia as much as in Italy and Spain—and in Germany and France and Britain, and (I might add) in Brazil and China. It's on its way to becoming something of a philosophical lingua franca, a modest shadow cast perhaps by the spread of the English language itself—and, also, by the empiricism and liberalism embedded in its Kantian/Hegelian sources. But it will have to earn its reprieve if it is to survive a closer, more global scrutiny.

It's become naggingly clear to me that all of my previous efforts to understand the new impulses of what still remains inchoate in pragmatism risk a serious charge of mere idiosyncrasy, philosophical dabbling, inert nostalgia if I (or others pursuing similar intuitions) fail to provide a suitable "genealogy" of (our) present (pragmatist) efforts. This is because nearly everyone puzzled and impressed by the recent turn in pragmatism's fortunes finds himself or herself all but speechless with wonder. Yet, there's a danger in such inaction, of course: it looks too much like the continuation of the near-fatal, self-deceptive complacency of American pragmatism in the first decades following the end of World War II. I'm persuaded that there's a genuinely worthwhile answer to be given: we must overcome our own disarray.

The book you hold is an abbreviated stab at that answer—perhaps, then, a preamble to the answer: a prophecy, as I say. In the sense in which it's a genealogy, I mean it to venture beyond anything like Michel Foucault's well-known specimen genealogies, in the direction of actual legitimation—hence (if I understand Foucault and Friedrich Nietzsche rightly), not beyond Nietzsche's original sense of the notion, however now more prosaically cast. In that sense, genealogy begins to assimilate the function of Hegel's historied critique of Kant's own transcendental turn.

I don't expect that these last remarks will be entirely clear until you agree to read the first chapter of what follows. But if the opening chapter is credible at all, you will begin to see that I believe that philosophical genealogy and prophecy go hand in hand as a replacement for or attenuation of the transcendental turn, which, I take it, rightly introduces what I've come to call "modern" modern, or Eurocentric, philosophy—which, of course, begins with Kant and Hegel.

Genealogy, in Foucault's hands, is largely used to confirm the sheer diversity of the relatively disjunctive forms of life of different parts of the Western tradition that follow one another in historical time. For Foucault, they are no more than brute presence: they do not wait on legitimation. Foucault waves his hand at the "transcendental" unity that lies behind this scatter, but he makes no effort to recover the meaning of the human presence that informs the diversity he collects. To my mind, this is the inverse of the weakness one finds in the ingenuities of figures such as Edmund Husserl, Martin Heidegger, and Hans-Georg Gadamer, in spite of their seeming efforts to ensure the reassuring presence of the universal human within the threat of radical historicity, which, in its own ambiguous way, rightly challenges the problematic unities of the analytic scientisms of the same period (prepared to risk the disappearance of the human altogether in their efforts to secure an impossible form of objectivity). I say "ambiguous" because the "continentals" inevitably hold on to a more robust sense of the a priori or transcendental than they are prepared to admit (which they apply to the human self), whereas the "analysts" have never relinquished their own adherence to the most attenuated versions of the Kantian search for universality (naturalized to disallow the sui generis distinction of the human, attenuated distinctly enough to make the transcendental seem no longer relevant).

It's there that I find the new promise of pragmatism and the other principal movements of Western philosophy, which now seem to me capable of a worthwhile rapprochement; and it's there that genealogy/prophecy affords a historied legitimation of what, formerly, might have been characterized as a transcendental argument. I have no a priori argument of my own. What I offer instead, I daresay, is a descendent strategy argumentatively (or genealogically) derived from the transcendental turn turned pragmatist by refusing to concede any strong disjunction between broadly "empirical" first-order inquiries and broadly "rational" second-order speculations about the legitimacy of both the first *and* the second. Philosophy has and requires no uniquely distinctive domain to plunder. But it needs the "genealogies" it constructs ad hoc, which I take to be akin to Nietzsche's contribution. That's in part due to the companion truth that the sciences themselves can no longer be thought to function as sciences in their own right if they are not also thoroughly engaged in what, in a simpler world, was once thought to be a separate discipline (philosophy). You have only to think of relativity and quantum physics to realize that there cannot be a disjunctive difference between science and philosophy—not merely epistemology and metaphysics (in the old sense) but, as Peirce, Dewey, William James, and George Herbert Mead were perfectly aware, moral theory (in the same old sense) as well. The intelligibility of the world and of our role in it is an indissolubly single target.

That is Kant's theme, of course, and the theme Hegel gladly accepts in his critique of Kant, the theme analytic scientism rejects in the same breath in which it endorses, in deliberately impoverished terms, the entire sweep of human understanding. By contrast, the pragmatist variant of our own future-present, which seems to me to catch up in the most perspicuous and promising way the strongest directives of the Eurocentric trajectory, converges (in my opinion) on the sense of a motto and manifesto that I take from one of Peirce's book reviews published in the *Nation* at the end of the nineteenth century: "Darwinizing Hegel and Hegelianizing Darwin."

We can't be sure what Peirce intended by that banner: it was an early pronouncement. But now, more than one hundred years later, there can be no doubt that it returns us to the theory of the human self or person, which, in the eighteenth century, neither David Hume nor Kant was able, finally, to define in any philosophically acceptable way. I believe their failure threatens in the most mortal sense the adequacy of their own best work: in precisely the same sense in which Plato's elenctic Dialogues and Aristotle's tracts fail (however gloriously) to bridge their age and ours. I mean, the sense in which the analysis of biology and culture must be seen to be very differently conceived but inseparably joined, following the eighteenth-century discoveries of figures such as Giambattista Vico and Johann Gottfried von Herder and Wilhelm von Humboldt and the sequel that takes form in Hegel and the post-Hegelian (Eurocentric) world, *and* the decisive new lessons drawn from Darwin and post-Darwinian biology and paleoanthropology: namely, that the appearance of *Homo sapiens sapiens* is datable among the hominid species, as are also the appearance of true language and the transformation of hominid primates into selves, by essentially cultural means.

I collect these themes in the name of a future pragmatism no longer parochially bound to its American provenance but unwilling to deny its genealogical engine, committed to the naturalism of the motto (and manifesto) just mentioned and, if I may now add, committed to the radical thesis that the self is a hybrid artifact of biological and cultural evolution that makes possible the entire run of the uniquely enlanguaged forms of human intelligence, thought, understanding, reason, feeling, experience, activity, conduct, creation, and knowledge that marks our race for what it is. There's the prophecy in a single line—but not the inquiries that it makes possible. I promise those as well, to the best of my ability. But they will require a fresh beginning.

Frankly, I see no incipient theme in Eurocentric or global thought that is philosophically more compelling or comprehensive. I bring the enabling narrative to the edge of its prophecy, and I bring the prophecy itself to its ready resources. That is to say, the argument that follows is the end of a long reflection. What ought to follow *that* is something entirely different.

1

The Point of Hegel's Dissatisfaction with Kant

HERE, WITHOUT PREAMBLE, is a version of the central paradox of modern philosophy—in effect, the paradox of the whole of Western philosophy, ancient as well as modern: to know the world, to have knowledge of "what there is," implicates at some level of understanding "knowing" what it is to "know," knowing what knowledge is; so that, justified in the way we view the second distinction, we rightly take ourselves to be able to justify our claims with regard to the first. And yet, we cannot say that we ever achieve a greater precision moving from our first-order intuitions to a critical analysis of our second-order concepts: the grammatical difference (so to say) in the levels of discourse seemingly invoked here obscures the slack identity of the cognitive sources accessed at the two levels.

Even in these first sentences, the term "level(s)" is already fatally equivocal: we cannot assign (in any discernibly principled way) the putatively superior cognitive power accessed at the metalogical level to exclude any matched first-order discourse involving truth-claims about the actual world. There is no second-order science of science (or of knowledge) that can claim a higher source of objectivity, though there are indeed second-order questions and second-order answers. (If we required such a hierarchy, we'd be caught in an infinite regress.) There you have the pons of transcendentalism and rationalism alike.

I take the dictum to be common ground between Hegel and the pragmatists, the touchstone of resistance to the deepest convictions of "Cartesian" thinking contested by both—not only in René Descartes but, perhaps more fundamentally, in Kant as well. Furthermore—and this is especially compelling "transcendentally" or in accord with whatever strategy might replace Kant's way of explaining the "possibility" of human knowledge—that finding is *not* a necessary or universal truth; it's hardly more than a faute de mieux concession that may, so far as we have managed to secure the second-order query as an option, suggest an alternative way of answering Kant's original question—that is, relative to our supposed knowledge and ignorance. Otherwise, we should never be able to escape Kant's transcendental*ism*, which, by determining (as it claims to do) the conditions of "possibility" of our understanding the world constrained within the space of our own experience, does indeed also claim to yield universally necessary conditions (though always and only from the vantage of the inquiring subject), which then constrain the "rational possibility" of reality or the entire cognizable world being intelligible at all. I take this to be the deepest puzzle of Kant's "Copernican" revolution (see, for instance, Kant's *Critique of Pure Reason*, Bxvi).

Here, now, a decisive paradox struggles toward clarity. The new option arises because Kant is committed to his transcendentalism even where he views the transcendental question as qualified (however it may be) by the inherent limitations of the human form of reason![1] Hegel, of course, rejects Kant's transcendentalism: hence, he calls into mortal question Kant's right to draw from his "Critical" inquiry any of the resources of "canonical" (rationalist) accounts of reason thought to yield genuinely universal or necessary enabling powers of, or limitations on, cognition *sans phrase*. There's a *reductio* there—or an insuperable mystery. The viability of the transcendent*al* question (apart from the fortunes of transcendental*ism*) makes no sense unless we also concede that the viability of empirical realism cannot be separated from "idealism" (the "Idealism" already implicated in the transcendental question itself): *that* consideration already signals the importance of deciding whether the human version of "reason" reflexively affects what we affirm to be possible regarding "what there is" in the whole of reality independent of human cognition. (There's a puzzle there that I must come back to regarding the relationship between realism and Idealism. Let me say for the moment that I take "realism" and "Idealism" to be inseparable within any "constructivist" form of realism—it being the case that there is no other viable form of realism. I take that to be both Hegel's and Peirce's view.)

Wherever knowledge is tethered to perception and experience—"presuppositionlessly," without privilege (as Hegel supposes, in the *Phenom-*

enology)—strict universality and necessity are either false objectives in the human world, impossible to confirm, or no more than presumptive targets that will have to change with evolving experience. The essential paradox (in Kant), then, is this: that although Kant abandons canonical rationalism's epistemological and metaphysical presumptions (restricting his own reflexive analysis to what is "possible" for humankind alone), he manages to recover the universalism of the rationalists "by other means," by reclaiming it (illicitly) in the work of human reason itself. There you have one way of formulating the essential premise that Kant's transcendentalism cannot possibly supply, that Johann Gottlieb Fichte and Hegel (and, in effect, Peirce and Ernst Cassirer) confirm from entirely different vantages.

Let me intrude here, without preamble as I say, a devilishly clever challenge addressed by Stephen Houlgate to Robert Pippin's Kantian-inclined reading of Hegel's "logic," that is, regarding the analysis of the intertwined first- and second-order questions (already broached) that fixes the inseparability of epistemological and metaphysical questions post-Kant (and post-Hegel), which, nevertheless, Houlgate manages to treat as separable. Houlgate charges that "in Pippin's view, [Hegel's logic] sets out 'all that "being" could *intelligibly* be,' but it does not set out 'all that "being" could intelligibly *be*.'"[2] Houlgate is right, of course; but that's because the would-be separable (second) question is entirely idle, impossible to distinguish (pragmatically) from the first.

Put in the most unguarded way, the best reading of Hegel's undertaking (perhaps not always textually perspicuous or interpretively reliable) commits us to the following constraints: (1) that Hegel adheres to a Kantian vision of a "critical metaphysics" (qualified by our theory of specifically human powers and limitations) rather than a "canonical" (rationalist) metaphysics such as Kant himself rejects; (2) that Hegel unconditionally abandons transcendentalism (all a priori assurances of necessity and universality); (3) that, in confining inquiry within the bounds of experience, the distinction between the analysis of intelligible being and being tout court proves to be completely empty (as both Hegel and the pragmatists would insist); and (4) that, under the constraints of evolving and historied experience, claims of necessity and universality are, wherever pressed, never more than faute de mieux contingencies. In short, Kant's defeat lies *not* with the demonstration that his claim is false—which would require (at least in arguing to a stalemate) a cognitive power equal to the one Kant himself affirms a priori—but, rather, with an argument weaker in cognitive presumption, yet adequate to the task, to the effect that neither Kant nor we know of any argument by which to confirm the transcendentalist power Kant claims. Indeed, we are not even clear that we possess a reliable criterion by the use of which we can distinguish, in Kant's sense, between transcendental and nontranscendental claims. (There's a difficulty there more serious than that of mere error—regarding Euclid or Isaac Newton, say.)

Perhaps, then, I may as well add: if Hegel exceeds these constraints, so much the worse for him; also, nothing on this score is likely to restore any form of Kantian transcendentalism—which always defeats itself, in the sense just noted. (I admire Hegel's daring, but his concessions in the *Phenomenology* already make it impossible to validate any recovery of Kantian apriorism by historied means.)

Thinking ahead to the use I mean to make of this penny survey of Hegel's continuation of the Kantian project, I daresay that Peirce's fallibilism, the continuum of finite and infinite inquiry, and the inseparability of realism and Idealism (in the spirit of acknowledging the transcendental question) define the sense in which pragmatism—initially Peirce's, but read conformably, Dewey's simpler account as well—cannot fail to be construed as an ingenious and especially promising spare variant of Hegel's own undertaking, now naturalized, shorn of Hegel's extravagances, and qualified by Darwinian and post-Darwinian considerations. Construed this way, contemporary philosophy has never (in my opinion) bettered the promise of the pragmatist retelling of the Hegelian correction of Kant's grand innovation. (This is not, of course, to ignore *Peirce's* extravagances!)

If, as Kant implies in the second preface to the *Critique of Pure Reason*, we cannot do better than offer the work of our strongest and most reliable sciences (shorn of apriorist assurances) as the least quarrelsome specimens of what to count as knowledge, we cannot draw then on any such contingent posit for (any) necessary or necessarily adequate conditions of what it is to "know": proceeding thus, we would make any would-be a priori presumption about what knowledge "is," fatally hostage, incurably subject a posteriori, to the contingencies of evolving experience.[3]

Knowledge appears, then, to be a contingent construction fitted as plausibly as possible to our would-be sciences and ordinary practice. There is no ready sense in which what knowledge is is a matter of empirical or transcendental discovery. I take this to be the most strategic—though perhaps not the most important—Hegelian theme that, retrospectively applied, could possibly effect the most congenial "correction" of, say, the whole of twentieth-century and the new century's analytic philosophies, both Anglo-American and continental European, in the spirit (finally) of abandoning all the vestigial sources of foundational and privileged conceptions of knowledge that the joined (hardly, joint) work of Kant and Hegel unquestionably demands.

Hegel saw in this the insuperable weakness of Kant's analysis of knowledge: he saw unblinkingly that whatever features of our actual sciences might seem to require synthetic a priori truths, in order to secure the bare conceptual "possibility" of their particular cognitive success, might also (for all we know) be no more than an "accident" of the contingencies of clever thought wrongly taken to be the enabling posit of the necessary and essential conditions we require! The Kantian program fails, Hegel supposed, at least because it cannot demonstrate in a principled way the difference between genuinely synthetic a priori truths in the body of confirmed science and opportunistic, even arbitrary or mistaken, empirical conjectures that a later advance in the sciences might easily eliminate.[4]

Accordingly, "knowledge" appears to be an unavoidably contingent and informal construction fitted as well as possible to the evolving work of the sciences themselves. But if that is true, then Kant's entire undertaking could never escape a decisive *reductio*—nor could Descartes's or Gottfried Leibniz's or our own (if we elect to follow these or similarly exhausted exemplars)—without yet denying or disallowing the immense importance and fruitfulness of Kant's original invention. It's just that, beginning in Kant's way, there can't be a science of knowledge tout court, and Kant can't have discovered the a priori conditions of any such science.

Hegel embraces this deep contingency, the sheer historicity of the search—and so must we. It's the constant theme of the *Phenomenology*, which, improving on Kant, implicates at one stroke the multiple blunder of Kant's first *Critique*: namely, (1) Kant's failing to acknowledge the unprivileged presence of whatever appears as "actual" in our perception and experience of the world; (2) his failing to match at the very start of his undertaking the subjective and objective sides of whatever we report as the content of experience; and, as a result, (3) the insuperable contingency of our reflexive, continually reconstituted constructions of what to regard as provisionally *actual*. (This is, of course, a Hegelian phrasing.)

It's for such reasons as these that Kant (according to Hegel) could never escape the incoherence of his completely subjectivist account of empirical realism. But it's also the reason that Hegel's own rhetorical identification of (say) the necessary and the contingent, the infinite and the finite, the essential and the accidental, the absolute and the actual—that is, the entire play of what he presents as the dialectical logic of thought and being—is either a complex ideology sublimely contrived or a new version of Kantian blindness writ large. It must be the first, since the first is Hegel's way of escaping the second—in which case it makes a splendid contribution to all the viable movements of contemporary philosophy. But, in the same sense in which Hegel corrects and replaces Kant, history manifests an appetite for even more diverse forms of resolution than Hegel's own rhetoric might seem to favor: for instance, along the lines of historical discontinuities, plural perspectives, fragmentary narratives, and incompatible interpretations. (Consider Nietzsche and Foucault.) The upshot is that we cannot count on validating any constant cognitive principles or assured practices mediating between our fluxive selves and our fluxive world. Which is to say: Hegel and the pragmatists make common cause. In any case, we glimpse here the master contest of the modern era down to our own day—affecting "analytic" and "continental" philosophy in equal measures.

This, then, is my charge; or, rather, its principal part. But it confronts Kant and the post-Kantian tradition eccentrically.

. . .

The first *Critique*, you realize, rests on Kant's grave concern that Newton's splendid achievement requires a cognitively validated commitment to "absolute space" and "absolute time," which could never be justified on empirical grounds alone (say, in accord with empiricist assumptions); the entire *Critique* thereby acquires (Kant would have us believe) its transcendental right to determine what is needed for a complete account of the necessary conditions of the empirical knowledge embedded in Newton's physics. Kant's purpose here was to come to Newton's rescue; so that the *Critique* presumes to investigate the possibility of hitherto unnoticed necessary structures in the understanding (of a cognizing subject) answering to the requirements of Newton's science and thereby justifying Newton's much-disputed provisions—by means of conceptual resources not otherwise accessible.

Kant's transcendental critique is meant, therefore, to be a science in its own right. But then, the cleverness of Kant's abandoning the "rational metaphysics" of thinkers such as Leibniz and Christian Wolff is, as Hegel plainly believed, hardly a perspicuous spelling of his own question and the answer he provides. As we might now say: couldn't a normal change in physics obviate the seeming need for anything as presumptuous as Kant's transcendental strategy?

If you grasp the point of the suggestion, you see at once how Kant's transcendentalism shores up his subjectivism; hence, then, how the defeat of his transcendentalism leaves his subjectivism completely undefended. The appeal to the empirical work of the sciences confirms, therefore, the presuppositionlessly "objective" cast of phenomenological reportage. (Thinking ahead to the purpose of my entire argument, this is the nerve of the Hegelianized reading of Peirce's phenomenology, however it may be that Peirce came to see himself and Hegel at first as opponents and then, gradually, in good part—many claim—under Josiah Royce's instruction, as distinctly convergent.)

How could Kant's maneuver fail to be ad hoc and question begging, given that it relies, transcendentally, on the strength of this or that potentially excessive claim *in Newton*, in inferring the validity of its own Critical effort to recover the synthetic a priori conditions on which just such claims (in Newton), assumed to be true, are shown to be "possible"? Hegel took Kant to have been fatally deflected by the "inessential" (purely "accidental") question of how, relative to his knowledge of physics, Kant might concoct a plausible account of the enabling "subjective" (not, however, psychological) conditions matching what Newton's physics (or Euclid's geometry) might "require." Whatever is "essential" ("internal") to knowledge or reality, Hegel supposed, could never be fathomed in this way: it could never escape being historically blind. Kant's a priori "necessities" obscure Kant's reading of the facts.

The deep (Hegelian) lesson I draw from this review (dependent, of course, on a reading of Fichte) is perfectly straightforward: philosophical arguments cast in terms of abstract concepts primarily, arguments *not* thoroughly and defensibly grounded in the concrete phenomena of the experienced world (and not demonstrably apriorist), are both implicitly privileged and utterly vulnerable to historicized changes in the drift of science itself. I take this to be the effective center of "all" subsequent valid philosophical work—whether analytic or continental—that marks the true beginning of "modern" modern philosophy: for instance, in the profound doubts (voiced by figures as different as Søren Kierkegaard and Foucault) embedded in our noticing that Hegel's *Geist* never seems to lose its sense of the continuity and unity of interpretive thought, an abiding consistency of perspective, a relatively totalized conceptual inclusion of experience that no mortal historian could possibly confirm, an absence of any experienced discontinuity of time or history, or the diversity or fragmentary nature of any particular person's sense of the actual play of individual and aggregated experience. (We cannot accord Hegel greater cognitive powers than those he rejects in Kant.)

Seen thus, it hardly matters whether Hegel was himself mistaken in thinking he knew what would be necessary and adequate in coming to know the true nature of knowledge: the charge against Kant would still stand. This hints at the relationship between Kant's transcendental and Hegel's dialectical logics vis-à-vis the relevant analysis of "necessity." But it's also reasonable to read Hegel as championing a careful sort of historied constructivism that Kant never seriously explored.[5] In any event, it's the most interesting of the viable options Hegel can offer the modern world.

Of course, as we now understand the matter, not only is the a priori necessity of Euclidean geometry subverted by relativity physics, but the whole structure of absolute space and time turns out to be a piece of excessive (illicit) rhetoric regarding the would-be separability of the "pure intuitions" of space and time and the nature of the physical world itself. On such considerations, and given the inseparability of our first- and second-order questions, we cannot fail to see that the contingency of our first-order answers ineluctably infects the conditions of validity of all answers to our second-order questions. Hence, faute de mieux—hardly a priori (in Kant's sense)—we find ourselves obliged to abandon, unconditionally, any transcendental strategy of Kant's unyielding sort: otherwise stated, we find we must construe synthetic a priori arguments as a posteriori constructions. Here, then, we gain a confirmation ("by other means") of Hegel's extraordinary intuition and compelling critique of Kant. (In reaching even this provisional finding, I have, of course, introduced a sense of "constructivism" that exceeds Kantian subjectivism; but that is precisely what Hegel's and Peirce's corrections require.)

Science claims (in principle, with whatever caveats) effective access to all that's true about the world: conjecturally, it collects what it takes to be reliable evidence of its would-be claims and is committed (in its evolving way) to various promising confirmatory strategies that diverge quite strikingly among themselves from time to time, not always in a measurably progressive way, sometimes even opportunistically.[6] But there is (and can be) no comparable procedure for determining or validating, empirically or transcendentally, the truth about the nature of *knowledge*, regardless of what our favored sources may recommend. Here, "knowledge" is not the subject of any first-order inquiry—or, what comes to the same thing, any determinately neutral or demonstrably privileged second-order inquiry.

On this argument, legitimation cannot be conceptually independent of what we take our first-order sciences to encompass: the "subjective" and the "objective" must be functionally inseparable if the primary concern of either is to succeed at all. Both Kant and Hegel admit this much; but Hegel, of course, finds that Kant neglects the robust form the "objective" focus requires—in his excessive effort to avoid the noumenal and his impoverished account of representations and mere appearances (*Vorstellungen*) as far as empirical realism is concerned.[7] Hegel takes Kant to be incoherent here,[8] and Kant's famous letter to Marcus Herz seems to anticipate the charge and something of its validity.[9]

Like truth, knowledge is not a suitable topic of empirical discovery, or of discovery, however strictly conceived, within empirically embedding contexts; it's hardly a datum for a determinate science, although its conjectured analysis provisionally yields the conceptual grounds on which the sciences themselves are said to proceed successfully. Cast in Kant's transcendental terms, the linkage becomes fatally circular, whereas it is never more than benignly ideological (perhaps, better, opportunistic) in Hegel. That is to say, the "prejudice" of belief cannot rightly be read as signifying that such belief fails to be "presuppositionless" (in Hegel's phenomenological sense).

The meaning of "presuppositionlessness," the key to Hegel's *Phenomenology* (a fortiori, the key to the *Encyclopaedia Logic*), is decisive here—decisive also for the fortunes of pragmatism. Its best reading must be opposed to Descartes's method of "universal doubt" and to Kant's would-be reflexive confirmation of the apriorist (necessary) standing of the categories of the understanding (which, prejudicially, may be deemed to be a "pragmatic" variant of Descartes's method). Neither Hegel's nor Peirce's treatment of doubt nor the resolution of doubt signifies an end to the "prejudices" of belief; presuppositionlessness is, effectively, the rejection of the Cartesian and Kantian (and related) assumptions, *not* the elimination of prejudice or the like.[10] Both Hegel and Peirce reject the possibility of "universal doubt" (effectively, a self-defeating or sham skepticism) and distinguish the advent of real doubt as occasional, contingent, motivated, contexted, concrete rather than abstract, fraught with a sense of encountered impasses to pertinent action, and capable of being resolved within the span of evolving experience though without assurances of any kind against further such doubts.[11]

The difference between Kant and Hegel depends on the presumed (cognitive) accessibility of strict necessity (Kant's premise) applied among synthetic claims; whereas Hegel, addressing the same linkage, admits in every way that the connection between first- and second-order answers must be continually constructed and reconstructed to accord with evolving experience and to gain anything like the ring of truth. Our answers, Hegel seems to hold, remain thoroughly contingent, no matter how persuasive they may prove to be within the endless flux of thought. Accordingly, Kant's deepest claims remain completely unconvincing.

Evolving convictions about what the sciences have achieved (empirically) may suddenly alter our analysis of what knowledge itself must be: think of the great shift from Aristotelian to Galilean physics; or, for that matter, of how epistemology swings from Descartes to Locke to Leibniz to Hume. Correspondingly, changes in our conception of knowledge may decisively affect our tolerance of strong theoretical discontinuities that "normal" science might well oppose: consider for instance Albert Einstein's resistance to the heterodox speculations of his own day regarding quantum physics. There are no fixities in *Vernunft* for the same reason there are none in *Verstand*.

There's a reciprocal dependence between the work of our first-order sciences and our second-order analyses of truth and knowledge; there is no clear way to demarcate such inquiries within any well-defined system of conceptual priorities (whether empirical or transcendental). But if this is so, and if (as is generally conceded) the empirical sciences begin (informally) with the palpable contingencies of experience or with what, without tendentious intent, we characterize as our sensory experience of the actual world, we find ourselves confronted (reconsidering Kant's Critical practice) with various problematic options regarding the relationship between the work of the physical sciences and their supposed cognitive foundations. Transcendental necessities, then, are illusions of meta-reflection: chance impressions of conceptual necessity artifactually projected from an overly sanguine trust in contingencies of theory that, for the nonce, somehow appear unalterable.

We find ourselves unable—or unwilling—to pretend to recover anything like Kant's transcendental confidence. Kant's confidence depends (at best) on a spectacularly brilliant but hugely wrongheaded conceptual gamble that has proved a strange mixture of dubious persuasions: for instance, a way of invoking unearned argumentative advantage ultimately as unacceptable as that of the Wolffian rationalists whom Kant repudiates (always on the scruple of never itself claiming cognitive privilege); or an ad hoc response to meet the essential lacuna noted in Newton's physics; or the saving application of transcendental rigor without providing a transcendentalist justification of the alleged necessity of invoking any such rigor; or the promise of a conceptually closed system by which to explain the "possibility" of empirical science itself, a system oddly deficient in failing to provide adequate grounds for confirming the objective standing of a realist science as such; or a would-be a priori catalogue of all the facultative elements that must function together in order to yield a complete table of all the kinds of judgment accessible to an objective science, though without any comparably ramified account of the dynamics of actual cognition; or, finally, the effective but unacceptably a priori disjunction between the theoretical powers of science and the would-be practical autonomy of moral judgment and moral commitment. Kant was immensely skillful, but he backed himself into a transcendental(ist) corner for reasons that now seem patently impossible to validate. His boldest "necessities" seem remarkably improvisational and undefended—and much too easy to dispute.

There are, however, reasonable conjectures that may be retrospectively and prospectively pursued about how (according to our lights) the history of the sciences might convincingly sustain our evolving conception of their objective work. But once we admit the novel mode of explanation Kant introduces in the first *Critique*—shorn of its obsessive and indefensible apriorism, committed (instead) to the historicity of thought and experience, centered on providing a constructivist answer to the question of how we might still speak of ever knowing when we actually arrive at objective knowledge—we realize that our answers can never be more than provisional, contingent, artifactual, open-ended, plural, diverse, possibly conflicting, reflexive, evolving, hopefully self-corrective, ad hoc, opportunistic, deprived of any principled rules of final validation, horizoned, ideologically committed, fragmentary, often narrowly contexted, practical, disposed to favor changing saliencies, and unable to approximate to any closed or absolute system of understanding. These, I say, are findings as close as any that might be thought to be insuperable (under currently prevailing horizons of thought): that encumber, let us say, every responsible form of contemporary philosophy and that cannot be explicated in terms that evade Hegel's innovations. Hence, the fact that Hegel is characteristically read as alien, or inimical, to analytic philosophy is itself a symptom of a thoroughly avoidable confusion. (I cannot deny, I concede, that Hegel is forever engaged in convincing us of the "necessity" of his endless, dialectical construction of knowledge—what, in accord with his own intent, may fairly be called the *Bildung* of knowledge: "the *education of consciousness itself*," as Hegel affirms (emphasis in the original); but the enthusiasm of the introduction to the *Phenomenology* could never support any literal such reading.)[12]

You cannot fail to see that the trajectory of the indicated "revision" of Kant's transcendental strategy leads inexorably to what we may correctly call *pragmatism* (without meaning to endorse thereby, or not endorse, the noticeably thin American version of pragmatism's possibilities): that is, one or another fluxive or historied form of what may be fairly judged to have devolved from Hegel's original critique of Kant—strangely missing (all but missing) in the American version. Of course, C. I. Lewis's pragmatic treatment of the a priori, signally influenced, apparently, by Josiah Royce's reading of Hegel (but chary of "absolute idealism"), provides, at a very late date, the decisive step in the pragmatic formulation of the needed correction of Kant's original question.[13] Hegel is more than doubtful about the fixity of Kant's categories of analysis: the predicates of dialectical reason, Hegel makes clear, cannot but be improvisational, tending toward the transient, contexted to the here and now, and impossible to rely on in terms of any canonical account of essential or universal or necessary regularity. But if that is so, then plainly, dialectical logic cannot be more than persuasive or consensual: there cannot be any asymptotic path to "absolute knowing."[14] Here, Hegel surely anticipates the validity of the eclipse of what I shall call his own "prototype" of dialectical reasoning along pragmatist lines. The argument is implicit in the paradox with which I first began: dialectical reasoning is bound to take any number of plausible forms, once we acknowledge its heuristic use in support of whatever we select as the nerve of the actual. Furthermore, it's easy enough to see that to treat knowledge (a fortiori, truth) this way is to bring knowledge (also, truth, meaning, confirmation, even number) within the bounds of naturalism—in the sense that though these concepts are not themselves concepts of natural "things," they are managed entirely in terms of the capacities of human agents; so that if human agents fall within the space of nature, so too must this *practice* of knowledge. (Naturalism, of course, need not cleave to reductionisms of any sort.) In Lewis's hands, the Kantian a priori, applied to specifically human contingencies of perception, experience, and thought, cannot escape being manifested in a succession of a posteriori posits.

. . .

No one believes that Kant was unaware of the paradox of his own position (for instance, in the preface to the second edition of the first *Critique*) if he was aware (as he surely was) of the epistemological authority of Newton's *Principia* with regard to the prospects of an objective physics. Kant was struck by the fact that the categories of absolute motion and absolute space, so essential to Newton's achievement, were not empirically accessible in any way; so that, as he construed matters, *Principia* stood in mortal need of some sort of nonempirical "resource" adequate for explaining the validity of Newton's claims in the context of their empirical relevance. Extraordinary![15]

I put the point in this roundabout way in order to close off certain tempting possibilities of escape. Kant's way of salvaging Newton's treatment of space, time, and motion is, perhaps, the only way open to him if (as we know) he *also* rejects the privileged resources of Wolffian rationalism but insists on the a priori nature of geometric proofs.[16] He cannot then have favored a transcendental account of the cognition of "independent objects" without restoring the privilege he repudiates.

Kant was indeed unable to capture what he needed—by "subjective" means alone. He distinguishes instead, *within* the manifold of experience, *between* mere (experienced) representations ("appearances" construed as representations), which belong solely to the subject of consciousness, and their selectively correspondent "objects" (distinct, somehow, from representations as such). Objects in the "objective sense" must also in some sense be distinct, however, from the "subject" *of* consciousness, since the representations of objects (but not independent objects) belong to such subjects (if they are intelligible at all) even when objective truth is thought to obtain.[17] For his part, Hegel might have said (indeed, did say) something to the following effect: first, that Kant's account is inherently paradoxical, since it fails to introduce at the very start a working distinction between appearances and the objects they are the appearances of;[18] and second, that the provision of would-be synthetic a priori conditions, meant to secure the possibility of validating Newtonian physics empirically, plainly depends on favoring "inessential" features of Newton's actual achievement.[19] Kant's "subjectivism" does indeed defeat any cognitive reliance on noumena (when Kant is not careless in his formulations); but just this construction makes it impossible for Kant to recover any robust form of empirical realism (the unresolved weakness of the A and B versions of the first *Critique*). Hegel's indissoluble union of the "subjective" and the "objective" at every point of cognitively pertinent perception and experience completely outflanks both puzzles, by replacing Kantian *Vorstellungen* (subjective representations) with *Erscheinungen*, which, in the *Phenomenology*, may be rendered as "the appearings-of-the-world-to-us," in a sense that claims no foundational privilege at the same time that it ensures an exceptionless but uninterpreted (constructivist) grip on realism. That is: Hegel rejects the primacy of representationalism but also insists on the (ontic) presuppositionlessness of his phenomenology.

I might add here that the epistemological inseparability of the subjective and the objective is not tantamount at all to admitting any "idealist" or "Idealist" construction of the real world—in any metaphysically pertinent sense. That is a non sequitur that has produced a good deal of philosophical mischief: the post-Kantian "objective" Idealist (Hegel, preeminently) means, rather, that the realism of the experienced or encountered world ineliminably implicates a relation to the cognizing subject (at once epistemological and metaphysical) within the terms of which, alone, determinate realist claims make coherent sense. In this regard, German Idealism (but not "subjective idealism") is able to preclude both noumenalism and cognitive privilege. Realist philosophies of the analytic sort often fail to perceive the dependent nature of their own posit if they themselves mean to avoid invoking the noumenal or the privileged. Objective realism is not constituted subjectively, but it cannot fail to be read in terms of the contingencies of the human forms of inquiry.

What appears as Hegel's ultimate telos belonging to the totality of knowledge is never more than the contingently totalized (hence, teleologized)—rhetorically projected—guesses at what, at any given moment of historied reflection, seems best at promising to lead us toward "absolute knowing." It cannot mean more, and Hegel's own concessions cannot vouchsafe more. In any event, the presumed absolute telos cannot literally draw us to itself: we are responsible for its projection, which, understandably, we may advance as the "final" goal of all our scattered inquiries. In Peirce's hands, a similar conjecture expresses itself as the progressivist form of realism itself. (Peirce's fallibilism is certainly one of the most inventive treatments of the puzzle—not because he solved it convincingly but because he demonstrated, by his own contrivance, that it can be solved without sacrificing its most important and daring challenge.)

Effectively, Hegel abandons explanatory closure (in anything like Kant's way), except (perhaps) rhetorically, as in the deliberate idealization he calls "absolute knowing" (that is, philosophy's putative rational grasp of the inclusive whole of reality); but then he cannot hold (in epistemically operative terms—and, arguably, he does not commit) to any unique telos collecting all valid inquiries about the way the world "is." That is precisely what I mean by the inevitably pragmatist fragmentation of Hegel's recovery of realism: objectivity becomes historicized and constructivist, and the naturalistic reading of the realism of science may be fairly construed as a metaphysical economy answering to something akin to Hegel's Idealist treatment of the indissoluble unity of the subjective and objective aspects of our cognitive engagement with the world (*Erscheinungen*). Once we are clear about Hegel's compelling strategy, we are hardly bound to confine alternative "Idealist" options to Hegel's own metaphysical extravagances: if, for instance, we abandon "Mind" or "*Geist*" in nature or at any "level" above nature (metaphysically), there may not be (in that sense) a need to admit any vestige of Idealism itself (or, of nature's telos), as late pragmatism makes clear.

But realism's cognitive dependence on historied *Erscheinungen* (or something of the sort) cannot be convincingly denied, since *Erscheinungen* can claim no cognitive primacy, though they are indeed the "primary" (epistemological) data on which cognition depends. There's the sticking point that analytic realism (naive realism, really) regularly scants. The persistence of Idealism is the consequence of adhering to Kant's transcendental question under all its variations—including Hegel's and Peirce's. Peirce is "persuaded" that inquiry converges toward a unique finding at the end of the long run of infinite inquiry; but he is persuaded that *that* is no more than a reasonable Hope. That's all! The direct realist reading of Peirce neglects this caveat; the analytic objection to Peirce's extravagance ignores the epistemological constraint intended by Peirce's Idealism. (Nonetheless, Peirce's "progressivism," read as "a rational Hope," may be fairly challenged, without thereby challenging the link between realism and Idealism.) If these findings are reasonably close to our current understanding of what the natural sciences have accomplished and what knowledge may be said to be, then, for all its brilliance and admirable scruple, Kant's Critical project was from its inception an impossible undertaking—profoundly regressive; question begging on essentials; incompatible with the reciprocal dependence of so-called transcendental and empirical considerations; committed (without compelling argument) to certain changeless, innate, a priori structures of cognitive competence; disproportionately demanding in isolating the would-be necessary conditions of what appears to be the insuperably informal nature of empirical inquiry; and demonstrably self-defeating.

I hasten to add that my reasons for rejecting Kant's transcendental strategy are neither textual nor concerned with Kant's deeper objective regarding the relationship between science and morality.[20] They are, in fact, "external" reasons intended, faute de mieux, to show that Kant's specific project was both impossible and profoundly misrepresented by Kant himself—without denying that Kant provoked a great flurry of closely related accounts of knowledge that we ought not to be deprived of.

After Kant, the question of what knowledge "is" is best answered by answering the question, What (in a nondisjunctive sense) "might knowledge be": that is, by defining and defending every conceivable inquiry, theoretical or practical, deemed capable of sustaining first- and second-order questions analogous to those prompted in the inquiries of Kant's explicit paradigm and among (what I call) the "prototypical" alternative strategies (Kant's own, and those of his critics, his opponents, his reformers, his continuators, and even those of more distant innovators who have caught fire from his example), especially those that strengthen our command of what the validation and legitimation of empirical realism may require.

Nothing (as far as the argument now before us goes) hangs on whether there is, or are, one or several new paradigms regarding what knowledge "is" or "might be." But the pervasive influence of Kant's seminal invention and Hegel's reactive innovation suggest an important economy. (There's the point of distinguishing between "paradigm" and "prototype," though the distinction remains entirely informal.)

Hegel, I would say, was obviously occupied with an "external" critique of Kant's *Critique*, even where he considers the consistency and internal adequacy of Kant's actual arguments. Kant himself was remarkably well-armored against his detractors (current as well as past), even where the most profound discrepancies have come to light. Everyone who admires Kant is aware of his almost unmatched resourcefulness. I have no quarrel with that. Nevertheless, Kant's grand undertaking fails, though it fails in that commanding way that warrants and demands revision in both paradigm and prototype.

Kant's great effort confirms (against his own devices) that the inquiry required could never convincingly begin with presumptions of cognitive privilege. It must first concede some relatively uncontested body of knowledge (always open to revision and firmer validation), and it must proceed from there to construct (as plausibly as possible) a second-order account of what needs to be settled in order to legitimate our first-order claims to knowledge. Every such effort, you realize, will be completely conjectural—down to the supposed need for apriorist necessities.

Kant's answer is an immensely alluring reply to Descartes's question, beyond anything the early rationalists and empiricists had ever conceived: it is a response that deliberately abandons all appeals to cognitive privilege, assurances of divine support, forms of authority, noumenal presumptions, and all other similarly inadmissible resources. And yet, as Hegel argues, no such effort can possibly know in advance what *is* "essential" and what "accidental" in the sciences we begin with in fashioning our analysis of what knowledge "is." There's the clue to the inevitable "aposteriorizing" of Kant's a priori necessities—hence, to exposing any apriorist misreading of Hegel as well!

Kant's transcendentalist answer, therefore, is never more than one possible model or prototype of how best, or acceptably, to pursue the new paradigm (still incompletely defined) that he sketches at the same time he introduces the transcendental "instrument" of the first *Critique*. The actual evolution of physics confirms that Kant surely conflated the "accidental" necessities of time and space in Newton's *Principia* with the supposed a priori necessities of the would-be form of legitimation required to match *Principia* itself—hence, to define, in turn, the "essential" structure of Kant's new paradigm of legitimated knowledge.

There is no settled name for the new paradigm and inquiry that Kant and Hegel share—and share with Husserl and Heidegger and Cassirer and even Dewey and Ludwig Wittgenstein.[21] But it has obviously come to dominate a large part of the philosophy of the nineteenth and twentieth centuries through the remarkable diversity of its prototypical approaches to a seemingly common (if elusive) paradigm. At the present time, the historicity of science, on which so much depends, tends to favor options closer to Hegel's treatment of the underlying paradigm (or some Hegelianized version of Kant's conception) than to the version Kant offers in the first *Critique*.[22] (This, I'm prepared to claim, rightly constrains all contemporary efforts at the analysis of knowledge, whether pragmatist, analytic, or continental: it's the inescapable upshot of admitting the validity of Hegel's critique of Kant, which could be offset only by inventing a fresh contribution of the gauge of Kant's and Hegel's original arguments.)

Hence, the validity and revolutionary power of Hegel's conception are at their most compelling when we realize that Hegel's vision was meant to be a closely matched rival of Kant's. In the whole of Western philosophy, there is no other comparable pairing of such thoroughly opposed conceptual programs that have so presciently informed the work of the past two centuries. Kant had indeed created a new way of construing the analysis and legitimation of the concept and enabling practices of knowledge, but his operative model (his "prototype") presumes more than anyone could possibly deliver or justify. Think of a suggestive analogy here: Dmitri Mendeleev's guess at what we now count as the periodic table of elements obliged him to fiddle with empirical weights instead of atomic numbers, which had not yet been discovered. Mendeleev, then, mistook the accidental for the essential. Here, we may (choose to) speak of Hegel's "sharing" the search for a new paradigm, which Kant misdescribed by way of his transcendental prototype; or we may speak of Hegel's pursuing an entirely new paradigm, one utterly opposed to Kant's. I favor the first characterization, given the sense that the deep infelicity of Kant's transcendental strategy hardly brings to an end "post-Kantian" inquiry, even where Kant's apriorism is summarily dismissed.

I take this line of reasoning to specify the most obvious, most straightforward sense in which, to follow the salient debates of current philosophical fashion, Hegel may be shown to be helpfully reconcilable with analytic philosophy. This goes decidedly against the rather tortured alternatives suggested by Richard Rorty's attempt to recover Wilfrid Sellars's attack on the "Myth of the Given," which seems to have been inspired (at least in part) by John McDowell's and Robert Brandom's efforts at recuperating Hegel. For the moment, let me simply say that the defeat of the Myth of the Given, which Sellars and P. F. Strawson supported independently in very similar ways, at about the same time, marks a very odd episode in contemporary Anglo-American philosophy. This is because, for one thing, read in Rorty's way (and in the way of those he directly influenced), it actually deflects our attention away from the principal strength of Hegel's contribution—the strong exposé of the insuperable deficiency of Kant's transcendental paradigm, which has dominated so much of Western philosophy when not itself "Hegelianized" along historied lines, and the compensating historicity of Hegel's own philosophy when moderately liberated from any heavily metaphysical readings or misreadings of his reorientation of the original Kantian problem.[23]

Allow me, however, to seize the moment to say that Sellars's best inquiries are characteristically incomplete regarding whatever issue is apparently at stake; they are often unstable and conjectural, even tolerant of obvious paradox, and rarely are identified by Sellars himself as constituting a definite commitment on his part. Temperamentally, Sellars is an "experimental" philosopher: that is, he offers plausible "defenses" of a variety of incompatible (but important) "positions," which he then abandons. Almost none of these forays can be invoked to support, say, McDowell's or Brandom's arguments and undertakings; and Rorty's endorsements of Sellars's commitments—as a pragmatist, or in hinting at the fresh importance of the attack on the Myth of the Given after fifty years of relatively uncontested acceptance, or (very possibly) in suggesting the "Hegelian" import of Sellars's general drift (in the absence of sustained evidence)—can hardly be counted on to shore up Sellars's elusive confidence in the "rules" of "material inference" (which Brandom attempts to resurrect).

Most readers of Sellars's most important selection of his own papers (*Science, Perception and Reality*) will find themselves, I imagine, attracted by the daring of his formulation of the dialectical opposition between the "manifest image" and the "scientific image,"[24] precisely because his account links two unavoidable but seemingly very different contests: one, concerning the reconcilability of freedom and causality in the Kantian account (which McDowell takes up, obliquely, inasmuch as Kant is hardly willing to venture a plausible "bridge"); the other, concerning the reconcilability of a materialist reductionism (or better, an eliminativism) and an account of the world that unabashedly features the irreducible complexities of the life and concerns of human persons viewed as apt agents (which Brandom takes up, even more obliquely, in his attempt to recover a pragmatist form of inferentialism that would allow us to view Sellars and Hegel as kindred logicians).[25] Sellars satisfies us on neither count, nor on the integral bearing of Hegel on the themes Rorty features in suggesting a linkage between Sellars and Hegel (including the themes McDowell and Brandom separately prefer). I take the issue raised by Sellars's "Philosophy and the Scientific Image of Man" and "The Language of Theories" (in *Science, Perception and Reality*) to be more important than the problem of the "Given" or the "inferentialism" question (in Sellars's own writings).

But then, the fact remains that when Sellars suggests *adding* the concept of a functional self (concerned with action and normativity) to the "scientific image" (Sellars's eliminativism), he fails to air the paradox that must, on any plausible reading, concede that the scientific image is itself a proposal advanced by the same intelligence that, on his own argument, congenially offers the "manifest image." Sellars's tail-end advice is, therefore, simply incoherent: if the manifest image were permitted at all, it would of course preclude the scientific image—which itself precludes the concept "person." Nothing here, or, indeed, involving the Given or inferentialism, lends the least encouragement to the idea that Hegel and Sellars are kindred "logicians." Hegel's logic is an interpretive instrument applied to historied events in any space of intelligent life. It may, of course, be used in inferential contexts, but it is not (in any sense) an inferential instrumentality itself. (McDowell and Brandom, therefore, are entirely on their own, however they succeed in drawing inspiration from Sellars and Rorty.)

Hegel saw the Kantian issue quite clearly—a matter already promisingly glimpsed by others before him. But it was Hegel who first conceived and carried out, in the most detailed way imaginable, what philosophy has since judged to be the single most important, most original, and most daring intuition to date—absent in Kant himself, though dawningly accessible in Kant's time—that could support a radical rival to Kant's unanticipated transcendentalism. Hegel begins with Kant's own sources and puzzles and sense of rigor; insists on answering the deeper legitimative question he shares with Kant (which marks them as the well-matched opponents that they are); and, proceeding thus, demonstrates how the would-be necessities of transcendental explanation may be fairly converted into a posteriori posits in accord with the contingent processes of history.

In this way, Hegel summarily rejects Kant's apriorism, though without disowning its newfound legitimative function (if suitably revised). At the same time, Hegel attempts to redefine the inchoate paradigm he finds in Kant, which Kant's own transcendental "prototype" disables. Implicitly, Hegel deflates all the needless conceptual extravagances of the entire Idealist company (himself included), who (following Fichte and Friedrich von Schelling) correctly understand the intolerable muddle of remaining at the point of Kant's uncompromising subjectivism.

Hegel's new intuition, of course, is nothing less than the huge theme of historicity itself, the idea of the historied nature of thought (and human being), which, rightly grasped, signifies the evolving dialectical "identity" of the a priori and the a posteriori, the necessary and the accidental. Kant comes too late to this conception of history.[26] To concede its relevance, at once metaphysical and epistemological, is to expose the irremediable failure of Kant's original reading(s) of the paradigm shift he undoubtedly produced. Thereafter, the available prototypes can no longer pretend that there are any fixed categories to invoke—because, of course, concepts and categories will have gone historical. The contest is no longer one between commensurable opponents: it now rests with how we choose to read the profound discontinuity between invariance and flux.[27] (Husserl's retrograde phenomenology—as, say, in *Ideas I*—is perhaps the last large expression of the Cartesian and Kantian rationalism that Hegel "finally" dismantled avant la lettre.)

. . .

I won't deny that much is baffling in Hegel's philosophy—even more perhaps than in Kant's. But it is Hegel, finally, who salvages Kant's essential innovation by abandoning Kant's disastrous transcendental conjunction of an impossible subjectivism and an ill-conceived apriorism. It dawns on us that a solution along genuinely realist lines—one capable of securing a robust reading of the "objects" of perception and experience (so that such objects need never have been submerged within whatever answers to Kant's "unity of consciousness")—was always close at hand. According to Kant, that unity accounts in an essential way (even if only in part) for *whatever* unity perceived objects appear to possess; hence, Kant himself makes it impossible to free "objects" from his obsessive taboos against noumena.[28]

Hegel's exposé, therefore, remains a model of good sense (whatever the obscurities of the *Phenomenology*). Hegel demonstrates, for example, how easy it is to introduce "external" (or "independent") objects in the uncomplicated context of what is "given" in experience presuppositionlessly, without invoking noumena or privilege of any kind and without subjectivist contortions (for instance, regarding the "given" primacy of Kantian "representations"). Again, the *Phenomenology* is the proof.

Here, now, I venture to collect the leanest set of constraints advanced on Hegel's behalf—reasonably defended independently of Hegel, and not implausibly assigned, inferentially or interpretively, in a liberal reading of Hegel's own texts—and cast in terms of replacing Kant's transcendental vision: (1) that, even if transcendental claims are synthetic *and* a priori, they cannot be synthetic a priori;[29] (2) that putative a priori conditions of knowledge are best viewed as projected from the evolving a posteriori cultural innovations of one or another ethos;[30] (3) that the seeming necessity of any a priori conception of inquiry or knowledge is never more than a contingent artifact of one or another part of our *geistlich* history; (4) that cognitive, expressive, practical, and related competences are, similarly, artifacts of cultural formation, however idealized, teleologically unified, holist, or collectively entrenched they may be; (5) that relations between concepts cannot be disjunctively fixed as purely analytic or synthetic; their continually evolving use within the flux of history and interpretive context and intent baffles any such principle; (6) that, accordingly, metaphysical, epistemological, and even logical oppositions cannot be sorted in any canonical or changeless way but are continually "sublated" (*aufgehoben*) or "negated": for example, the empirical and the transcendental, the real and the apparent, the subjective and the objective, the universal and the particular, the necessary and the contingent (or accidental), the finite and the infinite; and (7) that, within the constraints of an evolving cultural history, metaphysical and epistemological dualisms remain patently untenable.

The influence of these genuinely radical changes may be traced in the work of figures as disparate as Karl Marx, Nietzsche, Wilhelm Dilthey, Peirce, Dewey, Heidegger, Maurice Merleau-Ponty, and Cassirer. Kant's belief that transcendental inquiry yields a uniquely (determinately) closed system of necessary constraints leads us inexorably to test its *internal* adequacy and coherence along the lines of Hegel's *external* question. The future of philosophy still yields in Hegel's direction, though usually not in Hegel's own terms, even where it returns to Kant.

In the introduction to the second edition of the first *Critique*, Kant tries to persuade us, passingly, that, even in relatively untutored thought and speech, we are made aware that we have an a priori concept of "an object in general." Kant affirms that "philosophy needs a science that determines the possibility, the principles, and the domain of all cognitions *a priori*. But what says still more than all the foregoing is this, that certain cognitions even abandon the field of all possible experiences, and seem to expand the domain of our judgments beyond all bounds of experience through concepts to which no corresponding object at all can be given in experience."[31] Kant seems, therefore, to be tempted to think of our possessing a certain ability (somehow) to spot a valid (a correctly applied) a priori constraint on judgments applied to empirically encountered objects—even though, of course, it cannot be the upshot of any merely empirical cognition. How this ability is to be defined and exercised vis-à-vis objects (in the "objective" sense), without confounding contingent or "accidental" and necessary truths affecting realism, is nowhere satisfactorily laid out, though Kant clearly believes he's made a proper pass at the problem. The entire *Critique* hangs in the balance.

Certainly, Kant turns Newton on his head in providing the a priori conditions he supplies to back whatever he draws from *Principia*. In this connection, Peter Strawson shows in a particularly lucid way just how, on the one hand, Kant argues for what he regards as necessary *and* a priori elements within experience and judgment; and how, on the other hand, he relies on "a kind of strained analogy" between the very different ways in which transcendental and empirical claims "depend" on experience itself.[32]

Strawson pointedly reminds us that Kant "believed without question in the finality of Euclidean geometry, Newtonian physics, and Aristotelian logic; and [that] on these beliefs he founded others, still more questionable."[33] I have no wish to champion Strawson's particular resolution of the transcendental issue. (Some readers believe that Kant gives evidence of a more provisional application of his own method. But in the end, how much is he prepared to yield?) Strawson clearly notes the insuperable defect of Kant's borrowings from Newton in the lax way he favors, as in his holding that the geometry that informs "the spatial and temporal systems of relations between particular items encountered in experience have their source [*a priori*] in our own mind alone." "Space and time themselves," he reports, "are declared [by Kant] to be 'in us'"—effectively, innate.[34] In this way, Kant makes empirical realism impossible to recover.

But that means that Kant's assigning synthetic a priori standing to the supposed geometry of experienced space and to the counterpart analysis of time is already part of a still-unsecured transcendentalist explanation of the very conditions of the possibility of spatial and temporal experience, without regard (yet) to the experience of "independent" objects—hardly, then, a compelling reason for claiming that there ever was a need for such an account or, indeed, that its credentials could remain unaffected by the inevitable eclipse or reinterpretation of Newtonian science. Obviously, Kant's transcendental claims are subject to empirical refutation, apart from realist concerns.[35] It's not the error that's decisive here, it's the absence (in Kant) of any criterion for distinguishing between empirical and transcendental mistakes.

Accordingly, we find ourselves obliged to concede the historicized nature of science in the very attempt to define the a priori geometry of physical and experienced space. If this bit of history affords a paradigmatic clue to the "transcendental" work of constructing a possible "metaphysics of experience"—fitted to one or another particular "moment" of philosophical reflection—then Kant's entire model will have been defeated hands down: not, let it be said, as a result of shifting philosophical loyalties but because we will have learned that there is no convincing way to vouchsafe Kant's choice of a method of defense—or a principled disjunction between the empirical and the transcendental.

If you favor this last line of reasoning, you cannot fail to see how the perceived trajectory of the history of science drives philosophy (without privilege) closer to Hegel's "revision" of the Kantian program than to any attempt to redeem the more than problematic inflexibilities of Kant's own conception. The evolving (dynamic) history of science decisively demonstrates its superiority over the static (kinematic) pretensions of Kant's philosophical practice. But that alone hardly validates Hegel's own "system."

If we favor a strategy like that of *Erscheinungen*, we must make room for reasonable improvisations of categories evolvingly needed in the descriptions and explanations that new sciences happen to provide; and if we favor *Vorstellungen* in Kant's sense, we may pretend to discover the fixed structures of the inquiring "mind." But we can never use the latter "criterially," in Kant's transcendental sense. The history of science betrays the historicity of thought, as in superseding Newton. *Erscheinungen*, in Hegel's sense, do not preclude the representational function of our interpretations of what is phenomenologically "given," but they do preclude Kant's representational*ism*. Hegel's argument makes our "representations" no more (and no less) than freely constructed, provisional guesses at what, passingly, to count as "presentations" of what is "actual," on the way to "absolute knowing." Kantian *Vorstellungen*, viewed, rather, as subjectivist representations, illicitly implicate noumena and, for that reason, utterly fail to ensure the "possibility" of their serving as realist "presentations" of any sort. But that means that Hegel rejects the canonical view that every form of constructivism is also a form of subjectivism. The epistemological inseparability of realism and Idealism consigns metaphysics to artifactual standing; but then, since noumena no longer have any epistemological role to play, the validation of our passing "pictures" of reality goes completely pragmatist. (We construct our "pictures" of reality, but not reality itself.)

. . .

There's little point in asking whether Hegel misreads the details of Kant's Critical proposal. Of course he does—perhaps deliberately, possibly at times maliciously.[36] We must ask, rather, what possible explanatory contribution could a successor inquiry make (against Kant's transcendental practice) if it must historicize thought itself?

Focused on the paradox of analyzing "knowledge," Hegel always favors an "external" rather than a merely textual critique: there's the key to the *reductio* lurking in Kant's reliance on the new authority of Newton's *Principia*. An evolving physics that displaces an earlier phase of the same inquiry cannot assure us that it will never be eclipsed in turn—in time—in an essential way. But if so, then the running "necessities" it itself advances from phase to phase are no better than logically contingent beliefs tethered to whatever "accidents" of historical thought it happens to fasten on. According to Hegel's model of rational inquiry—replacing transcendental logic by dialectical logic—there is no way to avoid the provisional "identity" of the necessary and the accidental, inasmuch as the "absolute" telos of historical thought and being cannot be discerned in any finite inquiry.[37]

Hegel obliges us to reconsider the question Kant cannot answer, which Hegel cannot rightly supply beyond the conjectured historicity of thought. That is, what Hegel shows is that Kant cannot disqualify the aposteriorist reading of his own a priori and that the rejection of apriorism fits the historicity of science (and Kant's rejection of rationalism) more plausibly than Kant's own affirmation. In Kant's account, the contest ultimately depends on the analysis of the subjective thought of the scientist himself, the cognizing subject, whom Hegel (quite rightly, in my opinion) treats as *gebildet* within one or another historical culture.

Here, the decisive force of Hegel's argument, actually not unlike the force of the argument against Kant's reading of Newton, requires a characterization of empirical data (as such) capable of supporting (1) an aposteriorist reading of Kant's transcendental question, (2) a presuppositionless acknowledgement of the "objective" import of what is "given" in experience (in the benign sense already supplied), and (3) a reflexively constructive (constructivist) criterion that, provisionally and self-correctively, justifies us in guessing at what to regard as acceptably (though fallibly) realist. Kant's thesis fails on all three counts. Hegel's succeeds, but at the honorable price of disallowing any viable disjunction between realism and Idealism. In this sense, Hegel lays the ground for pragmatism's continuation of his project along naturalistic and post-Darwinian lines. I'm persuaded that the most general evidence for a contemporary answer to Hegel's question had to wait at least for Darwin's discoveries and the post-Darwinian paleoanthropology that derives from it (see Chapter 3). Granting that much, there can be no solution to the problem of knowledge that is not constructivist—though, now, no longer subjectivist in Kant's manner.

The lesson drawn from Newton precludes anything but an opportunistic idealization of the dialectical identities mentioned above, since whatever we might then posit (from time to time) as "actual" (in the requisite sense) would arbitrarily invoke the inaccessible "absolute." If Hegel had meant to exceed the limits of any such conception, he would have restored Kant's transcendentalism beyond anything Kant had ever dreamed of (namely, a grasp of the totality of history): he would literally have transformed the accidental into the necessary—now, unlike Kant, with his eyes open. (I take this, I should add, to help us understand the unnecessary inflation of Hegel's discussion of "contradiction.")

Hegel remarks (in the *Encyclopaedia Logic*—in effect, ironically)—that

> one of the main points of view in the *Critical Philosophy* is the following: before we embark on the cognition of God or the essence of things, etc., we should first investigate our faculty of cognition itself to see whether it is capable of achieving this. We should first get to know about the instrument, before undertaking the tasks that are supposed to be accomplished by means of it; for, otherwise, if the instrument is inadequate, then all further effort would have been expended in vain. . . . But the investigation of cognition cannot take place in any other way than cognitively; in the case of this so-called tool, the "investigation" of it means nothing but the cognition of it.[38]

It may be fairly claimed, in the spirit of this passage, that Kant never examines the transcendental "tool" (his prototype) perspicuously, though he believes he has. But then, in what sense does Hegel succeed?

What Kant does is assume, as necessary a priori, certain synthetic truths determinative of empirical knowledge that, on their face, are profoundly contested, distinctly counterintuitive, impossible to confirm without knowledge of the noumenal world, undeniably committed in some measure to a source of privileged knowledge that Kant explicitly rejects, paradoxically confined within the interior (subjective) "space" of consciousness or self-consciousness (as an essential part of a transcendental argument designed to ensure a viable form of empirical realism), and conceptually intolerant of any alternative approach to the analysis of the conditions of objective knowledge.[39]

Kant equivocates (egregiously) on the "externality" of objects; his account of the causality of what is "given" (in some phenomenologically acceptable sense) in experience is ineliminably tinged in a noumenal way; and the "act" of the understanding said to account for "the unity of apperception" is unable to explain why objectual unity can never (in principle) be admitted to be given in experience (in accord with the doubtful claim of passivity and without confusing noumenal and independent "things").[40] Here, Hegel, like Charles Peirce, whom he influenced but perhaps not in this regard, emphasizes the "resistance" of the real world—Peirce's famous notion of "Secondness," which Peirce takes to be a rational (abductive) intuition rather than a metaphysical criterion or an a priori confirmation of what is actual and which he believed (early in his career) Hegel slights.[41] Kant manages his own argument rather poorly here.

If all this is true, then Hegel's worry about the incoherence of Kant's great effort to secure, by essentially subjectivist means, a perfectly viable form of empirical realism is amply justified. For, in confining empirical knowledge to "appearances" (as Kant puts it), we may as well say (with Hegel) that what are initially "given" are the "appearances-of-objects" (*Erscheinungen*)—in a sense of "externality" Kant would have regarded as noumenal but Hegel treats as merely innocent of privilege ("apparently existent," if I may suggest Hegel's intent). There's the difference between Kant's vestigial phenomenalism and Hegel's robust phenomenology. Transcendental representations are neatly replaced by phenomenological presentations—presuppositionlessly.

Secondness is a phenomenologically plausible clue to the independent existence of material or materially qualified "things": not, of course, a reliable criterion in itself of actual independence or of the actual properties of particular things, but a distinctly apt clue nevertheless for animals like ourselves conceived within an evolutionary continuum and a seeming dependence on the resources of a material world. We find ourselves spontaneously responsive to what (in, say, Peirce's sense) we abstract and idealize as a practical or heuristic "principle" of Secondness in a world interpreted in various orderly semiotized ways (not unlike what Peirce has in mind in terms of his "principle" of Thirdness: again, not in any determinately criterial way). What I insist on, here, is no more than the bare plausibility with which a Peircean view of how to construct an account of our discovery of the objective world, fitted for prediction and technological control as well as for coherent causal explanation, may be roughly reconciled with something akin to Hegel's account of what is phenomenologically "given," presuppositionlessly. The conjecture is remarkably straightforward and free of Kant's apriorism.

Kant failed to provide a proper sense of (independent) "objects" suitably contrasted with the problematic standing of their abstracted "appearances"—even if (1) we concede appearances that are the indissolubly intentional "appearances-of-objects" (reportorially indexed within subjective consciousness), and even if (2) the realist perception and empirical knowledge of independent objects depend on experiencing the "appearances-of-objects" (perhaps better: "things-appearing-to-us") in the first sense (just given). The equivocation and its resolution are decisive for Hegel but plainly lost in Kant.

Hegel goes further, since he completely disallows Kant's notion of transcendental necessity. As far as I can see, there is no fixed necessity in Hegel, beyond the minimal necessity of deductive logic; and even there, semantically, the analytic and the synthetic are never finally fixed in any uniquely interpreted sense. Broadly speaking, Hegel's dialectical logic is the "logic" of an encultured intelligence "discovering" its way (informally) through the need to "negate" the seeming truths of evolving history: its "necessities" are, then, continually relativized to the habituated practices of a given ethos. I conclude from this—many would disagree—that there cannot be anything like a canon for what, rather adventurously, Wilfrid Sellars (recently seconded by Robert Brandom) counts as "material inference."[42] Peirce's "abductive" logic is closer to the spirit of Hegel's vision. I don't mean to deny that we must rely, ineluctably, on something like material reasoning and "abduction": that is, even where science and philosophy remain essentially informal (which I take to be the nerve of Hegel's lesson regarding historicity). But here, we arrive at another strong discovery affecting the future of analytic philosophy, particularly where it admits the need to come to terms with Hegel. Material inference, I should add, seems to be inherently conjectural, heavily context-dependent, often concretely restricted to singular circumstances, more ad hoc than systematizable, intuitive rather than rule-bound, fickle in response to fine changes of detail, and largely collected as obiter dicta—though helpful, nonetheless, in assessing consensual reliability among informal inferences. Possibly, "pragmatic," there, but not in any robustly "rule-bound" inferentialist sense.

One instructive clue has it that "necessity . . . is an *actual* whose contradictory is not *possible*."[43] But even this makes sense only if you add that the "actual" reflects a salient response to what "there is" when viewed in terms of one or another perspectived grasp of the events of our world: the "actual" cannot be finally fixed, therefore; nevertheless, relative to the phase of history in which it is found to be compelling, it cannot be denied either. Dialectically, Hegelian "necessity" is, so to say, the moving "logic" of what we take to be actual in evolving experience. That is, "necessity," ascribed within finite inquiry, cannot be more than a marker for a provisional or heuristic guess at what, impossibly (for mortal investigators), may be found at the end of infinite inquiry. Hence, the proposed "identity" of the necessary and the actual (John Burbidge's reading) holds only at the end of "absolute knowing": it cannot be more than a rational conjecture that what is admittedly "contingent" (in our finite guesses at the "actual") will, in the limit, prove to have captured the actual itself, that is, that "whose contradictory is not possible"!

This is the shortest possible way to understand Hegel's identities between the finite and the infinite, the contingent and the necessary, the accidental and the essential. If you allow the argument, then, plainly, it's impossible to suppose that Hegel's dialectical logic—which trades on these and similar "identities"—could ever yield an effective canon of "material" reasoning (a logic) that could be rightly compared, operationally, with any deductive or any more informal "pragmatic" logic.[44] Hegel's "logic" is essentially holistic; "material inference" is meant, rather, to be an analogue of standard inference—hence, not holistic at all—certainly not in Sellars's sketch of what he means by "material inference."

Here, J. N. Mohanty provides a very useful summary of Kant's very different account of "necessity": "Extensionally, [Kant's] modalities coincide. One and the same thing is possible, actual, and also necessary—possible, when it agrees with the forms of understanding, actual when it agrees with the matter [that is, with what is given in experience], and necessary when it agrees with both."[45] Hence, Kant's counterpart treatment of what appear to be the same concepts is inescapably bound to his own apriorist conditions of the "possibility" of objective knowledge. (That is, of course, as it should be, textually.)

For his part, Hegel is contemptuous of arithmetic proofs and geometric "constructions" presumed (as by Kant) to manifest the unconditional necessity of what is "actual": both (arithmetic and geometry) fail to provide a genuine grasp of the "essence" of things; detached from the evolving whole of reality's process of "self-discovery" (as Hegel puts it), both are "one-sided" and "inessential." Hegel means, first, that Kant's would-be transcendental necessities are merely artifactually contrived, since Kant nowhere demonstrates that the soundness of his own reasoning follows any confirmed transcendental rule; and second, that there is neither a need for unconditional necessity nor a way of approximating to any such necessity when we reason among the endless "accidents" of history. Hegel offers his dialectical logic as a conserving schema for bridging the gap between insuperable contingency and inaccessible necessity, as we are drawn, both practically and theoretically, to the transient saliencies of evolving history.

That is what I meant to flag by contrasting Hegel's "dynamic" and Kant's "kinematic" logics. Hegel's "necessity" is no more than the "contingency" of the past and future effects of *geistlich* influence centered, interpretively, on whatever we designate as compellingly "actual." Kant's corresponding distinctions are "extensionally" identified (as Mohanty says), but they are definitely not subject to the informal oppositions and transformations of evolving history. The dialectic makes its ingenious way, more and more informally, among the extremes of Marxism, existentialism, pragmatism, hermeneutics, phenomenology, relativism, and historicism: that is, in nearly every important current of recent Eurocentric philosophy, except perhaps in the most ambitious pretensions of Anglo-American analysis.

. . .

Hegel's achievement, then, is itself no more than a limited phase of the larger transformation of the evolving conceptual economy that runs from Descartes to Kant to Hegel himself down at least to the diverse "pragmatisms" of our time that share the following constraints: (1) to abandon all forms of cognitive privilege; (2) to oppose all dualisms of cognizing subjects and cognized objects; (3) to reject all necessary, all foundational structures in the analysis of knowledge and reality; (4) to replace the transcendental primacy of subjectivist representations by the presuppositionless, presentational "givens" of phenomenological experience; (5) to historicize all aspects of what we conjecture is contributed to our knowledge of the world from either the "subjective" or "objective" side of their constructivist fusion; and (6) to concede that historicity itself has no determinate or unique telos, no rule of unity, no favored argumentative canon, and no sense of the likelihood of converging toward a closed and finally adequate system of the inclusive categories of objective knowledge.

Items 1–6 count as a reasonably convincing tally of philosophical gains made over the entire span of Western philosophy. I see no other plausible trajectory. Nevertheless, we must admit that none of this comes to terms as yet with other—more "alien"—ways of understanding the problem of knowledge and its correlates regarding the nature of the world: for instance (to press the point in the briefest way) Buddhist or Daoist views.[46]

In the Western tradition, relative to our own time and continuing along the lines just summarized, "progress" is (as I suggest) bound to take a distinctly pragmatist turn more radical than the forms that classic (American) pragmatism ever favored. If, indeed, Kant's fateful innovation and Hegel's critique of Kant are "dialectically necessary" phases of philosophy's "best" narrative, then, faute de mieux, the perceived resolution of the paired problems of knowledge and world must go increasingly fragmentary, parochial, fluxive, historicized, never final or fixed in holist terms, practical, perspective, partisan, agonistic, ad hoc, plural, possibly harboring incompatible and incommensurable options, consensually and informally constructivist, yet realist in intent, and endlessly revisable relative to what is given, evolvingly, in experience.

Kant's great influence springs from the extraordinary ingenuity and resourcefulness of his analysis of subjectivity, not from his ultimate arguments for launching the transcendental venture itself; there is no satisfactory argument from Kant's side that could possibly be compelling, unless it is the dictum itself—a variant, as Hegel realized, of the forms of "metaphysical reason" that Kant rightly dismissed in Leibniz and Wolff but that he also cunningly recovered as straightforward gains made possible by the novel powers of his Critical invention.

By contrast, the source of Hegel's counterinfluence comes from his original conception of the objective processes by which our cognizing powers continually evolve historically and publicly; so that, through dialectical inquiry, we gradually construct a convincing account of the whole of human knowledge and the true structure of the world we claim to know—without invoking any form of privilege or a priori fixities of any kind.

Hegel's language is often hopelessly grand, I admit. But its operative parts are surprisingly spare and informal. Here, for instance, is a passage from the *Encyclopaedia Logic* that is about as direct as Hegel ever gets: "thoughts can be called objective thoughts; and among them the forms which are considered initially in ordinary logic and which are usually taken to be forms of conscious thinking have to be counted too. Thus *logic* coincides with *metaphysics*, with the science of things grasped in *thoughts* that used to be taken to express the *essentialities* of the *things*."[47]

The fact is, the extraordinary innovations that Kant and Hegel first introduced have now, separately as well as conjointly, motivated other compelling innovations of what appear to be variant forms of a deeper, still evolving conception of philosophical work—for instance, Husserl's and Marx's and, in a more hybridized way, Peirce's, Cassirer's, Heidegger's, Merleau-Ponty's, and the Frankfurt Critical movement's—a conception that ultimately depends on a retrospective reading of the opposition between Kant's and Hegel's deepest intuitions, which now count as the polar but inseparable prototypes of a distinctly modern way of reasoning. Slowly, even tardily, Anglo-American analytic philosophy is threading its way back to the same sources.

This still-inchoate paradigm depends in part on Kant's original error (regarding the synthetic a priori) and the entailed failure to advance a transcendental argument to confirm the validity of Kantian transcendental arguments themselves! It also depends on Hegel's powerful grasp of Kant's brilliant failure and his own overly dense replacement of Kant's fixed but disjoint faculties of understanding and reason: that is, by construing reason (as Hegel does) as a conjectured continuum of constructed self-transforming powers incarnate in the flux of evolving history. Hardly any theorist of importance in the past two centuries has ventured an innovative strategy of any kind that is not primarily informed by the contest between Kant and Hegel, unless, as among twentieth-century analytic philosophers, we happen upon innovations that are pointedly "pre-Kantian." Here, I can only say that the argument against any principled disjunction between cognizing and cognized is about as final as philosophy ever gets. (That may be the most settled achievement of Kant's having introduced the "transcendental question.")

I must enter a small aside here, in the interests of clarity. I use the terms "constructed," "constructive," and "constructivist" in two quite different but hardly unrelated senses: in one, "constructive" means "artifactual" (or "hybrid")—in the specific sense in which the self and all things cultural are artifactual transforms of the biological or material; in the other, "constructivist" means "conceptually inseparable"—in the sense in which the contribution of the subjective and objective "parts" of cognitive states cannot be separately assessed. The first draws attention to the cultural dimensions of all forms of inquiry and human intelligence; the second, to the impossibility of outflanking the contingency of cognitive claims. Together, the two senses account for the "constructivist" nature of the realism of science (and metaphysics)—consistent with preserving the distinction between metaphysical and epistemological questions. Hence, constructivism need not, and does not, in the present account, entail the ontic construction of the whole of "reality" itself.

Kant's transcendental project was intended to defeat and displace the dogmatic resolutions of the "rational metaphysics" of Leibniz and the Wolffian school. But the evidence of the first *Critique*'s argument seems unable to dispel the complaint to the effect that Kant cleverly substitutes one dogmatic strategy for another, though he also muffles (as he must) its seeming self-deception. For if the subjective and the objective are indissolubly fused in the "given," then the structure of sensibility and understanding must be inferentially subject to the vagaries of the "given" itself; and, if so, then strict transcendental necessities are out of the question, or else they must go contingent (dialectically) in Hegel's way. (That may, in fact, be the very point Hegel has in mind in opposing any dualistic contrast between "perceptive understanding" and "thinking understanding.")[48] Put another way: the argument shows that there are good internal reasons for faulting Kant's insistence on the adequacy of any subjectivist account of perceptual objects. To accept the fusion of the subjective and the objective *is*, ineluctably, to favor phenomenology over phenomenality *and* to make the transcendentally "necessary" thoroughly contingent! Flux proves more resourceful than invariance. QED. Put another way: Kant defeats the realist metaphysics of the rationalists all right; but, then, he also obliges the "objectivity" of science and metaphysics to depend on transcendental (subjective) sources, and, in doing that, he makes "empirical realism" no more than an artifact of those same *subjective* sources: accordingly, he *cannot* separate, as Hegel can, epistemological and metaphysical constructivism.

Hegel is rather sarcastic about Kant's undertaking here: he mocks him for his barbarous use of "a priori" and "transcendental" as epithets of assured precision—even as he admires Kant's skill. But he certainly says (in no uncertain terms)—a number of times, from somewhat different perspectives—that Kant never completed the labors his own project required. Kant's philosophy, Hegel says,

> made an end of the metaphysic of the understanding as an objective dogmatism [the dogmatism of the rationalists, when he (Kant) favored instead the line of thinking of the empiricists to the effect that "nothing true can be known, but only the phenomenal"],

but in fact it merely transformed it into a subjective dogmatism, i.e. into a consciousness in which these same finite determinations of the understanding persist, and the question of what is true in and for itself [objectively] has been abandoned.[49]

Hegel then adds—it's worth a small aside:

Kant does not follow up further the derivation of [the table of] categories, and he finds them imperfect, but he says that the others [that is, other subsidiary categories] are derived from these. Kant thus accepts the categories in an empiric way, without thinking of developing of necessity these differences from unity [in effect, the unifying function of self-consciousness]. Just as little did Kant attempt to deduce time and space, for he accepted them likewise from experience—a quite unphilosophic and unjustifiable procedure.[50]

Hegel's complaint—an extraordinarily apt indictment—anticipates the objection that Strawson presses, which converges with the sense of Fichte's intuition. But its distinctive power lies in its simplicity and in that simplicity's being embedded in Hegel's competing vision. Neither Strawson's nor Fichte's alternative can make a convincingly comparable claim.

Hegel is absolutely lethal in exposing the paradox at the heart of Kant's solution; he says, summarizing Kant:

The matter of perception is only what it is in my sensation. I know of this sensation and not of the thing. But . . . the objective which ought to constitute the opposite of this subjective side, is itself subjective likewise: it does not indeed pertain to my feeling [sensibility], but it remains shut up in the region of my self-consciousness; the categories are only determinations of our thinking understanding. Neither the one nor the other is consequently anything in itself, nor are both together, knowledge, anything in itself, for it only knows phenomena—a strange contradiction.[51]

There's no escape for Kant: the argument is conclusive. Hegel means, of course, that (contra Kant) it doesn't make sense to speak of knowing phenomena (subjective appearances) without at once providing for the cognition of perceivable things, that is, the actual objects of which, at whatever level of experience we acknowledge, appearances are the appearances-of-something (*Erscheinungen*): appearances cannot, otherwise, be coherently admitted in whatever is phenomenologically "given" (whatever may be reported as given) without presumptive privilege of any kind. Kant's "objects" (*given*-in-experience) are never more than the internal accusatives of *subjective* experience itself: internal artifacts yielded somehow as the effect (in experience) of the use of the categories of the understanding applied to the passive scatter of what *is merely sensory*—in short, the putative "unity of apperception" (as Kant would say) that nevertheless falls entirely within the bounds of self-consciousness. Hegel is at his best here.

This is but another way of asking Kant to demonstrate that he's earned the right to claim that his transcendental strategy validly recovers the objective standing of the empirical sciences. There's a transcendental argument missing: namely, the one that would have shown us precisely how and why Kant's argument succeeds! According to Hegel, Kant never rightly surpassed the limitations of the "metaphysicians" of reason, though he showed the way.

. . .

I can now offer a quick sense of the genuine effectiveness of Hegel's dialectical logic—in terms drawn from contemporary sources congenial to analytic philosophy: the two clarifications I have in mind go a great distance toward offsetting the widespread impression that Hegel's logic is a mad joke of some sort. What needs to be shown is, first, that if we invoke Kant's transcendental reasoning, the synthetic a priori will prove to be an a posteriori projection that captures, for an uncertain interval, something closer to, and no stronger than, what is "necessary" according to Hegel's dialectical logic—certainly not the strict necessity that Kant requires; and second, that the first sort of necessity is, according to Hegel, the work of an "objective" rather than a merely "subjective" Idealism (à la Kant), that is, an Idealism applied to whatever is never more than passively or subjectively "given" to consciousness or self-consciousness in sensory terms.

Hegel regards the application of dialectical logic as rounding out the full implications of having construed human knowledge as ideally unified with respect to any and all the accidents of history, as "absolute" in intended scope and meaning, entitled therefore to objective standing across all pertinent disciplines. In this sense, dialectical "necessities" answer to whatever, among the acknowledged modes of cultural objectivity (art, religion, philosophy), yields its provisional, "material," interpreted counterparts of the uninterpreted, formal necessities and contradictions of deductive logic— never more than heuristically drawn from the contexts in which they are first encountered, constructed, and reconstructed, therefore, in accord with evolving experience or history, along intuitive, free-wheeling, plausible, enabling lines, cast in terms of progressively inclusive rational (*vernünftig*) "negations" and "negations of negations" in the direction of "absolute" knowing. Hence, the sui generis "necessities" of dialectical speculation need never violate (however they may question) the operative scope of any formal canon that would doom them (the former) to being no more than subordinate, entirely contingent, merely rhetorical instruments.

They *are* more than forms of rhetoric, however: namely, a run of exemplary "inferences" of an informal sort that, from different domains, appear to endorse the persuasiveness of material (interpreted) discourse; that rely on the historicized fluencies of their semantics but present their arguments in the guise of something like an abstracted syntax (which they could never yield). Dialectical "necessity" is, then, an honorific distinction: not inapt or arbitrary, to be sure, but never formal or algorithmic in any canonical sense. Its logic is opportunistic, analogical, or figurative: it informs our most reasonable "pictures" of what (according to our lights) to count as candidate "actualities." Where it is compelling, it draws on saliencies that are already somewhat in vogue and influential, though always in a way that might also yield along lines that advance new possibilities of conceptual linkage, as if in support of fresh hypotheses that need not be quite ready for inductive testing. The argument does not require any literal-minded Idealist metaphysics, and no true contemporary mind would find its "logical" concatenations objectively "necessary." (A cognate concession is required for Hegel's use of "contradiction" and "negation." These terms signal emphatic, if provisional, endorsements of conjectured "pictures" of what is actual or real.)

Hegel's Idealism signifies no more than the inseparability of metaphysics and epistemology: in effect, the stable adoption of Kant's transcendental question (qualified one way or another to disallow Kant's own transcendentalism). It does not require that reality be the construction of any human mind or minds (or of any larger Mind). It is primarily a constraint on how we picture (or should picture) objective reality, on the condition that knowledge is itself a construction from unprivileged phenomenological *données*. Thus construed, Idealism is entirely compatible with naturalism: I would say compatible even with a metaphoric characterization of causal or functional or other forms of order or nomologicality or the like viewed (somehow) as the "plan" of some Mind in nature writ large (as, somewhat congenially, also extravagantly) in Peirce's well-known (Schellingian) remark that nature is "effete mind."[52] (I cannot see that this commits us to anything like Anaxagoras's doctrine. But if it did, I personally would find the entailment arbitrary and therefore inadmissible.)

What Hegel demonstrates, therefore, is that contingencies of the historical or *geistlich* variety support an interpretive discipline that never pretends to grasp (or need) the impossible rigors of Kantian transcendental necessity or a realist reading of "absolute Idealism" at its absolute limit. (Of course, Hegel abandons the idiom of the "transcendental" because he rejects Kant's subjectivism.)

There is no entirely formal way of validating the provisional "necessities" of Hegel's dialectical conjectures without admitting their inherent contingency, their reliance on the consensually perceived saliencies of societal life, their fragmenting diversity beyond Hegel's overly sanguine confidence in the uniquely encompassing legibility of history, the (metaphysically) determinable but not strictly determinate meaning or significance of whatever belongs to the historical flux, and their ineliminable threat of paradoxicality.[53]

Hegel himself is aware that he must, for instance, overcome the potential scandal of admitting the "logical" (and "ontological") viability of propositional contradictions in the ordinary pursuit of dialectical reasoning. Some sort of conceptual trickery may be needed here: call it philosophical ingenuity, if you will. My sense of the best efforts to "save" Hegel requires (1) a plausible limitation on the scope of Hegel's use of "contradiction" (which Hegel signals); (2) an interpretive transformation (both logically and ontologically) of would-be "contradictories" as "contraries" (or logically benign oppositions) at some lower (say, sensory or experiential) or higher level of propositional dispute (articulated contradictories) capable of being endorsed as yielding reconcilably "partial" aspects of what, infinitely or absolutely, is, finally, said, in Hegel's idiom, to be self-identical: *Geist*, perhaps, or God or Objective Thought (which Hegel defends in his *Science of Logic*); and (3) a mythic rationale (Hegel's Objective Idealism) of the dialectically invented telic fulfillment of the infinite task of pure thought (or thinking) grasping itself. I find none of this entirely hopeless, except (perhaps) the ultimate Idealist pretension (which Hegel may be prepared to betray after he's mustered his own brief) that *Geist* has truly grasped itself (according to his instruction)!

In any case, constructivism is hardly abandoned, and of course (for epistemological reasons) it remains bound to what is "given" phenomenologically; but then it is no longer subjectivistic, transcendentalist, representationalist (in Kant's sense), fated to achieve any final closure. Its "realism" lies, rather, with what the unending process of reason can afford, improvisationally, as it freely judges (according to its interests: improved predictability, conceptual coherence, and the like) how best to proceed in the way of superseding its apparent contradictions, inflexible conceptual truths, fixed categories of description and explanation, and premature telic conviction—read always in terms of its finite revisions of its transient pictures of the infinite ("absolute") end of inquiry. I find it impossible to call any naturalistic pared-down version of this sort of objectivity anything but pragmatic or pragmatist—in a sense that would invite a very natural comparison with Peirce and Cassirer.

To see the force of these "corrections" is to see that we must go beyond Hegel as well: first, by confirming Hegel's critique of Kant, and then, by grasping the leaner possibilities of Hegel's own strategy. We must, for instance, canvass the limited innovations of figures such as Marx, Dilthey, Heidegger, Jean-Paul Sartre, Dewey, the Frankfurt Critical School, Foucault, and (let me now add) Thomas Kuhn and Richard Rorty: that is, figures drawn to the hermeneutic force of Hegel's material reasoning, who are more or less disposed to tolerate even the rhetoric of necessity.

In short, what Hegel counts as the quasi-formal "necessities" of cultural self-understanding is little more than whatever is judged to contribute to its own sense of the objective standing of its own findings. These cannot be more than constructed, historicized, informal, contingent, fragmentary and transient, diverse and oppositional, consensually and provisionally confirmed, and superseded in the fullness of time.

Seen this way, Hegel favors little more than a carefully crafted sequence of dialectically narratized "moments" that are made legible by the continual interpretation and reinterpretation of the interminable accidents of societal life (in which they are incarnate) as entrenched "contradictories" collected as such and then "sublated" as the serial manifestations of the unified "thought and being" of a mythically nominalized—infinitely encompassing—intelligence (*Geist*) absorbed (according to Hegel's fiction) in understanding its own evolving career. Think of this (lightly, if you can) as a canny late replacement for Aristotle's first philosophy, one in which the biological (Aristotle's biology) is absorbed within the cultural, rather than the other way around.

The model is a metaphor, and the metaphor's a pretty one, though hopelessly misleading and much too contrived. But its interpreted "necessities" can hardly be more than whatever "actualities" are found to be consensually favored over *la longue durée*. Hegel's vision is more than a heuristic myth, since science is itself encultured; but it is also far less than a straightforward discovery, since dialectical reasoning is a partisan's discipline. It utterly lacks predictive or technological tests; it captures no more than the evolving, self-satisfying inertia of the apt forms of self-understanding. Perhaps Hegel saw no other way to capture the "essence" of the actual. Why not accept it as it is? It's the nerve, I would say, of Eurocentric "pragmatism," at a depth of analysis that captures, but cannot be captured by, the abbreviated American version.

Turn then to the first of the two final lessons promised. Hilary Putnam has recently thrown fresh light on the strategic peculiarities of so-called conceptual truths—viewed against the backdrop of contemporary disputes about the analytic/synthetic distinction. Putnam's remarks would make no sense at all if construed in Kant's apriorist terms—except, of course, as a telling critique of Kant.

Putnam is keen to outflank W. V. Quine's and Rudolf Carnap's accounts of the analytic/synthetic distinction; but, succeeding there, he obliquely undermines the central tenet of Kant's entire Critical venture. For he demonstrates that Euclidean truths (for instance), deemed necessary to the analysis of what is actual (rather than confined to what is merely conventional or at least distinguished from the empirical), must be relativized to the evolving history of what we report we can conceive. A historicized logic, let us admit, cannot accommodate any fixedly a priori truths. Viewed in Hegel's terms, which Putnam appears to tolerate but does not discuss, dialectical "necessities" are interpretively tethered to what (passingly) we take to be "actual" in our experienced world; but what is actual in this sense is itself changeably so favored from within the changing continuum of what is merely "possible"—which, for its own part, alters (evolvingly) our sense of what may yet be actual. What *that* makes possible may not (on Putnam's account) have been "conceivable" before.

"Conceptual truths," then, constitute an important subset of the defining conditions of our perceived stock of conceptual possibilities: they provide a perfectly reasonable sense in which the "contingent" and the "necessary" are treated (humanly, rationally, historically) as "one and the same"—without yet violating any of the usual constraints of conventional logic that we normally concede.

Putnam sketches a remarkably simple clue by which to join the resolution of the florid epistemological and metaphysical puzzles of Kant's transcendental and Hegel's dialectical logics and the sparer semantic puzzles of the analytic/synthetic contrast. What he demonstrates, I suggest, is that neither issue is a purely formal one; that they are inseparably joined and inseparably resolved; that they are, finally, one and the same; that the definition of the "rules" of logic, themselves embedded in real-world discourse, are not (by any means) the work of a purely formal discipline; and that the analysis of knowledge, the linchpin of any viable realism, is inherently informal, holist, not in the least arbitrary, and never more than constructively fitted to the evolving course of the history of the executive concepts embedded in both Kantian and Hegelian puzzles.

I take this to mean that, however problematically managed, Kant's great discovery of the internal duality of the unity of the subjective and objective aspects of knowledge is, even today, the most decisive "conceptual truth" of modern philosophy; although, contra Kant, it cannot serve as such, unless transcendental necessities yield in the direction of dialectical necessities. (Which is to say: Hegel trumps Kant; but in doing so, he trumps himself.) "Necessity" goes rhetorical when it is historicized—when it goes practical, when it responds to the demands of the here and now, when it turns pragmatist in its tolerance of the transience and diversity of our metaphysical schemes.

Here, then, is Putnam's answer:

> What makes a truth a conceptual truth, as I am using the term, is that it is impossible to make (relevant) sense of the assertion of its negation. This way of understanding the notion of conceptual truth fits well with the recognition that conceptual truth and empirical description interpenetrate; for when we say that the denial of a certain statement makes no sense, we always speak within the body of beliefs and concepts and conceptual connections that we accept, and it has sometimes happened that a scientific revolution overthrows enough of those background beliefs that we come to see how something that previously made no sense could be true.[54]

Putnam's example is drawn from Bernhard Riemann's discovery of the coherence (and applicability) of a non-Euclidean geometry in which triangles can exist "whose angles add up to more than two right angles." No more need be said about this: conceptual truths (in Putnam's sense) cannot accommodate any merely formal (or fixed) disjunction between analytic and synthetic truths. Putnam was obviously aware of his Hegelian affinities: the example shows the sense in which the logical status of the pertinent assertions Putnam has in mind can indeed be made to change under the conditions of an evolving history. There you have an absolutely decisive count against the Kantian venture and in favor of something closer to Hegel's logic. I find it perfectly convincing to think of the analytic/synthetic puzzle as a prime example of the need of a logic close to the spirit of Hegel's dialectical logic. But if so, there would be no reason to suppose it would take any simple, singular, or formulaically syntactic form. But it also means—and this has not been adequately grasped in the analytic literature—that the resolution (say) of the dispute between Quine and Carnap regarding the analytic/synthetic distinction and the logical positivists' "empirical" refutation of Kant's transcendentalism are ultimately grounded in the puzzle of historicity: hence, they require *some* accommodation of Hegel's critique of Kant. In that sense, all the arguments introduced at the very beginning of this account are already addressed to the deepest inquiries of analytic philosophy. That has to be admitted. (But no one would easily concede that Quine was a Hegelian in analytic dress!)

The second lesson, eked out textually, is also easily drawn. John Burbidge, probing a distinction already introduced, offers a compellingly plausible reading of the "necessity" Hegel ascribes to valid judgments in accord with his dialectical logic. Here is a much abbreviated summary of what (in an already abbreviated way) he offers (reading Hegel):

> Necessity is an *actual* whose contradictory is not possible. . . . An actual is whatever is; a possible is that which is not self-contradictory; and what is necessary is anything which is in fact actual. It would be self-contradictory for anything that is to be other than what it is. Therefore, if it is, its contradictory is no longer possible. . . . An actual is something that exists; and its possibility is articulated in a set of existing conditions that ground its existence. Any one condition by itself is only an element of its possibility, and requires the others in order to be sufficient. But when the set of conditions is complete, the actual must come to be. . . . The necessity [of the actual] is thus relative.[55]

Because, of course, what evolves as "possible" may then defeat what may have earlier been perceived to be "necessary." (Here, I must admit, I find Kuhn's notion of a paradigm shift gliding into view behind Putnam's disclosure.)

This is indeed a soft analogue of Putnam's stronger claim. Moreover, as soon as you sense the ease with which the would-be necessity of any proposed "actual" can be outflanked, you see why dialectical reasoning must go completely informal if it is to anticipate the provisional and piecemeal in accord with opposed interpretations of what is actual.[56] Nevertheless, the eclipse of Hegel's penchant for an all-encompassing narrative of history cannot but weaken even further the inflexibilities of the Kantian system. We cannot possibly return to a Kant whose categories are not historicized.

I must add a final clarification to ensure a suitable measure of closure. I'm recommending that Hegel's notorious dictum about "contradiction" be read in the rhetorical spirit Hegel favors—that is, "dialectically," in the service of his account of how, in historied terms, we arrive at a reasonable picture of the actual or the real. Paul Redding reports Brandom as construing Hegel as "*affirming*, rather than denying [the law of non-contradiction]." He also notes that Graham Priest, the well-known champion of "paraconsistent" logics, "applaud[s] Hegel for his percipient views about logical systems capable of *tolerating* contradictions." He himself acknowledges, textually, that, at the very least, Hegel defends the "law of contradiction," which needs to be carefully contrasted with the "law of non-contradiction"![57] I find myself prepared to support all of these views, though I'm persuaded that there's a much more informal, more convincing, rather lax way to read Hegel's doctrine, without risking any loss of rigor or textual fidelity, or philosophical scruple, for that matter.

In his *Science of Logic*, for instance, Hegel actually formulates the "Law of Contradiction" as follows: "*everything is inherently contradictory* . . . [it's a] law [that] expresses . . . the truth and the essential nature of things. . . . Contradiction is the root of all movement and vitality; it is only in so far as something has a contradiction within it that it moves, has an urge and activity."[58]

Certainly, the "Law of Contradiction" is *not* the same as the "law of non-contradiction" and need not violate the latter; and certainly, Hegel's "law" is meant to entitle us to interpret seeming "contradictories" (or oppositional distinctions)—whether with regard to the logic of terms (say, à la Aristotle) or of propositions or judgments (à la Gottlob Frege or Kant)—as incompatible (in thought or reality), as predicatively inconsistent, or as propositionally contradictory, or the like—as yielding, provisionally, partially, passingly, perspectively, and otherwise, limited but pertinent information to be collected that, at a "higher" level of rational reflection (*Vernunft*), may contribute to a more rounded picture of what to regard as closer to what is true about the world. Hegel offers a number of examples of what he means, for instance: "External sensuous motion itself is contradiction's immediate existence. Something moves, not because at one moment it is here and at another there, but because at one and the same moment it is here and not here, because in this "here," it at once is and is not. . . . Motion is *existent* contradiction itself."[59]

How can there be any concern about Hegel's threatening the principle of non-contradiction? Brandom is safe enough in his conjecture: Hegel supports non-contradiction; Priest is entirely within his rights to enlist Hegel as an ally, but he must have better allies; and Redding ventures far beyond what the traffic requires, though it's useful to have his careful review of a more sprawling literature. All in all, I can't see that Hegel's account of contradiction can be counted on to lend much in the way of support for Brandom's "Hegelianized" or "Sellarsian" pragmatism—along the lines of "material inference," say. Hegel's own emphasis is obviously focused on the historied *déroulement* of fresh (unsorted) information about the world we claim to know, it's very likely that much of what he brings together ("inferentially," if you like) is bound to be distinctly conjectural, quite informal, fitted (as far as possible) to supporting the most trusted coherences of what we've already collected. The very idea of searching for a "canon" that would make explicit what is "implicit"—roughly, rules embedded in human practices, "as [so to say] a generalization written in flesh and blood, or nerve and sinew, rather than in pen and ink"[60]—is, at an obvious level of expectation, already too easy to count as inferentialist. Certainly, we have inferences here, but whether we also have an unacknowledged set of inferential rules ("inferentialism" in a suitably sturdy sense) is hard to say. I don't find a strong enough clue of what to look for, in either Sellars or Brandom, to lead us beyond (say) what Peirce and Dewey have already (with both Hegelian and Darwinian credentials) informally suggested.

All this, I suggest, defines an inchoate pragmatism that runs largely unseen beneath Kant's and Hegel's respective strategies—the deeper project of the paradigm they share that has barely been acknowledged in analytic philosophy as it is acknowledged in pragmatism and continental thought.[61]

2

Rethinking Peirce's Fallibilism

I TURN TO CHARLES PEIRCE AND JOHN DEWEY, to recover the "Hegelian" spirit of classic pragmatism. The entire movement, so bafflingly scattered by the divergent impulses of its original voices, came very close to exhausting all its energies by the 1940s and 1950s. Revival, as I read the minor skirmish between Richard Rorty and Hilary Putnam, which unpredictably restored the academy's interest in pragmatism's deeper promise, signifies (for me) the need to reexamine what Eurocentric philosophy achieved in the interval spanning Kant and Hegel that was caught up by figures like Peirce and Ernst Cassirer (see Chapter 1).[1]

The history of the Eurocentric movement from the middle of the eighteenth century to the first decade of the twenty-first (the range of what I call "modern" modern philosophy) seems to me to have moved only a little beyond the epistemological and metaphysical puzzle of the relationship captured in the realist/"Idealist" unity confirmed so insistently by the entire post-Kantian sequel. I take the trauma of World War II and its aftermath to have led the best energies of late-twentieth-century thought into a kind of stunned impasse—too often a merely futile, excessive, largely contrived repetition of the best energies of the philosophies of the first half of the century. As a consequence, certain latent themes in American pragmatism remained largely neglected until they were effectively revived (according to my tale) in taking up again the promise of the post-Hegelian theme of historicity and the post-Darwinian theme of the artifactuality of the self. That, as I've briefly noted, is what I believe to be of decisive interest in the unforeseen convergence between Peirce and Cassirer, important spokesmen of two kindred but very different movements.

I don't believe Hegel is quite the "post-Hegelian" that the pragmatists need; nor is Darwin the "post-Darwinian" they need: the trick is to spell out a reading of both Hegel and Darwin that accords reasonably well with the lengthening reception of their own themes, defended (first) in terms of separable doctrines—the historicity of the human world and the artifactuality of the self—that grow stronger in the *post*-Hegelian and *post*-Darwinian world and are plausibly traced back to Hegel's and Darwin's original texts. I'm opposed, that is, to "genealogies" read in terms of a supposed search for the true meaning of the original texts, though I find it terribly important to assess just how plausible it is to read both figures in a way congenial to what, on the argument I'm deploying, suits the best philosophical fortunes of current pragmatism and late Eurocentric philosophy as a whole. How reasonable is it, for instance, to read Hegel as capable of yielding to a naturalistic interpretation hospitable to pragmatist undertakings without merely abandoning a proper sense of his distinctive rigor and invention? I've offered a sketch (in Chapter 1) of "how to read" Hegel in accord with the liberty I'm taking—in an effort to understand the historically construed philosophical gain by which, say, Peirce and Cassirer may be regarded as "Hegelianized Kantians." I don't believe there's any prospect of arriving at any uniquely correct reading of either Kant or Hegel (or the German Idealists); I think the entire inquiry of the period was construed by its own principal players as a profound thought-experiment in which they themselves were quite willing to revise their own commitments as the lengthening debate turned up fresh options; and I think the essential mark of any distinctly *philosophical* interest in a now-contemporary recovery of their perceived best insights rests with arguments of just the sort I mean to examine here. In that sense, we ourselves "belong" to Kant's and Hegel's philosophical world and they belong to ours.[2]

If I may put my intuition somewhat mysteriously at first, I would say that Peirce was captured very early by an inchoate insight of considerable grandeur, which he labored to master throughout most of his career. He succeeded incompletely and in an awkward way—one that saved his puzzle for a better version of his own solution but that misled some of his most devoted readers. The answer to his puzzle, the heart of fallibilism, must go through Kant and Hegel, though probably not as perspicuously as it might have—if it goes in the way Peirce actually contrives. I find the clue to a better explication in Cassirer's more up-to-date reflections on the history of physics post-Kant and post-Newton, which could not have been easily caught by Peirce in his ailing years approaching the discoveries of early-twentieth-century physics; and yet, though I don't pursue the alternative more than a little—sufficiently to assure ourselves that Peirce and Cassirer were on to the same discovery—Cassirer really does help us understand Peirce's larger pragmatist motivation in a way that (to my mind) suggests the promise of a rapprochement of all the strongest currents of Western philosophy; and yet, ironically, Cassirer himself retreats at the last moment in a (failed) attempt to salvage Kant's untenable disjunction between causality and freedom, which none of the pragmatists would ever have accepted, with or without Peirce's solution to his fallibilist puzzle.[3] There would be no point to bothering, after all these years, were it not for the fact that pragmatism has proved so extraordinarily attractive, philosophically, in our time, for just this reason.

I owe you a more explicit clue regarding what I'm up to, here. I take Peirce's fallibilism to be the fullest vision of the master themes of classic pragmatism: not always perspicuously rendered, as I expect you'll see, but unfailingly focused on the conditions of realism fitted to the endless inquiries of the sciences. That is Peirce's abiding theme: the link that catches up the "Hegelian" cast of the pragmatisms of both Peirce and Dewey, which took form, in Peirce, even before he was explicitly aware of his attraction to a good number of Hegel's notions and which captured something of the direction of post-Newtonian physics even before Heinrich Hertz's innovative reflections appeared—which, in turn, profoundly influenced Cassirer's improvement over Peirce's pragmatist approximation of the "infinite" continuum of inquiry applied to the radical changes introduced by relativity and quantum physics in the opening decades of the twentieth century—that is, shortly before Peirce's death.

I find a very clear narrative thread here that permits us to salvage Peirce's master theme beyond his own extravagances, in much the same spirit (if you can believe it) in which, currently, attempts are under way to save Hegel from his own extravagances: pragmatism is, prospectively, the leanest naturalistic mode of inquiry, hospitable at once to the sciences and practical life, that hews closest to Hegel's fundamental critique and continuation of Kant's innovations shorn of apriorism, to the realist/Idealist import of the thesis of the infinite continuum of scientific inquiry, *and* to the further innovations, now already seriously delayed, that may (and need to) be enhanced (by pragmatists) by conjoining the essential lessons of Hegel and what, independently, has been made of Darwin's and post-Darwinian inquiries. There's the new theme of the evolving trajectory I have in mind, spanning the decisive sources of pragmatism, its essential achievement in its classic phase, and what now is possible and required if pragmatism, no longer restricted to its original gropings, ought now address in our globalized world, in order to fashion a rounder vision of its principal contribution. (Bear this in mind, please, as the argument proceeds.)

All the best currents of recent Western philosophy seem to me to allow themselves to be redirected along these lines, however inexplicitly. I see very little else of comparable promise and power. But to concede the point is to reread our Eurocentric issues in a global spirit able to escape the older hegemonies. It was, of course, Kant's mishandling of pre-Critical representationalism (Locke's theme, for instance) that obscured the strategic importance of the very different benefits yielded by embracing the opposition between realism and *i*dealism and by acknowledging the new unity of realism and *I*dealism focused in Hegel's critique of Kant.[4]

The clearest evidence of how difficult it has become to disentangle the two sorts of pairing can be drawn from a close reading of Max Fisch's well-known pioneer essays regarding Peirce's "progress" from nominalism to realism with respect to predicative generals and, thereupon, from a comparison between Hegel's and Peirce's systems. Fisch's influential verdict—to the effect that Peirce abandoned "idealism" (effectively, subjectivism) for "realism" (some sort of objectivism)—decided the matter for a great many pragmatists, without ever explaining how the resolution of the first issue (countering nominalism) could, when separated from Peirce's analysis of the laws of nature, have had more than the slimmest bearing on Peirce's adherence to the unity of "realism" and "Idealism." There's a serious lacuna in Fisch's argument regarding Peirce's larger realism.[5] Remember: Peirce's metaphysics, like the nerve of German Idealism, entails the inseparability of realism and Idealism; Peirce was not a realist *and* an Idealist, though he presents himself in both guises.

The finding I favor is not so much the reverse of Fisch's judgment as it is the larger claim that Peirce saw no viable disjunction in pressing the realism of science and the need for an Idealist metaphysics: for he believed that it was *only* within the terms of his Idealism that the realist thesis would prove compelling at all. In short, Peirce was committed to the inseparable unity of what (quite misleadingly) have been separately called realism and idealism—that is, *not* any disjunctive choice between a very differently defined "realist" and "Idealist" metaphysics. He held a view that could only be drawn from initially united *relata*: he was not a realist *and* also, independently, an Idealist. He would have found that option incoherent. (He held a view that had no separate name—unless it was fallibilism.) But I have no wish to deny that Peirce's Idealist flights may have been needlessly extravagant—indeed, they were: for instance, in the well-known pronouncement that "matter is effete mind." If, as seems more than reasonable, *that* banner must be Schellingian or/and Emersonian, the Idealism Peirce vouchsafed was tethered to whatever he required regarding the continuum of finite and infinite inquiry—which also bears on Cassirer's "Marburg" union of realism and Idealism (respecting the sciences). To grasp the point is to see the permanent contribution of Kant and Hegel continually strengthened and reinterpreted down to our own day.

This, then, is the leanest précis I can offer of the argument that follows. Its best strategy—which I endorse, but which I cannot claim the great German Idealists ever explicitly adopted—holds that, for one thing, we must, as realists, replace representationalism with some form of constructivism; for another, we must, again as realists, avoid characterizing reality as itself constructed (apart from the Vichian sense in which the cultural world is "made") and hold instead that what we construct are only conceptual "pictures" of what we take the real world to be, which have their own heuristic or instrumental value for that reason (in a sense not unlike that of Wittgenstein's notion of the use of "pictures," in the *Investigations*); and, for a third, we must acknowledge that the realism thus achieved is itself cognitively dependent on, and embedded in, our constructivist interventions.

Alternatively put: to admit this latter sort of Idealism is to retire the idiom of the determinate and disjunctive options of realism and idealism favored (for debate) in the heyday of analytic metaphysics, as in P. F. Strawson's empiricist reading of Kant's first *Critique* and G. E. Moore's would-be refutation of Kant's Idealism.[6] (There's the source of much of the verbal confusion, in Anglo-American analytic circles, about the right way to read "realism" and "Idealism.") In *this* sense, Peirce is the seminal pragmatist of the Eurocentric narrative. Dewey favors many of the benefits of such a way of co-opting Hegel (as in *Experience and Nature*), with or without endorsing Peirce, but never, except marginally, by venturing his own reading of the realist/Idealist knot. On a Peircean reading (though not Peirce's),

Dewey gains conclusions without committing to their enabling premises; on his own reading, he abandons the exhausted vocabularies of academic philosophy (that is, the disjunctive reading). But if all this is fairly inferred, then the insistent disjunctive reading of Peirce's "realist" commitment regarding science and inquiry (for instance, Cheryl Misak's, as, also, Fisch's) misses the essential agon.[7]

As we shall see, this double thesis—namely, (1) that realism and Idealism form a single, indissoluble doctrine in Peirce's metaphysics, and (2) that accordingly, a pragmatist test of what is true about the world is itself mediated and interpreted (to that end) by our best "pictures" of however confirming evidence and explanatory theory are deemed to be objectively matched—cannot fail to affect, decisively, any tenable account of Peirce's realism. I give fair notice, here, of this important complication early in my argument, because its bearing on the prospects of otherwise very strong "realist" readings of Peirce's own doctrine characteristically ignore its force. It draws, of course, on the affinity between Peirce's line of reasoning and that of Hegel's, but the pertinent details need to be correctly assembled.

I begin, therefore, with another bit of indirection that brings us back to the essential nerve of "modern" modern philosophy: at the very least, the inseparability of realism and Idealism (however minimized) in the Eurocentric tradition.

. . .

In an address before the Charles S. Peirce Society (2003) and in other writings, Nathan Houser examines some questions I've posed about pragmatism's future:[8] specifically, the difference between Dewey's and Peirce's contributions and, in particular, the merit of a suggestion of mine to the effect that "Peirce's doctrine of fallibilism is a linchpin of his philosophy." Houser favors the more usual view that what Peirce called synechism might prove a likelier linchpin. I see no reason to object; but the fact is, Peircean fallibilism entails the doctrine of continuity and extends it to the "outcome" of infinite inquiry. Synechism does not require the fallibilist addition, and it's really the role of what is "fated" at the infinite limit of inquiry that marks what is most puzzling and novel in Peirce's theory.[9] By synechism (or synechism informed fallibilistically), Peirce intended a regulative principle "of philosophical thought" that construes generality (or generalization) in terms of a rule of continuity modeled on a "true [mathematical] continuum"; Peirce regards the resultant generality as harboring a kind of transcendental *ouverture* in which well-formed hypotheses are open in principle to infinitely extended testing (6.170–173).[10] The thesis entails a version of the doctrine of the unity of realism and Idealism that I've just introduced. It's in this sense that I treat fallibilism as Peirce's "linchpin": I have no wish to deny the immense scatter of Peirce's arguments. ("Linchpin" does not signal a closed system of any kind.)

I am doubly bound to answer Houser, because in answering I answer Fisch's charge as well. But I answer opportunistically: because Peirce cannot be shown to be a realist or Idealist in the usual disjunctive sense; because, in decoding Peirce's deliberately laid false leads, we understand the point of his subterfuge; because pragmatism's effectiveness depends on outflanking any such disjunction and arriving at a deeper picture of our inquiries into truth and reality; and because we are made to see the inexorability of constructing one or another successor to Kant's problematic transcendentalism, successors that abandon all pretense regarding the sufficiency of any finitist conditions of objective science.

Viewed this way, Peirce's fallibilism is a remarkable demonstration of how Kant's insistence on the necessary closure of his transcendental system exceeds the resources of its original purpose; hence, then, it deflects us from discerning how Kant's mistake may (and even must) be corrected. Here, Peirce is as effective in righting the account as any post-Kantian Idealist— as effective as Hegel, say, except for the telling fact that, like Hegel, Peirce *is* (and plainly declares he is) an Idealist, responding to the validity of Kant's original question qualified by Hegel's charge: very much (though with a noticeably different answer) in the same sense in which the question confronts Cassirer.[11] Without Peirce's contribution, we might never grasp pragmatism's "advantage" correctly.[12] Nevertheless, in gaining that advantage, we may be willing to replace Peirce's extravagance with a leaner correction.

Actually, I've come to an even more controversial reading of Peirce's fallibilism than I offered earlier (in the original paper that Houser reviews). I now count it as the true nerve of Peirce's entire output: present, then, in the earliest of his published papers as well as in the characteristic metaphysical speculations of his most mature work. Without displacing the earlier reading, the new proposal catches up Peirce's grand sense of the equivocal possibilities of science's finite grasp of the whole of reality. I would myself yield (here) in the direction of a benign skepticism or, perhaps better, a carefully fashioned relativism. Peirce favors instead a metaphysics of Hope. In relying on Peirce's early formulations, I think we must concede that the textual links to Hegel are somewhat uncertain. Those linkages were clearly strengthened after Peirce's sustained exchanges with Josiah Royce (the full significance of which, quite frankly, I'm unable to gauge). But the Idealist thesis itself seems (to me) to run through Peirce's entire oeuvre—possibly, then, to an original reading of Kant not (at first) indebted to a direct reading of Hegel's texts.

I capitalize "Hope," then, to flag the fact that Peirce does not intend "hope" in any merely mental or psychological sense: he prefers a rational or abductive doctrine ("Hope") that we can live by—that is, a reason that, at its best, justifies us in construing, as "real-independent-of-our-beliefs," what, in finite inquiry subject to the indissoluble unity of the subjective and objective in phenomenological experience, we treat as real in a sense *not* independent of our beliefs! Here, the first sense of "real" presupposes Hope but *not* evidentiary confirmation; and the second entails a limited form of finite confirmation but not independence from our beliefs—a fortiori, *not* independence from hope (as in Dewey) or a finite commitment to Hope (as in Peirce). This is my clue regarding what Peirce should have held—and may actually have held. (Many would not agree.)

If I'm right, there should be at least three independent foci in accord with which some form of Idealism is ineliminable: first, the point at which the first sense of "real" (which presupposes Hope) depends on the second; second, the point at which any appeal to Hope is inherently "Idealist" (because it exploits an infinitist expectation); and, third, the point at which the would-be confirmation—that's too strong a term; perhaps better: the rally of conviction in any regard that does not presume to draw on actual infinite resources—serves to define what we take to be "true" and "real" (to be thus "fated") only at the end of infinite inquiry: hence, only under the finite auspices of Hope. The only pertinent Idealist option that is not *un*avoidable in advocating a realism along post-Kantian lines is any variant of the doctrine that holds that the whole of reality is, or includes, a "Mind" or "*Geist*" that yields or generates or is the source of the emanation of the whole of physical nature and human life—which thereby partakes of the being of that Being.[13] Naturalism must, of course, abandon any literal reading of *Geist*.

Peirce's Hope precludes Cartesian certitude and cognitive privilege, because whatever we imagine may be accomplished in infinite inquiry cannot be assuredly accessible, evidentially, in finite inquiry. There is no literal approximation to the infinite end of inquiry: there can only be a rational Hope that we are coming closer. That is the point of Peirce's *ouverture*: the rejection of any methodological progressivism that can, quite literally, be brought to a determinate end. This is the shortest explanation of the reason Peirce cannot secure a realist doctrine separable from Idealist constraints: he believes realism cannot be confirmed on finitist grounds; though we may have reason enough (he adds) to treat selected beliefs in a realist way. (Effectively, canonical realism can be obliquely accommodated, though not in its own voice.) Even the methods for ascertaining what to regard as true in finite time are subject to changes that may exceed any finitely assignable limit. Peirce and Cassirer effectively agree about this. Variants of this argument constrain any and all modern epistemologies that admit the pertinence (the infinitely open-ended pertinence) of Kant's a priori question (without admitting apriorism itself). Post-Kantians can no longer fall back to Kantian or pre-Kantian options: anyone who would dispute the finding must answer the arguments (against Kant) that construe the a priori as an a posteriori posit within an endless history. Remember: Kant's a priori speculation is meant to respond to a contingent moment in the history of science (at the very least).

That *is* what I take to be the import of Peirce's fallibilism, though it's also true that Peirce presents his doctrine "officially" as a strong form of self-sufficient realism. Hence, when I say that Peirce fails to validate his fallibilism, I mean he's aware that he cannot isolate the (merely) "realist" reading of his fallibilism so that *it* can be validated; though his argument does indeed favor securing the realist aspect of his larger doctrine. He does vindicate his fallibilism in the sense of the Idealist reading of *its* realism; but that would never satisfy contemporary "realists" who invoke "realist" and "idealist" (read to include Idealist) options disjunctively—in something like the pre-Kantian sense—believing (erroneously) that the disjunction applies as well to Peirce's discussion of *his* realism within the space of his discussion of Idealism.[14]

The post-Kantian sense of "what is" or of what is "real" makes it easy to distinguish between the noumenal (which answers to nothing that can be known to be real) and what is known to be real in some mind-independent way: the latter, I say, is *not* independent of our beliefs (in cognitive regards); it makes no sense to deny that we believe (for good reasons) that we sometimes (indeed, often) encounter what is (ontologically) independent of our beliefs. But that's also the master theme of post-Kantian Idealism: what is determinately real in the Idealist sense presupposes the ability of a cognitive agent to discern the fact. Nothing, there, *requires* that the real world must be constructed by human agents: what *is* constructed is one or another picture of the world. When Hegel, for instance, assimilates the realism of the world to the "self-discovery" of Absolute (or infinite) *Geist*, we pragmatists must unpack his rhetoric naturalistically. The inclusive holism of Absolute Knowing is, in the human sense, infinitist: a rational myth, an article of Hope.

This is an extremely complicated matter that reverberates through the whole of the post-Kantian Idealist movement. I emphasize particularly the ease with which it exposes contemporary forms of scientific realism to the charge (too late in the telling) of favoring one or another form of noumenal self-deception of just the kind Kant had already handily defeated. But it also defeats Kant's utterly indefensible representationalism, as Kant's famous letter to Herz makes clear; it thereby signals the need to explain how we establish the realist standing of our conjectures about the real world. I trust it helps to say that to secure *the reality* of what is metaphysically independent of any opinion need not be epistemologically independent of any such opinion. Peirce himself remarks that "Reality is an affair of Thirdness as Thirdness, that is, in its mediation between Secondness and Firstness."[15] But, of course, *that* means that Peirce's *realism* is a constructivist posit supported in terms of what we rationally Hope holds true at the end of infinite inquiry. Here, Peirce and Hegel hold similar views. But you cannot fail to see that Firstness, Secondness, and Thirdness are very unreliable categories when applied criterially.[16] That is, Peirce simply permits any "firsts" or "thirds" he is impressed with to count as (yielding) "seconds"! He fits his trichotomous schema to his scientific and philosophical tastes: he does not test them first—he cannot—in any directly accessible way. Particular experiences are phenomenologically avowed; conjectured generalities are subject to abductive Hope.

Peirce's charm lies in his unique ability to bring into final order all the conflicting possibilities of a finite science in search of the benefits of an infinite inquiry. The final vision seems to be demonstrably "rational." Nathan Houser fixes on certain textual matters in challenging what I take to be the ineliminable paradox of Peirce's fallibilism, a paradox fatal on any canonical reading of his "realist" pronouncements—but otherwise benign. I'm persuaded that I must meet Houser's objection; though, truth to tell, Houser advances thoughts of his own that are distinctly favorable to my reading of Peirce but are nevertheless not prepared to allow the argument to rest on the strength of my original textual source.

Nevertheless, there's a perfectly straightforward explanation of the seeming infelicity Houser remarks, which, once rendered, actually strengthens my reading of Peirce—in both its earlier and now-intended sense—and collects the spreading significance of Peirce's fallibilism even more tellingly than before. I apologize for the infelicity: Houser's is a fair objection, and the infelicity (a minor matter) is entirely my fault. The correction needed—and offered—recovers without loss or revision the whole of the original claim and restores the relevance of the paradox by way of a closer look at the context in which the original citation appears. The argument shows convincingly that Peirce couldn't have supported, consistently, the extreme realism he's often assigned—and provocatively claims for himself—*and he knew it*. More than that, what Peirce concedes (in order to remain consistent) weighs on us as well: the "success" of fallibilism requires the "failure" of a disjunctive reading of realism and Idealism. (The point of the dispute still waits to be spelled out.)

My view is that Peirce was well aware that he could not disjoin the realist and Idealist aspects of his fallibilism but was reluctant nevertheless (possibly in recruiting public and professional support) to permit himself to appear in a seemingly compromised or paradoxical position. The fact remains that the rejection of the disjunctive option is far stronger, philosophically, than the adoption of either disjunct. The matter is of the greatest importance in simplifying the lesson of the innovations spanning the work of Kant and Hegel; so that the rapprochement of Eurocentric philosophy and the advantages expected to accrue by embracing historicity and the artifactuality of the self are put at risk by Houser's challenge, though that was never Houser's intent. The puzzle has been with us since Kant's *Critique* and Hegel's correction: as we shall see, Houser's worry makes it possible to gain a better grip on the matter by the smallest possible labor. There's the nerve of the correction needed.

The only pertinent resource Peirce could have drawn on would have been an a priori maneuver: *not* transcendentalist in the Kantian sense, which Peirce effectively outflanks, but an "instinctive" or "mythic" intuition (as I prefer to say), an abductive guess that cannot be evidentially confirmed, that conveys no more than a rational Hope, which Peirce ingeniously applies to the cosmos. Textually, all of this would count as a very small quarrel. But it bears in a strategic way on gaining a correct reading of Peirce, on appraising the resources of pragmatism, on the inseparability of "realism" and "Idealism" in the inventive work of post-Kantian constructivism (which pragmatism inherits and which affects the prospects of the whole of twentieth-century philosophy). The infinitist idiom helps us understand the impossibility of reaching any rational closure on truth and knowledge within the limits of finite inquiry. There's the point of Peirce's heroic contribution—pragmatism's radical reading of the transcendental question: the effective vindication of the "infinite" openness of the categories of finite understanding, an anticipation of what an adequate conception of what the endless evolution of modern science requires.

Houser honors the fact: it's the point of his concession regarding Kuhn. But he doesn't acknowledge that the literal correction he offers (against my reading) masks a deeper qualification on Peirce's part: a qualification embedded in the very context Houser recovers in the interest of strengthening the extreme realist position Peirce deliberately claimed as his own—which (I'm convinced) Peirce meant to be read as if it were a scientific finding (of a finitist sort), *not* therefore drawn from the *infinitist* extension of the encompassing continuum of inquiry to which, indeed, it rightly belongs. (Note, please, that synechism would not free us from the Idealist encumbrance.) Quite a muddle.

I assure you that all the answer that's needed falls into place very naturally: it's hardly a mystery, and it explains why Peirce's theory is so baffling, and so original, and how and at what price the imputed paradox is made entirely benign—*not* in a way that would make Peirce out to be the unyielding realist he took such pains to claim he was, the thesis theorists such as Max Fisch supposed eclipsed his earlier "idealism" (Idealism) around the 1890s. We cannot escape the Idealist's "infinite" extension if we accept a constructivist account of (scientific) realism under the condition of history. (Think of Cassirer and Kuhn—apart from Peirce.)[17] Would that signify that Peirce failed or succeeded? Well, perhaps a little of both. You will have to be the judge. The point of the labor lies in the dawning sense that Peirce's seemingly idiosyncratic speculation shows its true force as we approach the possibility of achieving a productive rapprochement among the principal divisions of Eurocentric philosophy—reunited by rereading the constructivist theme shared (in very different ways) by Kant and Hegel. Proceeding thus, we glimpse again the courageous frailty of one of pragmatism's most distinctive claims.

. . .

The discussion of Peirce's fallibilism, all must agree, has been remarkably slack—baffled, really—for all the attention it's received through the 150 years in which Peirce's grand output has been dissected. Progress here calls for a touch of daring, a risk (frankly) in favor of a seeming contradiction among uncertain readings, where much of the would-be confirming evidence is bound to be meager, tentative, equivocal, conspiratorially *zweideutig* (ambiguous) in the service of an evolving vision (Peirce's own) that could never (finally) afford to choose between one or the other of two seemingly competing claims—with disjunctive confidence. Too much, it might be thought, would then depend on mere accidents of argumentative advantage within a debater's space: gains too easily stalemated by the next opportunistic turn of evidentiary data. Peirce was clearly aware that his own largest regulative conjectures could never claim the secure fixity, universality, necessity, indubitability that belonged to Kant's transcendentalist apriorism—which he himself not infrequently co-opted in a verbally lax way. (That is to say: in spite of his admiration for Kant.) Of course, there's reason to believe that Peirce never sought to recover any such fixity—and neither should we.

Here, Peirce's argument becomes deliberately muddy—courageously lax, let us say—since it must find a way of controlling its infinitist needs within finite limits, without explicit contradiction and without abandoning the continuum of the long run. Peirce will not allow himself to be defeated here, but he "adjusts" (as much as he dares) his rationale of what to count as evidence along abductive lines (itself a continuum), so that there is no assured demarcation between what, as in the empiricist tradition, are sometimes distinguished as "past futures" and "future futures." (Think, here, of Hume and Bertrand Russell.) To his credit, Peirce never falls back to apriorism or privilege.

For instance, in a short paper, "Immortality in the Light of Synechism," submitted to the *Monist* in 1893 (but never published), Peirce offers a provocative list of some very large metaphysical options: "*materialism* is the doctrine that matter is everything, *idealism* the doctrine that ideas are everything, *dualism* the philosophy which splits everything in two. In like manner, I have proposed to make *synechism* mean the tendency to regard everything as continuous." Of the latter, he adds: "I carry the doctrine so far as to maintain that continuity governs the whole domain of experience in every element of it. Accordingly, every proposition, except so far as it relates to an unattainable limit of experience (which I call the Absolute), is to be taken with an indefinite qualification: for a proposition which has no relation whatever to experience is devoid of all meaning." Yet, speaking of this qualified thesis, which he applies to his well-known speculation regarding immortality (and which, in turn, entails, on his own account, the suggestion of a metaphysical continuity among distinct selves), Peirce refuses to probe further, saying only that he will not go "into the extremely difficult question of the evidence of this doctrine."[18] But he's already introduced his *Allgemein*, his "everything"—his rational Hope that penetrates every phenomenon.

We are entitled to some telling findings here: for one, none of the options mentioned (a fortiori, no others of the same gauge) can be taken to be true a priori; for a second, each seems coherent enough, and sufficiently "related" to "some" range of experiences, to be able to be shown to be true or false or "continuous" with what may be supposed true or false; for a third, none would be open to adequate empirical testing if it were construed as restricted, disjunctively, *either* to some infinite run of experience (the "Absolute") *or* to some strictly delimited run of mere accidents ("phanerons"); and, for a fourth, if philosophy were occupied with (and actually capable of) appraising the evidence for any of these (or similar) doctrines (the ones Peirce has enumerated, above), then philosophy would rank very high indeed among the *sciences*, because it would then concern confirming (in some measure) the "possibility" of one or another of the "special" sciences that are called on to apply the constitutive or constructivist constraints of these and similar doctrines to various circumscribed sectors of the experienced world. Thus, in the important 1903 Harvard lectures, Peirce straightforwardly declares:

> I have already explained that by Philosophy I mean that department of Positive Science, or Science of Fact, which does not busy itself with gathering facts, but merely with learning what can be learned from that experience which presses in upon every one of us daily and hourly. It does not gather new facts, because it does not need them, and also because general new facts cannot be firmly established without the assumption of a metaphysical doctrine; and this, in turn, requires the cooperation of every department of philosophy; so that such new facts, however striking they may be, afford weaker support to philosophy by far than that *common experience* which nobody doubts or can doubt, and which nobody ever even *pretended* to doubt except as a consequence of a belief in that experience so entire and perfect that it failed to be conscious of itself.[19]

Here, Peirce explicitly identifies philosophy as a "high" science—a pragmatic *a posteriori* variant of the Kantian *a priori*—empirically testable in principle when applied to any finite run of experience; but also, obviously, still supportable when generalized (in accord with abductive Hope, within "common experience") so long as we are clear that the infinite long run cannot be equated with any closed run of finite tests. It's here that Peirce affirms that

> Philosophy has three grand divisions. The first is Phenomenology, which simply contemplates the Universal Phenomenon, and discerns its ubiquitous elements, Firstness, Secondness, and Thirdness, together perhaps with other series of categories. The second grand division is Normative Science, which investigates the universal and necessary laws of the relation of Phenomena to *Ends*, that is, perhaps, to Truth, Right, and Beauty. The third grand division is Metaphysics, which endeavors to comprehend the reality of Phenomena. Now reality is an affair of Thirdness as Thirdness, that is, in its mediation between Secondness and Firstness.[20]

But, if the last doctrine is true, then, in one sense, what is real is strictly construed as independent of all thought and, in another sense, what is real is determined only in accord with the infinite conjectures of rational thought. Its determination makes sense, finally, only in terms of the fulfillment of "a rational experimental logic" infinitely pursued. But if *that* is so, then what is real cannot be actually confirmed (or approximated) empirically—because no conjecture about what (finally) "is," is free of abductive Hope: "the state of things which will be believed in that ultimate opinion [which, 'for the most part . . . will be general'] is real."[21] This particular scruple (essential to Peirce's Idealism and close to Hegel's Idealism, spanning the *Phenomenology* and *Encyclopaedia Logic*) never stopped Peirce from construing numerous (perfectly ordinary) experiences *as* "firsts"— feeling (pain), for instance, or perception (as of a color)—that present themselves *as* "seconds" and thereby become open to being interpreted *as* "thirds" (that is, *as* "real").

It's here that Peirce remarks that "phenomenology studies the Categories in their forms of Firstness."[22] But, surely the so-called universal categories *are* universal—infinitely applicable—only because they are as labile as you please and cannot really be falsified empirically. Correspondingly, the "singular" events of feeling and perception (or dreaming or believing-true) are (also) "real" (in Peirce's lax phenomenological sense) *as* (at least) what we are unwilling to disavow.[23]

The informality of Peirce's apparatus answers at times to the definition of the "phaneron" (or "phenomenon"), the supposed datum of phaneroscopy (or phenomenology), itself the most basic division of philosophy viewed as a positive science: Peirce says he uses "the word *Phaneron* as a proper name to denote the total content of any one consciousness (for any one is substantially any other), the sum of all we have in mind in any way whatever, regardless of its cognitive value."[24] It seems clear from this (and Peirce's subsequent remarks) that the trichotomous schema is simply fitted heuristically, ad hoc, to the data rather than being independently confirmed. Nothing is gained by treating (indissoluble) "firsts" of this sort as "real" qua the "seemings" that they are affirmed to be, since what they purport to be, as real (for instance, a pain felt in one tooth when its source proves to be in another, the seeming perception of a dagger suspended in the air when it proves to be a hallucination, one's believing to be true what proves to be false), requires investigative strategies that, in principle, involve would-be laws and pertinent generalities that implicate the continuum of the finite and the infinite and the interlocking unity of the phenomenological categories themselves. I see no way to override these caveats. Constructivism in cognitive matters cannot escape the historicity of thought or the continuum of the finite and the infinite or the sheer "givenness" of seemings: to say that our *vernünftig* or Idealist conjectures are "confirmable" is to say (with Peirce—and, I believe, with Hegel) that confirmation (in any plausible sense) entails a measure of transcendental (or abductive) Hope. But then, empirical realism cannot be adequate in itself; or else, empirical realism is *itself* inescapably colored by infinitist Hope! (Also, let it be noted, Peirce hints here at the imperfect separability of individuatable persons: a kind of naturalistic "improvement" of Hegel.)

Peirce understood perfectly well that the universality of his phenomenology—in particular, the ontic status of the categories of Firstness, Secondness, and Thirdness—was always, by design, more regulative than constitutive, though it was never meant to be merely heuristic. The phenomenology was never thought to be separable from the barest accidents of reportable perception and experience (as opposed, say, to anything like the pretensions of Husserl's pure phenomenology or Kant's doubtful reliance on the powers of transcendental analysis). It was also never meant to be more than dialectically compelling through the continually tested course of evolving experience, perhaps the single most plausible article of foundational regularity that abductive Hope could ever boast: stronger (in Peirce's eyes) than what he disdained as Hegel's ramshackle logic, certainly a better reading of categorical closure than Kant's apriorist speculation on the conditions of science—an account more modest and more scrupulous by far than either of those very grand undertakings. But it's the "scientific" standing of Peirce's phenomenology that remains troublesome.

My suggestion is that all the deliberately attenuated "continua" spanning the finite and the infinite, grounded in phanerons—Peirce's closest match to Hegel's *Erscheinungen*—support the idea that we must fall back to an indissoluble, ultimately informal, perhaps even inchoate resource of experience more fundamental and more lax than anything that could be articulated as the disjunctive doctrines of realism and Idealism. Given such a finding, it remains entirely open to Peirce to plead realism or Idealism by turns, wherever his rhetorical needs lead. The Peircean realists of our day (Fisch and Misak, most unyieldingly) have probably mistaken Peirce's clever rhetoric for an explicit metaphysics. I think we must consider that Peirce's fallibilism is meant to explain just why we *cannot*, post-Kant and post-Hegel, fall back again to any separate realism or Idealism; hence, also, why Dewey's fallibilism commits us, conformably, to something close to such a verdict, without conceding the need to champion Idealism again. In any case, such a phenomenology may be the sine qua non of any pragmatism that concedes the robust standing of Peirce's questions about the choice between realism and Idealism (which Dewey avoids engaging). It needs to be remarked emphatically, however, that though the "realism" that Peirce comes to favor over nominalism shares common ground with the "realism" he was convinced could not survive being disjoined from a descendant form of Kantian Idealism (historicized—"corrected"—by Hegel), the two doctrines are not close enough to permit the first to assume the burden of confirming the validity of the second. The common ground shared concerns the reality of "possibles," which at any given moment of emergence may not be actual, may in time become manifest (and yield further possibles). But this of course affords an additional insight into the baffling idea of infinite inquiry: what may be "tested" in infinite inquiry may not as yet have been possible to test in *any* finite extension of practical inquiry! (Fisch, I believe, does not take up the question.)

Let me add that, as with most of his fundamental notions, Peirce's phenomenology affords two very different kinds of claim, even where they seem to serve one another: on the one hand, they are cast as the work of some fledgling or neglected science under the usual condition of fallible experience; on the other, they gather the largest "instinctive" or abductive intuitions about infinite inquiry that guide the finite work of particular sciences. This is certainly how the categories of Firstness, Secondness, and Thirdness are presented. I linger a little on these details because they strengthen the sense in which Peirce could not possibly have favored a disjunctive reading of realism.

This is not to speak of "two Peirces"; the contrast signifies, rather, two very different kinds of claims that cannot be validated by the same method or "science." Here, I remind you of a characteristic caution in Peirce's 1890s *Monist* papers (which include "The Law of Mind" and "The Doctrine of Necessity Examined"), which seem (to me) to press something of the contrast I have in mind. Peirce says: "Try to verify any law of nature, and you will find that the more precise your observations, the more certain they will be to show irregular departures from the law" (6.46). Peirce means to disallow attributing such irregularities to error alone; he thinks they signify a deeper source in reality itself; and, running with that idea, he is (nevertheless) inclined to invoke a seeming invariance, necessity, universality and the like, of just the kind we've just seen he disallows. To speak of "continuity" here is to equivocate over finite and infinite continuities. The objection bears directly on the problematic realism of exceptionless laws of nature and constitutes a pons for pragmatists. For, of course, read literally, "infinite inquiry" signifies an indigestible paradox. Correspondingly, abduction takes two very different forms: one fitted to deduction and induction in finite inquiry (often read as the remarkable power of proposing fruitful hypotheses), the other cast as certain persistent "Hopeful" intuitions that guide the largest direction of our inquiries but cannot be tested in any evidentiary way, except negatively (that is, as never actually failing).

Peirce, I would say, was instinctively committed to a cosmic flux out of which arise, benignly, the potentially conflicting grounds and claims of realism and Idealism, of truth and the postponement of assured truth relative to human inquiry, of the final lawfulness of the natural world and the indefeasibly brute presence of originating chance, of closed conditions of intelligibility and the endless improvisation of human understanding, of cosmic teleology beyond Darwinism and human constructivism that invents its own evolving telic narratives, of the temptation of seeming invariances and the problematic interplay of Secondness and Thirdness, of the separability and inseparability of mind and matter.

All such oppositions evolve from the selfsame source, flourish without any need to achieve exclusionary resolution or overcome the deepest interpretive divergences on the way to self-consistent unity. But the options tendered are not usually submitted to the same critical methodology:

they are already bifurcated choices at a deeper level of reflection. *That*, I suggest, is, at least roughly, what Peirce's fallibilism comes to—that is, what it brings into focus.

I find it impossible to resist the idea that Peirce provides (here), in the most oblique way imaginable, an extremely lean interpretation of Hegel's *Encyclopaedia*—the *Encyclopaedia Logic* in particular. (This may be my own fancy.) But broaching the idea permits me to acknowledge that the distinction between realism and Idealism does not require, as the canonical distinction between realism and idealism surely does, a principled disjunction as well. If you ask, then, why Peirce persists in his extravagant metaphysics, the answer must feature the advantage of joining in one doctrine (fallibilism) (1) the seeming tendency of finitely observed regularities in nature to approach lawlike fixity only asymptotically; (2) the realist Hope, supported by such discoveries, that governs our practical life best; and (3) the realization that the paradigmatic rationality of science rests on a similar continuum of finite and infinite inquiry, which no finite strategy could possibly confirm against the threat of chance and existential doubt. Fallibilism is an argument against transcendental closure and the need to rely on cognitive demonstration.

Dewey, I should add for the sake of a pointed contrast, would probably be as much committed to the flux as Peirce, but he would see it only in the scatter of occasioned observations, not as a compendious pronouncement on the whole of the cosmos itself. Is that agreement, finally, between rival pragmatist temperaments? I think it helps to explain the sense in which Peirce appears among us as a sort of transplanted German Idealist, whereas Dewey appears to be in perpetual flight from his Idealist origins; all the while the pragmatism of each betrays an undeniably Hegelian-inspired novelty that neither would be willing to admit without strenuous correction. We seem to have, here, a mixture of two kinds of findings that do not belong together as disjunctive choices of any kind.

I shall come back to the contrast between Peirce and Dewey. But, for the moment, may I suggest that Peirce's "Hegelian" theme centers on the infinite long run and its importance in producing an adequate theory of science; whereas Dewey's "Hegelian" theme centers more on episodes within the means/ends continuum (construed in animal terms, in the here and now) within the processes of practical reason and its bearing on the instrumental, often discontinuous nature of theoretical analysis. I think this may account for the prominence of the realist/Idealist issue in Peirce's work and its marginal presence in Dewey's. (You may guess at the gulf between Peirce and Dewey by merely reflecting on how natural it would be to compare Peirce and Cassirer on the sciences and how profitless it would be to compare Dewey and Cassirer conformably.)

Admit this much and it's hardly surprising that fallibilism should be the linchpin of Peirce's sprawling "system." It also begins to explain why Peirce does not fit the disjunctive classification of "realist" and "Idealist" any more than Kant or Hegel.

The deliverances of phenomenology and of what I am calling the "instinctive" or "mythic" reflections of abduction may both be necessary (according to Peirce) to ensure the realism and pragmatist relevance of any would-be objective science (that is, the standard sciences); but the conditions on which they are brought to bear on the work of those sciences does not make *them* convincing sciences in their own right—though Peirce does indeed speak of phenomenology as a "primal science." In an obvious sense, they cannot be disciplined by empirical or transcendental or larger metaphysical constraints; for *they* constitute the most basic "grounds" (of experience) on which depend whatever serve as the data the usual sciences must interpret and apply in arriving at our picture of the world. Think back to Peirce's notion that the "habits" of the original flux of nature might evolve (in an infinitely distant future) into exceptionless laws of nature. Talking about theories of evolution in the context of the sciences and a "scientific metaphysics," Peirce famously affirms that "the one intelligible theory of the universe is that of objective idealism, [the theory] that matter is effete mind, inveterate habits becoming physical laws. But before this can be accepted it must show itself capable of explaining the tridimensionality of space, the laws of motion, and the general characteristics of the universe with mathematical clearness and precision; for no less should be demanded of every philosophy" (6.25).

Here you have the confirmation of the immense gulf between Peirce and Kant, for Kant would have acknowledged the intolerable incoherence of his own argument if empirical realism and transcendental idealism proved incompatible (or inadequate to their respective functions) within his encompassing system: the logic of "rational instinct" (abduction, let us say, at its most fundamental) cannot, therefore, be the same as the logic of rational apriorism; it is a resource that cannot be captured by any system. (Nothing "in any way or in any sense present to the mind" can be excluded from his phenomenology, Peirce says.) Peirce is certainly an admirer of

Kant—as Dewey is not—but he is not a Kantian or, for that matter, a systematic Hegelian.

Peirce's phenomenology (in much the same sense as Hegel's), whether primal or reported, cannot play a directly realist role in the standard sciences, though whatever serves evidentially in our sciences may be construed as (somehow) constructed (interpretively generated) from what we posit (but cannot possibly test or confirm empirically). Speaking very loosely, then, there are "two" sorts of abductive data: the basic intuitions of reportable phenomenology that appear to conform with the categories of Firstness, Secondness, and Thirdness (which the natural sciences draw on), and our best guesses at what we take to be the nomological regularities of the domains our special sciences investigate. The relationship between these two "orders" of inquiry is never adequately explained by Peirce, though they must be systematically linked. Nevertheless, there is no pristine phenomenological beginning and there can be no "absolute" or infinitely inclusive test of what is finally real. Peirce and Hegel are in agreement here: both orders are profoundly affected by the continuum of the finite and the infinite. What Peirce's argument makes clear is that the transcendental strategy requires a phenomenology; hence, that the Hegelian correction of Kant's apriorism requires the avoidance of phenomenological privilege. But then, though realism remains our best Hope, it plays no part in the confirmation of the laws of nature—precisely because it's no more than an abductive guess. Is that enough for the success of science?

. . .

Houser's principal criticism of my account of Peirce's fallibilism focuses on a "contradiction" I examine in an earlier paper (noted above)—which Houser says appears to undermine the force of my would-be argument—by exploring a textual infelicity in the citation from Peirce that I depend on. This is entirely reasonable, at least as a first pass: *except* that I believe the "contradiction" is important, needs to be explained, and is explained only by a reversal of Peirce's apparent intent. The textual infelicity is no more than skin deep; and Peirce's insistent affirmation of his own strong realism (in the text in question) marks the deeper truth that there, at the same time, he himself subscribes to an inseparable Idealist qualification regarding the same run of experience.

The two doctrines are never more than the indissolubly matched features of the same abductive posits that *we can never directly confirm* in any evidentiary way; Peirce's phenomenology is not a transcendental epistemic resource, but a series of spontaneous, seemingly contingent, interlocking *données* of experience, very possibly qualified by the play of our "rational instincts" (abductions of a sui generis kind) that guide but do not govern in any discernibly rulelike way the work of the working sciences themselves. The discipline of phenomenology is at times, and must be, clinically vague. Furthermore, the very idea of a phenomenology holds the key to the linked fortunes of realism and Idealism.

Perhaps you already see why the contradiction dissolves, *and* why it's a misleading exaggeration to hold (as admirers of Peirce sometimes do) that Peirce was finally a realist *rather than* an "anti-realist" of the Idealist stripe—or, a realist opposed to the realism of the Idealist sort (which the German Idealists considered). I don't believe the mature Peirce was at all uncertain here. It became quite clear to him that it would be a mistake to favor either extreme exclusively. Houser—in his Presidential Address—cites Peirce's important statement on fallibilism (from 1893), somewhat in support (as it turns out) of my own reading: that is, that, as Peirce says: "The first step toward finding out is to acknowledge you do not satisfactorily know already. . . . Indeed, out of a contrite fallibilism, combined with a high faith in the reality of knowledge, and an intense desire to find things out, all my philosophy has always seemed to me to grow" (1.13–14). But, of course, *if* knowledge (fallibilistically construed) implicates an infinite long run, then realism in the abductive sense Peirce requires can never be confined to, or confirmed in, the inquiries of any finite interval of time: it must leave forever open the Idealist possibility—although that option as well can never be shown to be strictly true. Realism and Idealism are, finally, the linked elements of a single construction offered at the infinite limit of inquiry—that is, figuratively[25]—but then, also, as a result, the elements of a constructivism unfailingly invoked to mark the inherent, continuing limitation of finite inquiry.

In effect, Peirce diffuses the force of the "God's-Eye view" of realism in its most extreme (literal) sense by assigning it (if wanted at all) the standing of an article of infinite Hope—hence defeating (if that is the right term) Josiah Royce's arbitrary "absolute pragmatism" at a stroke and freeing himself from any realism that pretended to conflate (and thus resolve) the realist/Idealist opposition by magically embedding the finite world within the world of some assuredly unique, divine, a priori, necessary, actual, "absolute" intelligence.[26]

I take this to be a reasonable guess at what remains valid and viable, if (with Hegel and the pragmatists) we displace the false privilege of Kant's transcendentalism while still conceding the need for "a priori" but not privileged conjectures about how, rationally, we may continue to Hope that finite inquiry approaches truth and reality. That is, finite conjectures about the infinite import of our finite inquiries—abductions—themselves become pragmatist projections assessed in terms of evolving *finite* intervals of inquiry! Truth and realism, then, regarding the fundamental regularities of the world rightly belong (after Kant) to the limit of infinite (unendingly constructivist) inquiry; but they are always caught up in the here and now, in the pragmatist way, by the finite projections of transcendental Hope.

Between the rejection of Kantian noumena and the admission of the necessity of the long run in defining objectivity in science, the expectation of our ever reaching absolute truth in science utterly falters—there are no evidentiary grounds to be culled. Realism cannot be an adequate, free-standing epistemological option if inquiries about truth must be infinitely extended: it requires an Idealist supplement (best, at the present time, a naturalistic candidate for such a supplement). Hegel saw at once the force of the Idealist concession, both in evolutionary and historicist terms, and therefore grasped the fatal extravagance of Kant's *Critique*: Kant had simply gone beyond the limits of what he could reasonably claim, as the history of Newton's physics confirms. In one blow, infinitism defeats all appeals to necessity and apodicticity.

If I understand the argument correctly, Peirce's (and Cassirer's) insistence on an infinitist inquiry is, in effect, a leap beyond anything like the closed system of Kant's apriorist categories of understanding. The transcendental, or any surrogate replacement of its universalist objective, need function only as a tolerant regulative Hope. In that way, causal conjectures within the practice of a science may be nominally satisfied at the end of an infinite inquiry, at the same time any actual hypothesis (advanced under its colors) may be favored on the expectation that, rightly interpreted, it may prove to be instantiated in finite time. Since, on Peirce's view, judgments regarding what is true and real are assigned to what is "fated to be believed" at the end of infinite inquiry, his version of realism is surprisingly in accord with the open-ended nature of the history of science. There may be more perspicuous ways of rendering Peirce's insight than he himself discerned—Cassirer's, for instance—but the options that suggest themselves, including

Cassirer's, are noticeably hospitable to pragmatism (and the main thrust of Peirce's fallibilism).

A significant turn in that direction is already apparent in the work of theorists such as Otto Neurath, Richard Feynman, Thomas Kuhn and Nancy Cartwright.[27] This turn favors a practical reading of lawlike regularities strictly constrained by the provisional limits of effective testability and the interpretive intervention of decidedly artifactual explanatory theories; it moves then to our divergent interests and perspectives and is never committed to the necessity of changeless or exceptionless laws of nature. There's the sensible key to the pragmatist simplification of Peirce's florid doctrine. We cannot recover the assurance of Kant's transcendentalism (which, of course, exceeds its resources anyway). But if we adhere as well to our reading of Hegel's dialectical replacement—if we abandon the telic role of Absolute Reason, the cognitive privilege of *Vernunft*, any of the forms of a rationalist progressivism—we are likely to outstrip the "realism" embedded in the subjective and objective Idealisms that collect Kant and the German Idealists. But who now thinks that any of those options is still viable?

Peirce follows Hegel here but does not quite see the sense in which he does: for instance, he converts the critique of every impulse favoring a closed system—in effect, his fallibilism (especially the themes he calls agapasm and synechism)—into a pragmatist scruple and a courageous joke. But he also has too great an appetite for metaphysical extravagance to let the matter go at that: he becomes entangled in his own web, is tempted to assign his "mythic" themes a kind of shadow realism that he knows to be impossible. So he urges a distinctly rhetorical, a deliberately excessive realism that joins the empirical and mythic "phases" of the continuum of inquiry as a frank expression of his robust but unconfirmable Hope; while, at the same time, he never fails to embed *that* realism in the abductive myths that define his (Idealist) instincts about Truth. And he never confuses doing *that* with drawing on inquiry's sources of finite evidence and finite assurance. Fallibilism, then, is Peirce's way of linking the blindness and opportunism of the here and now of ordinary practice and the grander (finally blind) assurance of a form of cosmic optimism that interprets, but does not actually rest on, evidence—drawn from infinite inquiry.

Peirce might have been led to say that he had "evidence" for his transcendental Hope—that is, for its "rational" adoption. But that would have betrayed the benign trickery of his rhetoric. Shouldn't we say, rather, that Peirce and Dewey converge here in spite of their opposed philosophical temperaments? (Think of Dewey's notion of "warranted assertibility.") And isn't it reasonable to suppose, *post*-Kant (and *post*-Hegel), that the disjunction between the realism of the sciences and the Idealism of the methodology of science can no longer be made out—cannot constitute a serious choice?

I don't for a moment believe that this is the end of the story. Far from it. But it demonstrates how puzzling Peirce's fallibilism really is. For the moment, I wish to confirm only that Houser, who seems to favor the strong realist reading of Peirce (and, in doing so, effectively collects the authority of Fisch's opinion and the realist current of so many contemporary readings of Peirce), actually provides textual evidence for the counterthesis I'm defending and he opposes.

Houser explicitly says *he* believes that the "slightly religious sound" of fallibilism's emphasis on "humility" is probably due to the fact that "Peirce thinks that in joining the quest for scientific truth one must undergo a conversion of a Kuhnian sort and recognize, deeply, that we can only make progress together as a community of dedicated investigators." In saying this, he threatens the anticipated victory of any single-minded realism that we or Peirce could ever hope to vindicate. Think here of Peirce's favorite stage trick of dropping a stone in free fall as a sort of manly confirmation of a no-nonsense realism. (Ian Hacking shares Peirce's intuition.)

I remind you, also, that a Kuhnian resolution would entail something close to Peirce's "contradiction" between the realist and Idealist accounts of inquiry. But a Kuhnian concession would also make it impossible to be a realist in the sense Houser has in mind (and Kuhn originally favored). That is precisely what worried Kuhn and what Peirce resolved in his ingenious way. Certainly, Kuhn was not terribly sure about the compatibility of his own strong form of realism and the import of the severe methodological limitations of the finitist inquiries he analyzes. In fact, he (or Paul Feyerabend) might easily have supposed that the discontinuity of a "paradigm shift" certified the falsity of synechism as a settled element of scientific methodology infinitely extended. You may see in this sort of reflection, as I do, a very strong clue in favor of the idea that contemporary efforts to theorize about the physical "closure" of the universe—convergently subordinated by figures like Peirce, Cassirer, and Kuhn to the infinitist openness of inquiry—effectively confirm the profoundly pragmatist cast of science itself in our own day. (I offer this conjecture in the spirit of reclaiming Hegel's philosophical relevance and daring.)

There is a deeper issue lurking here: one that, in my own mind, begins to collect in a fresh way the converging strands of pragmatist, analytic, and continental philosophy as those strands have evolved after the fateful inventions that span the work of Kant and Hegel. Houser was prescient to suggest the link between Peirce and Kuhn: for Kuhn's discontinuous paradigm shifts *are* very much like manifestations of Peirce's transcendental Hope. That is, *both* answer to the need for naturalistic replacements of the epistemologically excessive pretensions of Kant's transcendental apriorism and the would-be options of his Idealist critics.[28] (But Kuhn, of course, confounds the synechism that Peirce and Cassirer share.)

Think of the matter this way: the fact that the first *Critique* rests on a very doubtful maneuver on Kant's part to justify the apodictic standing of his Transcendental Deduction hardly counts as disqualifying the need for an "a priori" (but no longer privileged) reflection regarding the "grounds" or the "possibility" of a valid science. Once (as with Hegel) you challenge the idea of a (Kantian) science of science, or a privileged knowledge of the nature of knowledge, you see the seamless argument running from Descartes to our own time that demands a "rational" defense of our conception of knowledge—on the strength of which what we regard as the compelling work of the sciences justifies the realist import we impute to what we examine reflexively.

Here, the sui generis nature of our "transcendental" (or "reflexive") inquiries needs to be made clear—against Kant's excessively strong proposal and (by a sort of comic relief) Richard Rorty's postmodernist excesses as well. There *is* a characteristic rigor in these "reflections," which address the question of what it means to say that the pursuit of knowledge and understanding is an entirely *human* affair. I see in this the key to the Eurocentric rapprochement I've been hinting at, as well as to the preparation of that world for the larger global undertaking that is already taking form.[29]

Let me add, more provocatively still, that I don't believe Peirce's advocacy of *any* robust form of scholastic realism (regarding "real generals," that is, generality independent of thought) could possibly be confirmed by known means (6.99–100), though I freely admit that nominalism is either incoherent or hopelessly question-begging. (I don't believe that scholastic realism is our best option here.) I recommend instead a constructivist (third) account of predicable "generals" just as I recommend a constructivist account of truth, knowledge, and reality read as known or confirmed. They're part of the same tale. Notice that Peirce affirms that "Platonic forms themselves have [by evolutionary processes] become or are becoming developed" (6.194). Imagine! Yet that cannot be conceded without making scholastic realism subject to the valid assurances of infinite inquiry that no one can reach (assuredly) in finite time. Thought and, let me say as firmly as I can, *all* of our conjectures are finitely and mortally constrained, even where they are intended to have an infinitist scope. Realism (in both the predicative and substantive senses) is as much an "instinctive" conjecture as is Idealism—*if* Thirdness is as ineluctable (universally) as Secondness is.

Could Peirce convincingly claim that Secondness and Thirdness were genuinely separable phenomenological categories? Could Secondness ever claim criterial standing in the realist sense? I doubt an affirmative answer can be given to either of these questions. Firstness, Secondness, and Thirdness are not reliable universal categories of phenomenological description: they form no more than an informally applied heuristic schema for collecting whatever, pell-mell, we may affirm in affirming the *données* of experience in whatever way we choose; so that nothing (as far as I can tell) need be finally precluded or prejudged. Peirce's schema can claim no categorical closure in the Kantian sense, though it obviously harbors persistent intuitions about the probable order of the world. It collects no inferential rules: at best, it's the expression of transcendental Hope, to the effect that we shall find a way to confirm that the world sustains our animal expectations regarding its discernible order. But the "categories" seem more like heuristic schemata than crisp criteria. Hence, even if you favor Houser's willingness to read Peirce along Kuhnian lines, you cannot possibly eliminate the infinitist reading of the Idealist option; or, if you think you can, you've changed the rules of Peirce's game and left him far behind.

Let me add here (for clarity's sake) that, by "constructivism," I merely mean to endorse the Hegelian correction of Kant's original thesis: namely, that the "subjective" and "objective" sides of our cognitive powers (leading to true and objective claims) can never rightly be disjoined so as to identify their determinate, separate contributions to whatever we suppose counts as knowledge of the real world. In that sense, our picture of objective science (not reality itself) is a constructed conjecture based on how we partition (abductively) the would-be contributions of sensory intuition and the rational structure of understanding extending along a would-be continuum that bridges finite and infinite inquiry. Peirce is aiming at a pragmatist defense of our rational tolerance of an infinitist extension of finite inquiry.

Scholastic realism is a form of exaggerated loyalty to the final teleological theme of Peirce's agapasm, hardly an empirically confirmed doctrine in its own right: it couldn't be. It's fitted rather freely to predicative practices already skewed by telic expectations. It's a risky corollary of an extreme abductive dare that looks for all the world like the findings of a special science, if only we could reach the end of infinite inquiry. So the realism of scholastic realism is no more than a manifestation of a would-be "native instinct" (for generality) that we (say we) capture in all our inquiries: it's equal to the presumption of the supposed "realism" of would-be universal laws of nature, but the two doctrines are not the same.

Scholastic realism nowhere vindicates predicative "generals" independent of human thought: that would require a privileged view from a resource beyond ordinary science. Realism, in Peirce's strong sense, is a rational (and radical) myth, an abductive guess that suits us through the whole of life—that cannot rightly be falsified if explanatory regularity obtains at all. But if there is any one such schema that fits the human condition, it's hard to see that Peirce could possibly be right in privileging it among its alternatives—in opposition, say, to the tolerant conjecture of someone like Houser who's willing to yield in Kuhn's direction. It loses its comparative force because it has no comparative force to risk. How can we measure rational optimism here? (Opportunistically, I suppose; retroactively.) And how implacable can our realist guesses finally be? (Pragmatism hangs in the balance.)

If you consider Peirce's account of the continuum of infinitesimals applied to inexorable scientific progress, you see the circularity at once, just where you see the sense in which Hegel's looser dialectical logic is just as sensible a guess at the trajectory of scientific progress as is Peirce's Schellingian excess.[30] Certainly, it suggests a whole raft of abductive alternatives that he or we may choose at will. Peirce's "developmental" evolution of lawlike nature by way of an overlapping series of soldierly infinitesimals is pretty enough, but it's also naive and mathematically more than ordinarily problematic (see 6.111). Inquiry remains open-ended even in infinitesimal space. Alternatively put: it's infinitude that counts (that is, the open-endedness of finite inquiry), not the extravagance of a continuum of "infinitesimal interval[s]" of perception or experience.

. . .

The force of Peirce's fallibilism can hardly be guessed from any formal sketch of its ordered elements. The concept remains inert—even banal—

until we breathe into any pertinent sketch something of Peirce's exceptional vision. Certainly it provides an analysis of what acquiring knowledge means, and certainly it must be perceived, philosophically, as a distinctly post-Kantian and post-Hegelian proposal. I've advanced the perfectly modest suggestion that Peirce's fallibilism may be serviceably summarized as a set of three "serially nested themes": (1) *fallibility*: that, with regard to any proposition, it is humanly possible to hold a mistaken belief; (2) *self-corrective inquiry*: that, for any mistaken belief, it is both possible and likely that a society of inquirers can, in a finite span of time, discover its own mistake (according to its lights) and move on in the direction of the true state of affairs; and (3) *an enabling metaphysics* (a hybrid union of empirical generalization and infinitist myth) that marks fallibilism as more than an epistemological doctrine and provides a metaphysical ground for epistemological confidence itself.[31] But there's nothing particularly arresting in saying only this; there's nothing yet that distinguishes pragmatism from its Eurocentric cousins: Marxism and existentialism might easily be construed as adopting a variant fallibilism of their own. What *is* important about the addition of item 3, which distinguishes Peirce's pragmatism from Dewey's, is its insistence on an answer that requires accounting for the linkage between realism and idealism (Idealism). Peirce's immense inventiveness is focused there, in his reading of the continuum of finite/infinite inquiry; and yet, as I read the issue, Peirce's answer is altogether different from the usual disjunctive options regarding realism and idealism and depends more on his account of truth than on his "synechistic" account of continuity. That, at any rate, is crucial to my reason for thinking that fallibilism, rather than synechism, is the linchpin of his philosophy.

Peirce's grand thesis, I must warn, has its problematic side; it's risked at its most daring point of entry. Its novel account of truth and reality, by which pragmatism was originally defined, generates a palpable, potentially mortal paradox as a result of two very different readings of item 3 applied to the sense of items 1 and 2; "fallibilism" is, then, Peirce's effort to "resolve" the paradox (not yet completely spelled out) along the lines Peirce (in a fit of pique) came to call pragmaticism. (The term never rightly caught on: Peirce had hoped to establish his proprietary hold on the correct use of "pragmatism," but he failed.) Furthermore, Dewey (as I've suggested) subscribes or appears to subscribe to no more than items 1 and 2 and admits no need and no further ground for cognitive confidence regarding the sciences—no need for versions of item 3. Apparently, no Peircean paradoxes arise for Dewey. (I am persuaded that this cannot possibly be all there is to the best way of distinguishing between the two.)

Dewey's retreat from anything resembling Peirce's conception of truth in the long run, in favor of "warranted assertibility" in any sequence of short-run encounters, is already an economy that risks making no sense if deprived of any sufficiently compensating account of our continuing engagement with the world in the sciences and in other cognitive ways. Peirce's conception is paradigmatically tethered to his attempt to understand, in jointly epistemological and metaphysical terms, what, precisely, we must mean in speaking of the laws of nature among the most advanced sciences. Dewey tends to be much more explicit in spelling out what he is unwilling to support in any canonical treatment of the sciences than in what he actually affirms in the way of a fully articulated alternative proposal. He yields up every formulaic constraint, maximizes risk and freedom, abandons anything like the rules of truth.

Nevertheless, *Experience and Nature*, perhaps the most sustained of Dewey's efforts at fashioning a comprehensive metaphysical alternative, goes some distance in signaling how to displace the standard habit of speaking of well-formed individual substances—for example, Aristotle's settled account of *ousiai*, ranging effortlessly over inanimate objects, animals, and human persons—favoring, instead, an informal treatment of persons as the nominal sites of those dynamic processes and powers that are distinctive of the human form of life (otherwise only loosely linked to the theory of natural kinds, essences, and the sciences themselves). Dewey views human persons as natural histories exercising powers deliberately cultivated and perfected in the characteristically human pursuit of freedom.

This is as clear a clue regarding the difference between Peirce's and Dewey's pragmatisms—and treatments of "truth"—as we are likely to find. In much the same spirit, Dewey's *Logic* abandons the primacy of analyzing the syntax of standard propositional forms and forms of argumentation in favor of grasping the inventive, living powers of fathoming and resolving human problems as, passingly, they arise in the sciences (as in practical life at large). The result is that Dewey has no central need for the notion of the continuum of the finite and the infinite (that decisively links, say, Peirce, Cassirer, and Kuhn—and the original Idealists). He has a very different perception of the open-ended nature of what human intelligence may achieve. But then, Dewey's version of fallibilism is not easily compared with Peirce's and cannot be read merely as an economy drawn from Peirce's undertaking.

My thought, here, is that Dewey features an episodic reading of the means/end continuum—hence, always, the primacy of the play of practical intelligence, viewed in terms of an evolutionary continuity with animal intelligence and the perception of central human problems as transforms of deeper animal needs. Dewey's emphasis, therefore, features instrumentally effective causal continua (discerning "cause" and "effect" as inseparably linked) in suitably contexted "problematic situations," rather than as canonically separable events (in Hume's sense) that may be justifiably linked, as by the discovery of natural laws within the theoretical arguments of a competent science.[32]

The result is a very different, sparer fallibilism that construes the "Hegelian" union of realism and Idealism in a largely episodic way (matching Dewey's instrumentalism); and since it also cleaves to a finitist vision of human inquiry, Dewey's fallibilism replaces the strenuous search for the ultimate unity of the true and the real, by positing the contextual sufficiency of "warranted assertibility" (favoring what is episodically effective in the here and now).

Accordingly, I am inclined to characterize Dewey's fallibilism—with regard to identifying something to match Peirce's item 3—along the following lines: (1) that the indissoluble union of realism and Idealism is replaced, episodically, by the existentially effective (practical) resolution of a "problematic situation," which is itself a humanly accessible, intelligently constructed, cognitive transform of some more fundamentally felt threat to the vital or animal fluency of a human agent's powers; (2) that all canonical categories such as "truth," "reality," "objectivity," "knowledge," "evidence," "proof," "confirmation," "causality," and the like are retired in favor of provisional, finitist analogues drawn from the indivisible process of undergoing, becoming aware of, and resolving actual problematic situations in the here and now; and thus (3) that the replacing distinctions are treated only as provisional *relata* grasped within the episodic holism of the problematic situation itself, which may be thought of as replacing James's blunderbuss account of truth (with James's blessing and a sigh of relief). On this view, "truth" yields to something like the instrumental "adequacy" of any propositional formulation of our understanding of a given "situation" and of our way of resolving it. Truth becomes embedded in an ampler, diversified array of effective ways of meeting the practical concerns of the living creature, not therefore marked for any particular distinction, precision, or methodological rigor of its own. Dewey's emphasis is always on the flourishing and viability of the integral human creature, along the lines of whatever form of life it favors. All other pertinent categories yield along similar lines, so that they are never more than functionally specified within the holist life of organisms. Here, theory is made to serve the singularity, the transient flux, and provisionality of our existential involvements. There are no fixed or universal norms to obey.

Dewey's fallibilism, then, is not meant to disallow our theorizing about the nature of the sciences or knowledge. Nevertheless, theorizing is itself instrumentally dependent on the primacy of existential "situations" that are initially noncognitive: the key lies with the idea that our theories afford "signs or evidence to define and locate a problem, and thus give a clue to its resolution."[33] Thus construed, the analogue that (in Dewey) matches Peirce's indissoluble union of realism and Idealism appears only at the safe remove of its being an instrumental sign, only as the cognitive transform of an existentially endured situation, as an instrumentally validated "picture" of that situation apt (or "adequate") enough to lead to its successful resolution.

Here, the Idealist theme yields, in naturalistic terms, along instrumentalist lines. This may suggest a further line of argument seeking to recover the disjunctive choice between realism and Idealism.[34] But if it does, it must still reckon with the fact that Dewey provides a naturalized, somewhat Darwinian reinterpretation of the same conceptual union (that Hegel and Peirce address) that originally defeated the disjunctive option that the fiercest realist readers of Peirce insist on. Quite frankly, Dewey's actual idiom does not lend itself easily to any fine-grained analysis of the laws of nature or the methodology of confirming lawlike generalizations. But that's not to say that such analyses are impossible—or implausibly associated with Dewey's vision. It means only that we must look elsewhere for more pointed contributions that glimpse a stronger convergence between Dewey and Peirce than might be drawn directly from Dewey. I find it explicit enough, for instance, in Ian Hacking's *Representing and Intervening*, Nancy Cartwright's *The Dappled World*, and Richard Feynman's *The Character of Physical Law*; hence, also, in Otto Neurath, Thomas Kuhn, Ronald Giere, Paul Feyerabend, Peter Galison, and others.[35] Here, notably, the conception of the laws of nature goes constructivist, pluralist, fragmented, and provisional, keyed to restricted contexts of effective human intervention and experimental and observational control: the very idiom of changeless and exceptionless realist laws is viewed as more than doubtful, and Peirce and Dewey are seen to converge in spite of their differences.

I take Dewey and Peirce to favor very different forms of fallibilism, therefore, which are not always easy to compare. Nevertheless, both treat the growth of knowledge in evolutionary terms, both are naturalists, and both are committed (in some measure) to constructivist accounts of realism and scientific knowledge.

Put more manageably: Dewey and Peirce are realists of a new kind. Dewey judges the metaphysics of substantive individuals to be conceptually inadequate in accounting for the effective process of acquiring knowledge under the conditions of human survival and experience; and Peirce remains a skeptical opponent of any reading of a full-blown scientific realism that converts its rigorous propositions into no more than ordinary empirical hypotheses. (Think of Peirce's insistence on the incomplete separability of individual selves.) Peirce and Dewey (I would say) converge as far as the eclipse of conventional realism is concerned. But then they also diverge—profoundly—in their reading of the pragmatist problematic.

For Dewey, philosophical adequacy mirrors animal survival and evolving human purpose (and the mastery of freedom) within the life of a viable society; for Peirce, our grasping the truth about the real requires an additional mythic reconciliation between what is "given" in experience in the here and now and what, in accord with our seemingly reliable instincts of inquiry (abduction), yields a plausibly spare but ample picture of how the "habits" of nature might evolve into universal laws (governing, in the limit, the entire cosmos). Both Peirce and Dewey are fallibilists and both are pragmatists; both are realists of an unusual sort and, in a way, both are Idealists: Dewey by subtraction, Peirce by celebration and addition—along very different lines. In the process, the pertinent oppositions of the originating paradox dissolve, although Peirce clings in a peculiarly insistent way to the unyielding realist manifesto that became his badge of honor (his public voice, his official rhetoric). There's reason to believe that Peirce worried that casually informed readers of pragmatism might always fall back to confusing his severe thesis (about the reality of truth) with the careless work of his good friend and benefactor—and nemesis—William James (see 5.552–554). (I'll touch on this again when I take up Houser's challenge directly.)

Dewey's fallibilism (a fortiori, his pragmatism) makes no theoretical or criterial use of the notion of infinite inquiry, though inquiry remains entirely open-ended, lacks assignable limit, and is thoroughly constructivist. Peirce's fallibilism invokes the prospect of cosmic closure but only teleologically or evolutionarily, beyond the settled competence of finite inquiry;

it invokes nomological invariance, once again only evolutionarily, beyond the limit of human inquiry; it insists on reality's independence of human belief but admits that actual inquiry depends on what is given as phanerons (on what is present to the mind phenomenologically, without metaphysical presumptions of any kind). What might otherwise count as independently real (exceptionless laws of nature, say, real "generals," noumena at the end of infinite inquiry) are beyond any standard form of confirmation but not necessarily beyond the rational resources of an imaginative interpretation of inquiry itself—hence, not beyond being endorsed by abductive Hope (which is the only way to bring closure to finite inquiry).

Peirce has no intention of slighting resolute judgment in the here and now, but finite inquiry cannot (by its own lights) yield an adequate conception of truth: it searches (endlessly, ingeniously, uneasily) for a rational bridge between the finite and the infinite and comes to rest in abductive Hope. Dewey trusts very nearly completely in the experimental courage and inventive responsiveness of individual selves within a supportive and generous society. Peirce shows us how to live rationally with an existential paradox that arises out of the complexities of science and practical life; Dewey risks abandoning all pretense at methodological instruction in order to collect our vital and political self-discipline required in every part of the flux of life itself. Surprisingly, they tend to converge from seemingly opposite directions.

If you think carefully about how to map the pragmatist's terrain, *any* robust admission of a phenomenological "given" at or as the true beginning of pragmatic inquiry precludes any principled disjunction between realism and Idealism, unless you suppose (as Husserl does, at least in *Ideas I*) that what is "primordially" given (and obscured or deformed by the "natural attitude" embedded in empirical science and ordinary practical life) can be apodictically recovered by transcendental means.[36] What is "constructed," therefore, along the lines that Hegel and Peirce share is entirely incompatible with the extraordinary assurance Husserl signifies by what he names "constitution." Nevertheless, Hegel and Peirce and Husserl all profess to be phenomenologists.

Short of his own mythic claim, whatever Peirce regards as robustly real in finite inquiry need not be independent of the influence of belief and cannot rely on epistemic criteria drawn (say) from our intuitions about Secondness. Because Secondness itself can claim no criteria of its own: none of the phenomenological categories can, and because what count as manifestations of Secondness implicate, in different ways, what count as instances of Firstness and Thirdness anyway. Peirce thinks of his categories as distinct and determinate but linked (by way of instantiation) in an ascending order of complexity, which he calls "valencies," by analogy with the combinatorial power of chemical elements (1.291). But the fact is, his usage is a good deal more informal wherever the question of the real arises in experience or finite inquiry. Firstness, Secondness, and Thirdness are largely notional or abstract: they have no genuine or genuinely separate criterial force. If they did, Peirce would have solved the paradox of the finite/infinite continuum. Also, the only way Peirce's fallibilism can function in the pragmatist manner requires that we admit that our mythic commitments are needed to give closure and rational coherence to whatever we are disposed to favor as true or real (independent of thought) *among* the accidents and contingencies of evolving (finite) experience: where, mythically, there is no principled disjunction between reality and thought. (Peirce's increasing convergence with Hegel needs to be noted.)

Remember: fallibilism is an abductive conjecture—in effect, a regulative optimism—presented as yielding an open-ended realism answering to what Peirce takes to be the work of a universal phenomenological instinct of inquiry. It's "scientific," in Peirce's eyes, but only in the sense in which science is already wedded to the inclusive holism of the fallibilistic vision—that is, to the indissolubility of finite and infinite inquiry initially applied without exception to the entire run of one's phanerons.

I don't fault fallibilism for that. On the contrary, both Peirce and Dewey confirm, in their very different ways, the impossibility of recovering—by ordinary scientific methods—any sort of cosmic closure, or "absolute" confirmation, or "real generals," or exceptionless laws of nature, or escape from the accidents of societal experience. Fallibilism in the pragmatist's sense, whether Peirce's or Dewey's (or Royce's, for that matter), problematizes truth and knowledge at every level of theoretical reflection that implicates the finite limits of inquiry; but it also manages to gauge their objective standing "probabilistically," in terms of their practical reliability within the finite (evolving, internalist) span of human evidence.

The obvious irony, therefore, confirms that Peirce's most strenuous insistence on reality's being independent of belief—for instance, regarding the universal laws of nature—is, contrary to what he actually says, not "independent of what anybody may think them to be" (5.405). If I understand the argument aright, this is part of the effective meaning of what

Carl Hausman (for one) identifies as Peirce's new doctrine of "evolutionary realism," though it is also a reading in which Hausman emphatically opposes an exclusively realist (nonidealist) interpretation of Peirce's position (against Fisch and Christopher Hookway, for instance)—chiefly because he (Hausman) believes "the status of the object of the final opinion or convergent conclusions of inquiry" must be consulted. I agree with Hausman in this regard; but the fact is, Hausman "agrees" with both Fisch and Hookway in treating "realism" and "idealism" as *independent* questions in Peirce's account, even if Peirce is both a realist and an idealist. I think the independence cannot be shown: my own reading has it that realism and Idealism are inseparably intertwined in Peirce.[37] I see no possibility of escape here. But the confusion is due to Peirce.

If you concede this much, Peirce and Dewey cannot be very far from one another as pragmatists—possibly even as fallibilists—although they are as different, temperamentally, as can be imagined. Here, James is little more than a secondary figure: both as an ideologue and a cosmologist. (His best contribution, I surmise, lies with the introspective psychology of *The Principles of Psychology*, including its links with physiology. His remarks on truth seem never to have touched on the complexity of Peirce's reflection, which, let it be noted, is hardly the point of Bertrand Russell's notorious disdain for the pragmatist account of truth.) For my part, the convergence between Peirce and Dewey seems inevitable—profoundly influenced by Hegel's critique of Kant—although the linkage is almost completely erased (see Chapter 1).

. . .

Let me round out the picture I've presented thus far before bringing the argument to a close. Peirce was obviously exercised by the need for a strategically positioned definition of "reality" already as early as the account in "How to Make Our Ideas Clear" (1878). There, he famously affirms: "The opinion which is fated to be ultimately agreed to by all who investigate is what we mean by the truth, and the object represented in this opinion is the real" (5.407). But he remarks at once that this appears to "[make] the characters of the real depend on what is ultimately thought about them." So he takes up the worry more directly: "the answer to this [concern] is that, on the one hand, reality is independent, not necessarily of thought in general, but only of what you or I or any finite number of men may think about it; and that, on the other hand, though the object of the final opinion depends on what that opinion is, yet what that opinion is does not depend on what you or I or any man thinks" (5.408). The answer is uncharacteristically evasive—though clever enough. In fact, Peirce speculates that even if our race should become extinct (and perhaps another, also capable of inquiry, arise), "the reality of that which is real does depend on the real fact that investigation is destined to lead, at least, if continued long enough, to a belief in it" (5.408). But does that mean that Thirdness is finally subordinated to Secondness or Secondness to Thirdness? Peirce is remarkably opaque about this, though we know where he means to draw the line. (And, by the way, what should we understand by that weasel of a word, "fated"?)

Peirce wants to be able to invoke within the scope of a viable pragmatism the following items: (1) "real things" independent of any human opinion, and (2) the "fact" that what is true about reality at the end of infinite inquiry must be uniquely what it is. Both these conjectures seem impossible to establish in any plausibly pragmatist inquiry; or, if we allowed them (in some nonvacuous way), pragmatism (or pragmaticism) would be seen to depend on the preemptive findings of some rather murky sort of rational (or abductive) "instinct" regarding what is real—which, often enough, Peirce finds irresistible (a usage never strictly confirmed or legitimated). Such an instinctive "science" (a "mythic" science, if I may call it that) could never be reconciled with any familiar form of science (as a single confirmatory practice), simply because no actual science would ever claim to confirm propositions like items (1 and (2)—or, for that matter, even understand such claims in terms of its usual practice. Pragmatism would be instantly converted into its negation.

The only other possibility seems to lie with the idea (which also attracts Peirce) that the addition of the resources of our "mythic science" (abductive hypotheses that need never be confirmed and could never be disconfirmed) could always be benignly fitted, "regulatively" (so to say) but not "constitutively," to whatever (otherwise) proved to be acceptable to an acceptable scientific practice. Yet, in spite of what Peirce says to reassure us, the claim is assuredly false (as well as unresponsive), as the usual questions about objectivism, the realist standing of exceptionless laws of nature, the historicity of evolving belief, and the seeming discontinuities of "paradigm shifts" confirm. The maneuver would also subvert Peirce's phenomenology: there'd be no conjoint role for Secondness and Thirdness to play. In fact, if Secondness and Thirdness are instinctual categories that answer to our phenomenological impulses—more regulative than constitutive (certainly not transcendentalist, but seemingly "close")—then *they* can have no "realist" standing independent of human thought. They may be mythic proposals (empirically unconfirmable, no more than instinctive abstractions) drawn from our phenomenological practice and never directly confirmed by it. Any stronger claim would exceed the finitist conditions of pragmatist theories.

Carl Hausman, who has examined the matter as carefully as anyone, suggests that Peirce means to leave "open the possibility of the identity of the object with thought in general" (this is Hausman's gloss on the expression, "not necessarily").[38] But what Hausman offers misses the point: there would be no "thought in general" (pertinent to pragmatism or pragmaticism) *if*—if there were no human inquirers to consult or if (*per impossibile*) human thought and belief would have to be effective at the end of infinite inquiry—we could never prise apart the meaning of the concordance between Thirdness and Secondness so that criteria could be provided for the separate application of each. Think only of the fact that where we believe we have been mistaken in our realist claims, we obviously believe that what we've treated in a realist way *is* adversely qualified by what we believe; but then, what is the sense (the pragmatist sense) in which what we believe true we believe accords with the way the world "is" independently? I think there can only be a constructivist answer. But that leads to the indissoluble unity of realism and Idealism—a fortiori, to the unity of Secondness and Thirdness.

The bare admission of the reality of "mind" in nature at large, apart from human minds, is never epistemically responsive; nor is the admission of the causal efficacy of the mental on the physical. The issue lies entirely with Peirce's (seemingly) verbal efforts to outflank all finite, constructivist forms of cognition and cognizable validity, which, admitting Peirce's Kantian and Hegelian proclivities, would require an arduous defense. (I think we may safely say that no such defense has been effectively advanced.) Read as Hausman suggests, the formula is no more than an empty repetition of whatever we may say we are prepared to admit in admitting (with Peirce) the exceptionless "truths" of Secondness and the other categories of Peirce's "phenomenology" applied to whatever an empirically constrained interpretation of experience may be said to yield.

I take this to be the compelling (if unintended) lesson of Peirce's reflection (in 1906) on the true meaning of the original "Fixation of Belief" paper (November 1877), which limns a *passage* from "the settlement of belief" (here and now) to the further impulse of inquiry ("then only") "to consider how the conception of truth gradually develops from that principle under the action of experience" (5.564). You cannot bring Peirce's "system" to a close at (or as if at) the end of human inquiry—under any one conception of inquiry; and you cannot be sure, here, what the right way is to "confirm" or "support" (in some sense laxer than confirmation) our rational reliance on the second-order conjecture Peirce sets before us. (Firstness, Secondness, and Thirdness are not entirely reliable; on the contrary, they are always phenomenologically labile and intertwined.) But you can certainly grasp Peirce's notion of how inquiry invariably *begins*, by understanding what Peirce means by what is "given"—*always* given-in-experience. The answer required requires an analysis of what Peirce means by "fated"; and that, I daresay, requires, in turn, an account of how the idea of a continuum of finite and infinite inquiry affects our being entitled to speak of what is "true" and "real" at the end of infinite inquiry. *How* is the opinion (said to be "fated" to be believed) related to our relying (and to our being justified in relying) on "the conception of truth" that Peirce supposes is aptly invoked at the end of infinite inquiry, when it is applied in any phase of finite inquiry?

If you find these musings reasonable, then we may agree about the pragmatist conception of truth. Peirce risks massive misunderstanding by insisting on his regulative conception of truth, fitted largely but not exclusively to the special work of the sciences, a conception that cannot be criterially invoked in any finite inquiry and, in any case, captures little more than his own progressivist abduction (Hope). Dewey dismantles the seemingly privileged importance of truth, by way of reducing the presumptions of science itself within the existential concerns of the human animal—hence, he disallows even Peirce's problematic distinction, favoring viability instead, by whatever means come to count as successful forms of freedom. And James, shuttling between Peirce and Dewey but tending to side with Dewey, insists on subordinating the propositional specialism of truth to whatever agentive resources the forms of satisfaction require in the way of intelligent and sustained interventions, however distant the latter are bound to be from canonical pictures of truth favored, more or less exclusively, in "analytic" treatments of the sciences. In that sense, Bertrand Russell's attacks on James and pragmatism at large are plainly due to intolerance. Nevertheless, what needs to be redeemed (regarding the matter of truth) belongs to the comparison between Peirce and Cassirer and between Peirce and such "pragmatist" allies as Neurath, Hacking, Cartwright, and Feynman, who address the sciences directly. (Pragmatists understandably attracted to James are themselves, I'm afraid, often unwilling to admit the damage of James's well-known, attractive informality, when much more is needed.)

There's the interlevel question no contemporary Peircean "realist" about truth has convincingly answered: *my* charge is that no plausible answer *can* be given that does not implicate the indissoluble union of realism and Idealism. That, I take it, is what fallibilism—a fortiori, pragmatism—comes to.

To understand all this is to understand why Peirce *cannot end* his account in the way he apparently does! Put in the slimmest terms: Peirce begins as a constructivist (in whatever nonvacuous sense may be conceded to be shared by Kant and Hegel), but he ends (he seems to end) as an extreme realist opposed to every form of constructivism. At this point in the discussion, it makes little difference whether Peirce actually believes there is a form of "science" that could confirm the outcome of infinite inquiry, or believes only that we have a rational right to "Hope"—abductively, blindly, by a kind of rational instinct, regulatively—and that progress in science beyond the findings of any finite inquiry will finally vindicate our otherwise unsecured confidence (see 5.565). For, on one option, Peirce must invoke the "mythic" science mentioned, which he cannot reconcile, cognitively, with any pragmatist method; and, on another, he must abandon the pretense of applying any further science at all. He's not prepared to rely entirely on finite inquiry or on finite inquiry freed from infinitist scruples. In my opinion, Peirce really does choose the second (by far the better) option, but then, perversely, he also expresses himself as if he favors the first. That is, he simply stonewalls in order to give the impression of an unyielding realism. (As I say, this may be meant, in part at least, to offset James's intrusive influence.)

In any event, here, once again, is one version of how Peirce thinks we begin with what is "given." In texts dating from 1904–1905, which bear on the "Fixation of Belief" paper, Peirce affirms:

Phaneroscopy [that is, phenomenology] is the description of the *phaneron*; and by the *phaneron* I mean the collective total of all that is in any way or in any sense present to the mind, regardless of whether it corresponds to any real thing or not. If you ask, present *when*? and to *whose* mind?, I reply that I leave those questions unanswered, never having entertained a doubt [a real doubt, of course] that those features of the phaneron that I have found in my mind are present at all times and to all minds. (1.284)[39]

Peirce explicitly associates this notion with the British empiricists' use of "idea," but he finds their use too narrow and skewed. (He's openly committed to universalist categories here.) He also says, mysteriously: "I know that there is another series of elements imperfectly represented by Hegel's Categories. But I have been unable to give any satisfactory account of them" (1.284). This is certainly strange, since "phaneron" seems to correspond best (though not precisely) with what Hegel has in mind (in his own *Phenomenology*) as what is "given," in the constructivist way, though without metaphysical presumptions of any determinate kind, as *Erscheinung* (*Erscheinungen*). In a word: like Hegel, Peirce opposes any privileged realist attribution to the "data" of his phenomenology (his phanerons); but, as against Kant, his phanerons implicate the inseparability of subjective and objective features. I put it to you that if you admit the finding, Peirce cannot be a realist in the disjunctive sense. *His* realism implicates his Idealism: he must be a constructivist with regard to truth at the end of inquiry.

Let me remind you once again that, as I read the matter, "*i*dealism" (lowercase "i") is either independent of or neutral with regard to "realism" or disjunctively opposed to "realism"; whereas "*I*dealism" (capital "I") is hospitable to incorporating some forms of constructive "realism" (as among the German Idealists). Furthermore, "idealism" (in the Kantian sense) holds that what is empirically "real" is actually constituted (in part at least) by what is subjective in origin and nature; whereas "Idealism" (in Peirce's best sense) is (so to say) construed "epistemologically" (in the constructivist way) rather than "metaphysically" (disjunctively), hence is restricted to our "picture" (our constructed picture) of reality rather than addressed to the actual "constitution" of reality itself. (Peirce's Schellingian temptation may be deemed to go in an opposed direction, though what Peirce means here by "mind" is problematic.)

I cannot pursue the link between Peirce and Hegel here; it would take us too far off our course. But it surely suggests that Peirce's penchant for the extreme forms of realism (and fallibilism) "collides" with the implicit constructivism of his semiotized and phenomenological treatment of thought and reality. Either Peirce never resolves the matter or he views the conjunction of the two tendencies as conceptually benign, or he is genuinely of two minds. I think the second possibility must be the right one, since the elements of his phenomenology—the trio of basic categories and the phaneron itself—are said to have no metaphysical import of their own, though they are (somehow) universally binding on "any future metaphysics." Note, too, that the paradox pictured by applying the categories of Secondness and Thirdness to what is "given" in experience effectively functions only at the infinite limit of inquiry where Peirce's seemingly immovable realism proves to be a "mythic" posit. There's the clue to the importance and intractability of the paradox I've promised. (We seem very close to exhausting all pertinent options.)

. . .

I come, finally, to Houser's objection to my account.

Here is the paradox I originally offered—drawn from Peirce's words—which Houser cites in his Presidential Address:

Claim 1: "the act of knowing a real object alters it" (5.555)

Claim 2: "the real thing is as it is, irrespectively of what any mind or any definite collection of minds may represent it to be" (5.565)

The resolution of the paradox (if that is what it is) is perfectly straightforward, though the argument that's needed cannot help meandering (and cannot elude the enabling equivocation I've been trying to elucidate). Houser is right to insist on a textual correction: I'm entirely at fault for having failed to provide the full context of Claim 1. I'm happy to make amends here—and I apologize. But I do so with the intent of recovering the deeper truth Peirce originally obscured and cannot explicate, except equivocally (or circularly), which Houser more or less acknowledges by way of other considerations—without, however, bringing them to bear on the texts before us. On my view, the correction actually strengthens the intended argument just where it sets out the sense of Peirce's account. But I'll need a little more of your patience.

Peirce ridicules the sense of Claim 1; there's no doubt about that. (It's Houser's ace.) Peirce understands the claim (narrowly construed) to be valid (if it is valid) *if* it is indeed the case that "True and Satisfactory are synonyms" or that the meaning of True "makes it to be *coextensive with* the Satisfactory in cognition" (5.555–556). This phrasing, you realize, is a sort of stage whisper (as late as 1906) against William James's (and F. C. S. Schiller's) disastrous account of truth.[40]

Peirce explicitly remarks (also in 1906) that James and Schiller "made up their minds that the true is simply the satisfactory"—and then adds wryly: "No doubt; but to say 'satisfactory' is not to complete any predicate whatever. Satisfactory to what end?" (5.552). (I don't believe Peirce ever got over the original trauma of James's immensely successful but misguided popularization of his own supposed theory of truth read as a kind of good—a "subjective" feeling of satisfaction, finally.) Now, the absolutely decisive point is this, a point Houser does not mention: namely, that Peirce was entirely willing (in the context of what I've cited) to countenance the verbal formula (James's in effect) *if* the meaning of "satisfactory in cognition" were brought into accord (whether in science or morality) with the *fallibilist* concordance between Truth and Reality.

Peirce is as explicit as he could possibly be:

> Men act, especially in the action of inquiry, *as if* their sole purpose was to produce a certain state of feeling, in the sense that when that state of feeling is attained [that is, satisfaction], there is no further effort. It was upon that proposition that I originally based pragmaticism, laying it down in the article ["The Fixation of Belief"] that in November 1877 prepared the ground for my argument for the pragmaticistic doctrine ["How To Make Our Ideas Clear" (January 1878)]. In the case of inquiry, I called that state of feeling "firm belief," and said, "As soon as a firm belief is reached we are entirely satisfied, whether the belief be true or false," and went on to show how the action of experience consequently was to create the conception of real truth." (5.563)

Peirce associates "satisfaction," generically, with "the fundamental properties of protoplasm . . . *virtually* directed toward the removal of stimulation"—hence, with the philosophically banal level of speculation he believed he found in James; whereas the "ideal" form of satisfaction needed (which the metaphysician, but not the logician, might be moved to claim is *real*) identifies, innocuously enough, "that at which inquiry [ideally and correctly] aims"—"the True" (5.557, 563).

There's the corrected sense in which what I had too hastily attributed to Peirce (textually) I nevertheless rightly did attribute to him (philosophically) in view of the deeper meaning of what he actually says; although, to be sure, it obviously suits Peirce's rhetoric, in context, *not* to pick that thread up just where he wishes to distance his pragmaticism once again from James's initial blunder. There's no reason, therefore, to abandon the argument. Peirce cannot make his case (even against James) if he cannot account (on the pragmatist's or, better, the pragmaticist's grounds) for the fallibilist's vindication of the final correspondence between truth and reality—that is, *at the end of infinite inquiry*. He cannot succeed if he cannot separate, methodologically, the would-be scientific confirmation of fallibilism's insistence on the unique realist payoff of the long run (as a working element in the method of scientific self-correction) from the merely "mythic" (or heuristic) affirmation within the terms of the realist/Idealist metaphysics he espouses.

I agree that it may be reasonable to argue, as a pragmaticist, that one should (at some point) turn away from finite, self-corrective methods of science to the mythic (*non*cognitive) assurance of the realist reading of the long run; but I cannot see the sense in which that can be confirmed to belong (on determinate, cognitive grounds) to science itself. Peirce turns away from the impossible necessity of completing infinite inquiry by mastering the infinite goal of Truth—by accepting the rational, merely notional closure of transcendental Hope. That is the only reasonable (the sparest) solution possible under the condition of history. It shows the way to retiring all the extravagances of post-Kantian Idealism and to reconciling empirical and transcendental realist expectations. The solution I recommend, then, is content to equate the legitimate appeal to Hope just where, approaching Peirce's sense of "satisfaction," we are inclined to speculate about what infinite inquiry might yield. But that is not a realism the "disjunctive" realists would allow. (Bear in mind that I'm trying to resolve the paradox within the terms of Peirce's idiom: I also have in mind Cassirer's leaner and trimmer formula, which I mean to compare with Peirce's.)

For the moment, let me collect the principal puzzles that have become hopelessly entangled. James never satisfies Peirce on the right restriction of his (James's) theory of truth confined to the sciences, in the regard that particularly interested Peirce. Nevertheless, Peirce was not entirely inhospitable to the laxer sense in which James applies his notion to what might prove fruitful (pragmatically) in the way of belief, even if not in accord with Peirce's notion of how a rigorous science works—whether applied to finite claims or reconciled with what is fated to be believed. Dewey, it should be noted, accommodates James's view rather more skillfully, since, effectively, Dewey drops the strong use of "true" in favor of "warranted assertibility."

But Peirce *is* committed to something akin to James's usage in his own papers of the 1870s. Peirce's strenuous theory of truth has its principal application wherever, in the context of science, he considers generalizations that may be treated as specimens closely linked to potential laws of nature. There, the infinitist context seems most reasonable: in a way, nothing is lost if we never bring the relevant inquiries to a final close. There,

Peirce seems (to me) to be very close to Cassirer and (often) very distant from James. But when he addresses beliefs about particular things—where, that is, the principle of Secondness seems to have its best inning (as in experiments and controlled observations)—it's quite understandable that he would be open to speaking in terms of a straightforward sort of "direct" realism. (I think this approaches Ian Hacking's sense of what is "real" in experimental circumstances.) Yet, even here, or at any rate among practical beliefs different from those commonsense beliefs regarding matters the sciences would normally address—religious beliefs, in James's usage—another sort of pragmatic fruitfulness seems to occupy James's theory and is viewed from Peirce's side as an unhelpful complication.

There's something that goes awry in Peirce's argument, palpable already in "The Fixation of Belief": Peirce obviously affirms the belief that rigorous inquiry pursued fallibilistically will lead "to the one True conclusion." Let me put this carefully. He writes as if he believes that, on the "hypothesis [which, he says] is the sole support of my [his] recommended method of inquiry"—namely, that "there are [indeed] Real things, whose characters are entirely independent of our opinions about them"—inquiry will, (or, more cautiously and correctly, would), when rightly pursued, lead "to the one True conclusion." He further says, defensively, that (even) "if investigation cannot be regarded as proving that there are Real things, it at least does not lead to a contrary conclusion. . . . No doubts of the method, therefore, necessarily arise from its practice" (6.384).

But Peirce is mistaken here. For one thing, his "hypothesis" *makes no determinate confirmatory difference in pragmatist terms* (which threatens its possessing any pragmatist meaning at all). For a second, if it leads (or would lead) to the "one True conclusion," it would do so only at the end of infinite inquiry, by the fiat of abductive instinct; that is, compatibly with its *not* leading to any "one true conclusion" *in finite time*! For a third, the account fails to explain the conceptual relationship that holds between "Real things . . . entirely independent of our opinions about them" *and* "real things" provisionally and progressively posited in the process of finite inquiry. (Among the latter, but not among the former, would-be "real things" cannot fail to depend epistemically on our contingent and evolving conceptions of what we take to be real: there's a clue to the intended *reductio*.) For a fourth, Peirce does not address the significance of the cognitive *continuity* between what we posit as real things in the sense just remarked and what Peirce calls "Real things" in his "mythic" (metaphysical) hypothesis. Finally, for a fifth, if real things (what are ideally or independently real) are themselves captured only in constructivist ways, by "picturing" them as we take them to be—in our inquiries—then either Peirce is caught in a *reductio* of his own making or his doctrine cannot be more than a variant of Hegel's essential critique of Kant's first *Critique* (which I take, in turn, to afford a *reductio* of Kant's *Critique*). But if that is so, the paradox I offer must be insurmountable.

I believe Peirce *is* best read as offering a variant of Hegel's strategy; at least I take him *not* to suppose he can (on scientific or philosophical grounds) escape a thoroughly constructivist account of realism (though he is obviously not a subjectivist). But if that is admitted, then, for one thing, there cannot be as great a difference between Peirce and Dewey as we ordinarily suppose; and, for another, fallibilism must abandon all the extravagant doctrines Peirce draws from the "mythic" version of his hypothesis, read literally, that is, in a manner incompatible with a strict constructivism. In that case, on Peirce's argument, we must acknowledge that there can be no assured concordance between thought and reality: agapasm and evolutionary optimism are doctrines too strenuous to hold to be true in any straightforward way, and a moderate skepticism about scientific realism may well be more convincing than the strong (disjunctive) reading of realism itself. Metaphysical realism is no more than an article of abductive Hope, if we reject all pretensions of privilege. But if you allow this, the advantage of Dewey's seemingly more primitive fallibilism is bound to dawn, though it's also true that Dewey's solution must then be a cousin to Peirce's.

I should also add, explicitly, that, even under the condition of abductive Hope, Peirce's faith in the unique convergence of infinite inquiry (the belief "fated" to be believed) is, finally, unpersuasive. But, contrary to Hilary Putnam's well-known charge that Peirce is committed to a "wrong theory of truth"—namely, that "it is metaphysically impossible for there to be any truths that are not verifiable by human beings," in effect, some form of "antirealism," the claim that "the limits of what can be true of the world [depends] on the limits of human verification-capacities"—I don't see that Peirce's extravagant "Hope" bears at all on the determination of what we treat, fallibly, as true in actual inquiry. "Infinite inquiry" is not, in any guise, a part of actual (finite) inquiry.[41] It's an interpretation of the import of finite findings, informed by our mythic conjectures, assigned to the end of infinite inquiry. Peirce is advancing a deeper paradox. His argument is primarily "epistemological": effectively, the would-be "metaphysics" provides a mythic rationale for the unending openness of finite inquiry: the realist Hope of infinite inquiry infects the operative Hope of finite inquiry!

. . .

This last conjecture suggests a further line of confirmation drawn from Peirce's account of the infinite continuum of interpretant signs—to turn to a late distinction of Peirce's that T. L. Short examines with considerable care.[42] My reading of this important enlargement of the realism issue will have to be cursory.

Short asserts, quite straightforwardly, that, in a late manuscript from 1907 (MS 318)—only small excerpts of which have ever been published and other excerpts of which Short seems to be the first to have cited—Peirce provides "a stunning reversal of his earlier view [on semiotics and, if I understand Short rightly, Idealism]. Meaning is not an endless translation of sign into sign. There must always, in every case, be an interpretant that is ultimate in the sense of not being yet another sign."[43] (I'm persuaded by Short's analysis, but I don't think it settles the realism/Idealism issue.) The argument, centered on the theory of signs, is construed by Short to apply to Peirce's Idealism—and therefore to the defense of the "strong" realist reading of Peirce's metaphysics, which (on Short's reading) advises us to separate the realism from the earlier idealism (Idealism). The link between the semiotics and the Idealism, which might otherwise strike an attentive reader as contrived, is briefly but briskly supplied by Short:

> There is a fundamental difference between ultimate interpretants and final, or ideal, interpretants. In the case of cognition, the final interpretant is the truth, as full as is sought, about the object signified and is itself of the nature of a statement: it is what Peirce elsewhere called "the final opinion" [sic]. But any statement, true or false, fixed or provisional, must be meaningful, hence, it must have an ultimate interpretant. Final interpretants, when verbal, must themselves have ultimate interpretants.[44]

This is Short's gloss (nearly the whole of it) on the import of MS 318 regarding the right way to read the standard passages drawn from Peirce's semiotics. The implicated realism rests with the force of the carefully crafted definition: "the final interpretant is the truth"—Short adds, "as full as is sought, about the object signified." This brings into play at once the crucial early essays from the *Popular Science Monthly* series that begin with "The Fixation of Belief" (1877). But you cannot fail to notice that Short's comment insinuates a functionally assured sense of our being able to *grasp* the ("final") truth (*sans phrase*, as well as "as full as is sought, about . . .").

One might say, not unfairly, that the formula covers the argument in "How to Make Our Ideas Clear" (1878), the second essay in the series, which introduces the infinite long run ("the opinion that is fated to be ultimately [or finally] agreed to"), as well as the argument of whatever (equally "final") short-run interpretants ("truths," in cognitive cases) may arise in accord with "the fixation of belief" doctrine of the first paper. So far, all of this is entirely programmatic: we have as yet no assurance of any kind that the "realist" reading of any seemingly successful semiotic process *can* be confirmed; or that if it may be conceded at least in story-relative short-run episodes, it must also be demonstrable for the (infinite) long run; or that any extended short-run inquiries, successful in the sense remarked, assure us that, as we approach asymptotically (so to say) to long-run inquiry ("truth, as full as is sought"), the "realist" reading of the "reversal" (of Peirce's earlier commitment to "idealism")—drawn from MS 318—may be counted on to apply, without let, to infinite inquiry as well. I find no mileage here as yet regarding the resolution of the realist/Idealist question. Short seems to me to be too sanguine.

There's no sleight of hand here. But it pays to bear in mind that, in Peirce's well-known passage from "How to Make Our Ideas Clear" (5.388–410), partly excerpted above ("fated to be . . . agreed upon"), on which Short relies, the terms "ultimate" and "final" are used interchangeably (as Short acknowledges). The essay itself provides the link between Peirce's semiotics and his Idealism; it also includes Peirce's most famous, most problematic pronouncement—namely: "The [fated] opinion is what we mean by the truth, and the object represented in this opinion is the real." This is the same paper in which the equally famous "pragmatic maxim" occurs, which Short also cites in the context of his running argument and which catches up Peirce's earliest formulation of what *he* means by "meaning"—thus invoking the central problem of his semiotics read as clarification of his would-be "realist" use of "true" (regarding the reliability of the "method of science") offered in the first paper of the series, "The Fixation of Belief" (5.358–387).

Short holds that "Peirce's realism" is committed to two theses: (1) that "the world is independent of any particular representation [or sign] of it," and (2) to denying that "a theory held at 'the ideal limit' of inquiry might yet be false." Short claims that to deny thesis 1 is "idealism."[45] Perhaps it is some sort of idealism. But it is *not* Peirce's way of securing realism, and it fails to capture the idea that realism and *I*dealism are indissolubly joined. Furthermore, neither thesis 1 nor thesis 2 is perspicuously formulated: post-Kantian and post-Hegelian metaphysics must be constructivist—which is to say, metaphysics cannot be separable from epistemology. In conceding Short's thesis 1 but avoiding (with Kant and Peirce) every form of noumenalism, we approach the "independent things" of thesis 1 by means of our epistemically informed "picture" of what we take to be real: according to Peirce, the Real answers, epistemically, to the True; furthermore, again on Peirce's argument, the metaphysical cannot meaningfully be separated from the epistemological. Regarding thesis 2, I think we may say, straightforwardly enough, that if Peirce affirmed thesis 2 under the epistemic conditions of thesis 1, he would have exceeded the reach of any and all finite resources; but, of course, he never advances thesis 2 except as an article of transcendental Hope! Short does not come to terms with these complications: it's not uncharacteristic of canonical realism.

I'm afraid that Short's inference is much too hasty: I don't find that he's demonstrated anywhere in *Peirce's Theory of Signs* that Peirce's new account of a sign strengthens the disjunctive version of realism. I myself claim (as I've already said) that Peirce is committed to a nondisjunctive reading of realism and Idealism; I've also explained the sense in which the "independence" of real objects is best construed as a construction based on, or an interpretive picture of, what we take as evidence of "what is"—which implicates Idealism. I don't see how it's possible, relative to Peirce's assumptions, to prove or demonstrate that what we *posit* as real *is* independent in the requisite way. Apart from what Short draws from MS 318, which we must consider, Peirce seems never to have settled on any assuredly "realist" reading (in Short's sense) of what a "final" or "ultimate" interpretant must be.[46] Thus far, Short is whistling in the wind. That is, the best I can say for Short's argument (with the greatest respect) is that Short has demonstrated that there must be a "realist" reading of the "ultimate interpretant" of a sign in a cognitive context; but that goes no distance at all toward answering the question whether, or how, what fills the role must entail (or can escape) the Idealist encumbrance I've been pressing.

Let me say again that though it's true that Peirce denied the second of the two theses mentioned—that is, thesis 2—*he does so only on the strength of abductive Hope*: he couldn't possibly have demonstrated that it was true or that it was false tout court. (I also think, as I've said, that Peirce's "Hope" is an extravagance.) In discussing Kuhn's theory, Short remarks that Peirce was himself aware that we cannot now claim to *have* evidence that "every question can be settled" or that a way of answering will always be found.[47] Nevertheless, Short claims that Peirce's *realism* centers on the possibility of affirming thesis 1 and denying thesis 2. This fails to acknowledge the constructivist standing of Peirce's realism and the unconfirmable but cognitional relevance of Peirce's abductive Hope.[48] My suggestion is that thesis 2 was never meant to posit a genuine inquiry open to pragmatists (that is, an actual infinite inquiry): it's really a device for introducing Peirce's ingenious solution to the problem posed by the finite/infinite continuum itself. It centers on the paradox of making scientific truths (general truths regarding candidates for the laws of nature) depend in some cognitional way on the "opinion fated" to be believed at the end of infinite inquiry.

Short's new argument notably revises Peirce's semiotic theory (drawn from MS 318) and brings the revision to bear on certain standard passages drawn from Peirce's theory of truth and reality. Here are two of those passages:

To satisfy our doubts . . . it is necessary that a method should be found by which our beliefs may be caused by nothing human, but by some external permanency—by something on which our thinking has no effect. (3.253)

Such is the method of science. Its fundamental hypothesis . . . is this: There are real things, whose characters are entirely independent of our opinions about them; those realities affect our senses according to regular laws. (3.254)

These remarks (cited by Short) from "The Fixation of Belief" introduce Peirce's "realist" thesis in its earliest phase: which is to say (as Short acknowledges), in the form it takes *in* Peirce's "idealism" (the earliest phase of what I identify as Peirce's *I*dealism), which, in "How to Make Our Ideas Clear," brings the argument to the point of yielding the doctrine (already cited) regarding "the opinion which is fated to be ultimately agreed to by all who investigate," that is, Peirce's (early) definition of "the true" and "the real."

The key to the latter passage is, of course, this: that the definition of "true" and "real" would be false to the admitted facts *if* the phrasing "all who investigate" were *always* taken to signify no more than a finite company; it could then never exceed James's definition of truth (which Peirce rejects); and it could claim no way to distinguish between truth and settled belief (belief that brought doubt to a "satisfactory" end, belief that was "satisfied"). In that sense, the reading would have abandoned (without cause) Peirce's issue regarding infinite inquiry. In fact, the expression "entirely independent of our opinions" effectively distinguishes between what we deem to be "independent" and what Kant means by "*Dingen-an-sich*." As far as I can make out, neither Peirce nor Short ever explains what "entirely independent . . . real things" *means*, pragmatically. On the argument I've been developing, what we *say* is independent is, always, *dependent* on some theory about how we know such things; although we may indeed conjecture that it's unreasonable (or worse) to doubt that there is an "independent" world. *That*, however, is no more than an abductive guess, a piece of abductive Hope. If the dependence is admitted, then, as I see matters, the canonical "realist" fails hands down.

The realism Short assigns Peirce requires some further thesis distinct from theses 1 and 2—which would be unacceptable if it required a form of cognitive privilege: any fallibilist doctrine would eschew such an addition. But then, the metaphysical schema that features theses 1 and 2 is already inhospitable to Peirce's choices. Furthermore, I'm not persuaded that it makes any sense to *claim* that, if inquiry were infinitely extended, thesis 2 would have to be read bivalently. Short, you remember, faults Peirce for denying thesis 2. Short is not opposed to the bare concept of an infinite continuum. But when he thinks of continua in cognitive terms, he construes them in terms of "unactualized potentialities": thus, he says, "we do perceive what is merely possible, the counterfactually possible. For it is unactualized potentialities that comprise continua, and we perceive continua."[49] Short simply opposes the idea that an infinite inquiry could have any cognitional bearing on our theory of science if it couldn't have any determinate cognitive standing in its own right. But *that* idea tests the very nerve of Peirce's treatment of the notion of infinite inquiry and the saving grace of abductive Hope regarding finite inquiry. The shift is essential to Short's account of Peircean phanerons, but it rests on an equivocation.

Consider, now, the passages from MS 318 that Short introduces, in good part to confirm that where semiotics is concerned, infinite continua cannot be essential to valid interpretation, though there may well be no need to reject the possibility of an infinite inquiry as such. Put in the sparest terms, Short draws from MS 318 Peirce's new instruction to the effect that the early semiotic thesis—"signs are to be interpreted [only] by signs," hence, ad infinitum (2.203)—is neither correct nor acceptable any longer.[50] The argument is perfectly straightforward but understandably busy. For one thing, Peirce is thinking in the broadest way (in MS 318) of signs in cognitive contexts: there, signs are variously called "intellectual," "mental," and "logical," though, as such, they may also be "immediate," "ultimate," or "final."

Short's advice is certainly helpful: "Pragmatism is not a general theory of meaning but pertains only to the meanings of those signs—words, concepts, statements, beliefs—of which cognition consists, and only to such of their meaning as belongs to cognition ['logical interpretants']."[51] Peirce himself flatly denies (in an unpublished fragment of MS 318, which Short cites) "that a sign can be the 'naked,' that is, the ultimate meaning of a sign"—so there's an end to the earlier semiotic; he also explains in another (already published) fragment of MS 318 (1.493–494) that though "a concept, or general mental sign, may be a logical interpretant . . . it cannot be the ultimate logical interpretant, precisely because being a sign, it has itself a logical interpretant." So Peirce has caught the flaw.

The ultimate interpretant of a sign in a cognitive context must be something *other* than a sign! Here, if I understand Peirce's strategy, Peirce returns to the pragmatic instruction of "The Fixation of Belief" and "How to Make Our Ideas Clear." And there, explaining what it is to "possess" a concept—in effect, to form certain habits of expectation—Peirce (rightly) concludes (as Short very neatly explains) that "it is the habit itself, and not a concept of it, that is the ultimate interpretant of a concept."[52] I think this must be right. But I don't see that it settles at all the question of the right way to read Peirce's realism: of how, for instance, realism and idealism (or Idealism) are related in Peirce's theory or, for that matter, of how they should be construed on independent grounds responding to the work of Kant and Hegel. Also, of course, "the habit itself," as distinct from "a concept of it," effectively *selects certain signs* rather than others—for a special cognitive role or function: on Peirce's view, a "thing" may be both a sign and an "ultimate interpretant" of a sign.

In any event, the *semiotic* issue *is* resolved. The clinching argument (from MS 318), which Short cites, has actually been published: "The real and living logical conclusion *is* that habit; the verbal formulation merely expresses it. . . . The concept which is a logical interpretant is only imperfectly so. It partakes somewhat of the nature of a verbal definition, and is very inferior to the living definition that grows up in the habit" (5.491). There's no question Peirce must have realized the threatening absurdity of his promoting the earlier semiotic as a contribution to pragmatism (or to good sense or to realism). But then, there's no reason to suppose he wouldn't have seen the counterpart argument regarding the standing of infinite inquiry (if he had a use for the idea, which of course he did). Hence, from my point of view, Short's argument may be co-opted without the least adjustment in Peirce's account of the indissoluble union of realism and Idealism!

. . .

A few loose details remain. They won't bring closure to the huge question posed. But they confirm, in textual terms, that Peirce *must* have subscribed to Claim 1; that he *does* in fact do so in the context of the citation given, in spite of appearances to the contrary; and that his *not* subscribing to Claim 1 would have signified his rejecting the ground for his own pragmatism (or pragmaticism) as well as the ground on which any future pragmatism might collect the best discoveries of current Eurocentric philosophy—which might otherwise be lost for another generation.

Here, for instance, is one extremely telling passage:

> Truth is a character which attaches to an abstract proposition, such as a person might utter. It essentially depends upon that proposition's not professing to be exactly true. But we hope that in the progress of science its error will indefinitely diminish, just as the error of 3.14159, the value given for π, will indefinitely diminish as the calculation is carried to more and more places of decimals. If our hope is vain [for "logical" reasons] . . . in respect to some question . . . , then in regard to that question there certainly is no *truth*. But whether or not there would be perhaps any *reality* is a question for the metaphysician, not the logician. (5.565)

Now, there is no operationally determinate sense in which our approaching the "ideal limit" of independently "Real things" ever proceeds in the way the correction of "the error of 3.14159" is rightly diminished. The analogy is completely useless with regard to what is real and to what is true. (See 5.407.) This is a variant of W. V. Quine's charge, of course. But we surely cannot conclude from that that there's nothing real in nature and nothing that we can say about it that is true. Furthermore, the clever separation between questions of truth and questions of reality makes no sense at all, except in terms of flagging the Idealist grounds for and against the disjunctive realist reading (let us say, the "God's-Eye view") of "reality."

I've already touched on this in drawing attention to Peirce's excessively linearized intuition about overlapping sets of infinitesimals (applied to "reality") that might suggest a way of progressing toward a determinately ideal description of ordinary things: there is no such pertinent limit in speaking of what is encountered, and the would-be laws of nature have no fixed role of any kind regarding the fallibilist characterization of "real things" that bears any functional similarity to our progressively calculating the value of π. (In fact, any theory favoring the determinacy of exceptionless laws of nature would now probably count as an expression of abductive Hope.) So the canonical realist has lost some important ground. There is no asymptotically accessible ideal limit of *inquiry*. Peirce is off the mark here. (Note his expression: "depends upon that proposition's not professing to be exactly true.")

Here, secondly, is a pair of closely related, very telling passages:

> In ordinary life all our statements, it is well understood, are, in the main, rough approximations to what we mean to convey. (5.568)

> ... it has been held that a real object is that which will be represented in the ultimate opinion about it. This implies that a series of opinions succeed one another, and that it is hoped that they may ultimately tend more and more toward some limiting [convergent] opinion, even if they do not reach and rest in a last opinion. (5.608)

These seem to me to be intended as methodological hypotheses of a very general kind, but they are clearly infected with the sense of Peirce's "mythic" hypothesis about ultimately "Real things"—which can never be shown to exist though the hypothesis itself conforms with something akin to Hegel's "Absolute Knowing" (without any explicit textual connection and without any telic or cognizable convergence). Both betray an expectation that some probabilistic calculus may be applied, progressively, to sets of events or particular things, in anticipation of discerning the ideally "Real things" they "approximate." They intend a reasoned comparison between what, provisionally, we treat as real "in ordinary life" (or in some "opinion" formed in ordinary life) *and* what, by some supposed calculus, will enable us to formulate a further, relatively more accurate opinion or approximation regarding the *same* real "object" or "objects" *as we approach* an ideally "limiting opinion" or statement closer "to what we mean to convey" (about what is truly real).[53] Bear in mind that, in finite inquiry, we can never escape the interlocking instantiations of Secondness and Thirdness; but, at the end of infinite inquiry, we "must" do so (on the disjunctive or realist view).

I reject any such analysis. Peirce's tortured reasoning introduces the "provisionally" real objects of ordinary life, the right examination of which leads us (on Peirce's account) to what, semiotically, points in the direction of the "Real things" *they* approximate.[54] Peirce rarely gets beyond the formal, quasi-mathematical continuum that lends plausibility to a very unlikely picture. (The entire exercise may not really matter, if, as I suspect, the whole affair is essentially a charade meant to bolster the reception of Peirce's picture of what is "independently" real.) Not unlike Hegel before him, Peirce is unsure of what would follow if we abandoned altogether the "ideal" of what is "absolutely" real. (The answer, I suggest, is partly sketched by Dewey.) You realize that there are two very different sorts of projection here: one, close to the earliest of Peirce's remarks on pragmatism, regarding approximating to the final truth about what we claim to encounter here and now in practical life; the other, what continually emerges as presumptively real causal regularities, which may not have been manifested before, but which may affect the validity of our conjectures regarding the final laws of nature.

There's no question that Peirce favors a formal, quasi-mathematical formulation of what he surely understands to be inherently informal, inductive, and consensual in the social sense. Thus, in a telling third passage, he says:

> At any moment we are in possession of certain information, that is, of cognitions which have been logically derived by induction and hypothesis from previous cognitions which are less general, less distinct, and of which we have less lively consciousness. . . . The real, then, is that which, sooner or later, information and reasoning would finally result in and which is therefore independent of the vagaries of me and you. Thus, the very origin of the conception of reality shows that this conception essentially involves the notion of a COMMUNITY, without definite limits, and capable of a definite increase of knowledge. And so these two series of cognition—the real and the unreal—consist of those which, at a time sufficiently future, the community will always continue to re-affirm; and of those which, under the same conditions, will ever after be denied. (5.311; compare 5.605)

Here, you may glimpse the advantage of Cassirer's "idea of limit" over Peirce's bizarre meander with infinitesimals. (The passage just cited is decidedly muddled.) Cassirer forthrightly treats the mathematized explanatory models of physics as free conjectures, whereas Peirce treats the finite steps of any pragmatically responsible science as converging, mysteriously, toward its infinite goal. The one favors the contingencies of rational imagination and invention; the other, the comfort of rational Hope in the face of the insuperable limitations of every conjectured truth. The one improves our grasp of the methodology of scientific inquiry; the other reminds us of the constancy of mortal risk through all such gains. The one tests the possibility of revising the Kantian presumption; at best, the other confirms its endless pathos. Both, I would say, are pragmatists: Peirce, possibly freer, ultimately, than Cassirer; Cassirer, probably more canny, finally, than Peirce. But both secure the inseparably intertwined union of realism and Idealism against impatient ideologues.

There is, I now venture to say, no plausible reading of the admission just cited from Peirce regarding the (semiotic or informational) continuum of inquiry and the profoundly informal way in which consensual conjectures regarding "the real" can be shown to mount toward their "ideal limit." But, then, we are led to see that the idea of what is "independent of the vagaries of you and me" *is itself constructed by pragmatist means*. Does that validate James's original account of truth? I think not. But then, I should also say that, in *Essays in Radical Empiricism*, James is not at all bothered by anything like Peirce's hothouse questions about truth. There, James appears to be holding to a robust sense of the reality of perceived things and the general reliability of reported experience. He's a commonsense "realist" all right; but the questions he examines in the *Essays* presuppose an effective grasp of what is ordinarily taken to be "real": he does not answer that question in a way that would satisfy the careful "realist." Nevertheless, it is true, as I've already suggested, that he turns the question regarding truth in the direction of an important "paradigm shift."

So Claim 1 is confirmed in spades. The mythic science is completely retired as a science, and Peirce stands before us as a most ingenious Hegelian-like phenomenologist as he affirms:[55] "The science of Phenomenology is in my view the most primal of all the positive sciences. That is, it is not based, as to its principles, upon any other *positive science*. By a *positive* science I mean an inquiry which seeks for positive knowledge, that is, for such knowledge as may conveniently be expressed in a *categorical proposition*" (5.39).[56] We never rightly know the sense in which "the phaneron" *could* be the subject of a "positive science": Peirce is not sufficiently clear as to whether he believes, in addition to believing that the categories of Firstness, Secondness, and Thirdness are universally present in phenomenological experience, that the "phanerons" of experience itself could possibly yield any universal regularities on which some further positive science could build. He means his "primal science" to be presuppositionless, which of course puts the universality of his categories at insuperable risk.

I take the true force of Peirce's fallibilism to be simpler than these last conjectures suggest. I don't mean to say that the linkage between Peirce's phenomenology and his fallibilism is not important. It is. But since the relationship between the finite and the infinite in Peirce's theory of inquiry *can't* be cast as an analogue of the relationship between the finite and the infinite applied to the natural numbers, Peirce equivocates when he speaks of the limit of infinite inquiry *and* of what a community of inquirers will, "at a time sufficiently future . . . always continue to reaffirm." The vindication of Peirce's realism falters on that equivocation.

But if we suppose (as I do) that Peirce's fallibilism may be read more promisingly in accord with Cassirer's more up-to-date account of the evolution of modern physics from, say, Newton to Hertz and Hermann von Hemholtz and beyond, the aptness of Peirce's conception becomes clear at once. Here, Cassirer speaks of a decisive eclipse of what he calls the "copy theory of physical knowledge" (by which he means the theory, shared by Kant's first *Critique* and "Galilean-Newtonian dynamics," that holds that the "basic concepts of natural science . . . appear as mere copies and reproductions of immediate material data"), which has been irreversibly replaced by autonomously proposed mathematized functions abstractly invented in order to capture some hypothesized physical law that the pertinent data may (when rightly consulted) be shown to conform to. Cassirer regards this turn, initiated by Hertz, as decisive for the entire subsequent history of physics: it signifies (he says) a turn to "a purely symbolic theory," and it obviously requires a form of interpretation that cannot be bound to the seeming limits of Kant's account of sensory experience. This new dimension of conceptual freedom, in Cassirer's opinion, "constitutes the essence of physical theory."[57]

Seen this way, and applying Cassirer's explanation of the finite/infinite continuum of scientific knowledge that occupied Peirce's attention so strenuously, we see how easily fallibilism's advantage can be made to rest with *not* attempting to succor realism by appealing to the "outcome of infinite inquiry" (as Peirce does) but, rather, with the endless need to invent, again and again, *further* "symbolic" conceptions ("pictures," as I've suggested) of the would-be underlying laws of nature apt for replacing previous particular such inventions. Of this "new mode of formation and conceptual unity" in physics, Cassirer says:

Of course it is implicit [in its history] that the objectivity toward which it progresses and aims can never be conclusively determined. Whereas the "thing" of naive intuition may appear as a fixed sum of definite properties, the physical object by its very nature can be conceived only in the form of an "idea of limit." [This is essential to what Cassirer means by "a purely symbolic theory."] For here it is not a matter of disclosing the ultimate, absolute elements of reality, in the contemplation of which thought may rest as it were, but of a never-ending process through which the relatively necessary takes the place of the relatively accidental and the relatively invariable that of the relatively variable. We can never claim that this process has attained to the ultimate invariants of experience, which would then replace the immutable facticity of "things"; we can never claim to grasp these invariants with our hands so to speak. Rather, the possibility must always be held open that a new synthesis will instate itself and that the universal constraints, in terms of which we have signalized the "nature" of certain large realms of physical objects, will come closer together and prove themselves to be special cases of an overarching lawfulness.[58]

Peirce's solution entrusts the force of the argument to a thesis that cannot fail to be question begging, whereas Cassirer's solution shows a natural convergence between pragmatism and the Hegelian possibilities of neo-Kantianism. (Cassirer must have realized that his criticism of Kant's account of a closed system of concepts required an extremely liberal reading of Hegel's notion of the telos of "Absolute Knowing.") My sense is that that convergence affords the key to the best prospects of the whole of Eurocentric philosophy. It also shows Peirce a better reading of his own intuition: merely replace (it advises) the abductive teleology of the long run (whenever it gratuitously infects Peirce's realism) with whatever abductive open-ended concatenation of testable, finite, incremental guesses proves promising—and then admit that we have no other sources of realist assurance to fall back on. Wherever the historicity of inquiry is conceded, realism is inseparable from Idealism. But then, since on that score realism itself must take a historicist turn, pragmatism need never be compromised—and canonical realism will be eclipsed almost without effort. For Cassirer—here at least—the transcendental has ceased to be constitutive (in the Kantian sense), is now entirely "regulative"; but, then, it corresponds to the function of Peirce's abductive Hope, though (to be honest) it's far more straightforward.

Peirce is entitled—abductively—only to the generic Hope regarding realism: there can be no legible sense in which a particular general belief provisionally thought true now can be tracked through the continuum of finite and infinite inquiry in any way similar to the continuum affecting generic Hope. History cannot be constant in the requisite way. Here,

Cassirer may be a better pragmatist than Peirce. Peirce has too great a longing for the older universalisms. But then, as it may be argued, so, too, has Cassirer. In one respect, Cassirer's Kantianism may prove more resilient than Peirce's and, in another, more regressive. For present purposes, Cassirer's formulation provides a way of recovering Peirce's important intuition—fallibilism's central theme—in terms more congenial to the leaner history of science's modeling of reality than Peirce's more idiosyncratic idiom affords: in doing that, it suggests how pragmatism may improve its "picture" of its own principle by co-opting the emerging pragmatist prospects of pertinent solutions of cognate problems independently achieved. In that spirit, pragmatism begins to escape its more parochial limitations in its enlarged career. It's the historicity of inquiry and explanation that's decisive in resolving the question of the right way to read fallibilism's realist commitment. Once constructivism replaces cognitive privilege, once our grasping truth and reality is "located" at the end of infinite inquiry, the very idea of improving our approximation to either, incrementally, by way of finite inquiry, makes no sense at all in confirmational terms. Peirce, I would say, is explaining why Hope is needed everywhere in the rational pursuit of life and science.

3

Pragmatism's Future
A Touch of Prophecy

PRAGMATISM'S RECOVERY from its near demise in the 1940s and 1950s is nothing short of miraculous. It's a completely gratuitous reprieve, without warrant or explicit purpose, now exploited in a thousand insouciant ways worldwide. It may be the most improbable philosophical recovery of its kind in recent academic memory since it has no manifesto to proclaim that could account for its newfound attraction. In this regard, its recovery cannot compare with W. V. Quine's ingeniously pared-down retrieval of the remnant forces of logical positivism's failed vision, reconfigured transatlantically around the innovative spark of Quine's own "Two Dogmas" paper and freed (by Quine's wit) from the overly strenuous, now impossible ambitions of the Fregean, positivist, and unity of science visions that once joined hands to command analytic philosophy's sprawling empire in the first half of the twentieth century.

Quine extended analytic philosophy's hegemony another fifty years, though not robustly enough to improve the viability of the programs of its most daring progenitors. They've lost their triumphal edge, possibly forever, and now betray the impoverished results of the narrow strategies of analysis they once demanded. Failing there, analytic philosophy has lost its original fluency and speculative breadth, which might have kept its practice in touch with the best of pragmatist and continental ventures. Its reputation still rests with its rigor; but rigor is doubtful wherever its best efforts are too slow to admit the failure of its reductionisms, supervenientisms, eliminativisms, axiomatizations, systems of causal closure, or the rest of its utopian projects. Also, Quine's initiative arose to meet the willing responses of the faithful in support of his frontal attack on the canonical distinction (Rudolf Carnap's) between the "analytic" and the "synthetic" so essential to the faltering claims of the positivists themselves. The pragmatists never had such a cause; yet their own cause, hardly much improved over the past sixty years, now seems remarkably secure.

The most plausible explanation has it that the revival of pragmatism reflects a sense of the continuing respectability and limited gains of its original program—despite its obviously faded fortunes—when compared with the more precipitous decline of the boldest analytic programs of the whole of the twentieth century and the no-more-than-tepid interest on the part of the dominant moiety of the Anglo-American academy to draw any strength at all from the best work of post-Kantian "continental" philosophy. If pragmatism could but find a plausible new source of conceptual invention to "complete" the insufficient articulation of its classic trajectory, it would, I foresee, move to incorporate within that new vision selected intuitions from the best of the analytic and continental movements it's now well-placed to outdistance. That may explain both the unearned recovery of pragmatism's prospects and the contorted, oblique efforts among recent pragmatists and analytic philosophers to test the waters to fathom just how much of Hegel and Heidegger they dare risk absorbing without contamination. I would say the saving themes have already been accessible, however neglected, for a longish time: namely, historicity and the irreducible emergence of the cultural world.

There's a line of reasoning, barely bruited here, that I shall keep in my sights, in the recuperative effort that now beckons, which I'm bound to say requires uniting the speculative breadth of the preceding chapters and the characteristic appeal of a model of rigorous argument so dear to analytic practice. It's a commonsense clue that the analysts have slighted in their most impressive cameo specimens—those, for instance, focused in an admirably spare way in Quine's "Two Dogmas" paper, Saul Kripke's arguments regarding the "necessary a posteriori" and the brief for "rigid designators"—and, of course, from there, stretching out within a motley of similarly lean would-be "demonstrations," the best specimens on all the topics that belong to the analysts' habit of miniaturizing the gist of global speculation so that it yields what, when successful, presents itself as a jeweled paradigm for further definition.

I offer only a word of advance notice here. The analysts have been notably attracted, in the second half of the twentieth century and on into the twenty-first, by the possibility of recovering the still-viable force of their strongest philosophical programs. I doubt they can be recovered in anything like the daring of their original visions. (We may not agree about that.) But the specimen work of late Anglo-American analysts is uniquely marked by the guiding assumption of such a possibility. The result is that late analysis has produced a considerable body of extremely brief, seemingly autonomous, argumentatively transparent exemplars that are legible at once to the initiated without more than the least reminder of different parts of the original inspiration—which once commanded a very large part of the philosophical literature of the entire past century but which (I believe) has essentially failed at great cost. The cost has taken the form of a very definite atrophy of interest and attention to "metaphilosophical" debate pursued across all the most active movements of the Eurocentric world. I think it has left analytic philosophy peculiarly impoverished—almost deliberately uninformed about the prospects of a fresh recovery of so-called second-order intuitions and debate. I return, at the end of this book, to a brief sampling of the analytic literature in question—opportunistically, let me admit, in the company of an admirable, much more optimistic assessment of its actual achievement, which appeared in a recent, well-received review, in Gary Gutting's *What Philosophers Know*.[1] I mean this as a substantive aside in support of a more balanced rapprochement within the bounds of Eurocentric philosophy.

There's nothing in pragmatism and continental philosophy that quite compares with this analytic practice, though there's rigor enough. I find (as I say) that the analysts have risked too much, without sufficient gain, in the way of sharing and understanding the global context in which their own best specimens have any force at all. But for the moment, I mean only to hoist a warning against returning to the disparate practices of the principal movements of the tradition. To exaggerate: the cameo arguments of the analysts are blind when detached from their speculative contexts; pragmatist and continental speculation risks being empty or trivial when it fails to yield exemplary "demonstrations"; *and* the philosophical discipline fitted to these two foci of attention appear to invite very different ranges of rigor and precision. Finally, it must be said that philosophy continually discovers that it is informal, even where its effectiveness appears in the idealized idiom of deductive argument, with only the slightest concessions to the stray intuitions that seem to capture nearly the whole of serious argument among its principal opponents. I think the picture must be corrected, if anything like the rapprochement I'm recommending has any future.

My guess is that the new pragmatism will remain vigorous enough for a second inning, but if it cannot motivate its gift soon enough, it will fade again into the archival oblivion that was ready to receive it at the end of its first life. I do, however, see something (now) of the deeper meaning of reclaiming the early promise of pragmatism's classic phase. It's not a regressive sort of enthusiasm. I don't mean that there is or ever was a golden discovery somehow overlooked until the period spanning the 1970s and the first decade of the new century—that is, the start of pragmatism's second life. Of course not. But the philosophical world has changed its priorities. Nearly every movement of distinction that once flourished in the last century (chiefly, in the first half of the century) has failed or lost the bloom of its original promise by now—or is viewed very differently than in its prime—as a result of philosophy's disenchantment with disenchanted philosophy. In that sense, pragmatism's unearned recovery is the sign of a certain unspent resource (faute de mieux), an intuition of conceptual possibilities only hinted at, that the competing movements of its own prime could never build upon.

Pragmatism's recovery is in good part due to a dawning sense of the importance (still decisive in our age) of the philosophical revolution originally set in motion by the now-indissoluble contributions of Kant and Hegel. It begins with the earliest reception, in the United States, of the Hegelian critique of Kant[2]—in what, after the Civil War, marks the first flourishing of America's newly liberated philosophical imagination, as it entered the Eurocentric world as the unanticipated expression of a newly minted people.

Its recovery, now, depends on a new perception of the skewed work of the whole of twentieth-century philosophy; possibly, then, on a sidewise estimate of its original promise, not yet fully discerned but dawning, that senses its native advantage over the more nearly disabling weaknesses (approaching irrelevance) of its most famous competitors: for instance, in terms of the inapt collapse of positivism and the near exhaustion of Husserl's and Heidegger's notably unstable apriorisms. What, from our present outlook, Hegel achieved includes at least the abandonment of all that remained regressive in Kant's original defeat of the presumptions of cognitive privilege within the "pre-Kantian" world: the a priori of the transcendental question turned aposteriorist; it became, with its shifting interests, historied, provisional, constructed, diverse, and impossible to confirm except as plausible and congruent in a practical way; hence, it proved to be plural, open-ended, fragmentary, continually evolving, impossible to complete, and useless to think of asymptotically in naive-realist terms. That is already more than an incipient pragmatism. Have a look, for instance, at C. I. Lewis's "A Pragmatic Conception of the *A Priori*" and George Herbert Mead's account of the emergence of the human self.[3] You cannot fail to "anticipate" (so to say) Hegel's probable interest in their new naturalisms—if not his prescient approval.

Pragmatism *is* Hegelian, then, *and*, of course, Kantian for that reason. It eschews the prospect of a closed system of categories for any descriptive, explanatory, or normatively practical discourse. It concedes (or celebrates) the insuperable informality of rational and responsible legitimation; the contingent and functional adequacies of human judgment; the *vernünftig*, entirely reflexive, constructivist sources of conviction, bootstrapped by its refusal to exclude any *données* of experience; hence, also, it is committed to the primacy of the merely human self and its humanly accessible world rather than to the invented fiction of a Transcendental Ego and its supposed practice.[4] Hegel brings Kant back to the human world—so that the transcendental question cannot and need not be abandoned and can never again claim to justify any hierarchized order of cognitive competence. In championing all this, Hegel embeds the self in the internal *Bildung* of an enabling culture, itself historicized by the evolving work of its second-natured offspring. (This, I suggest, is the nerve of Hegel's emendation of the Aristotelian thesis, hospitably extracted in accord with the interests of contemporary philosophy.) But to feature such a theme within the naturalistic paraphrases of twentieth- and twenty-first-century philosophy is hardly to be obliged to concede, say, the telic holism of Hegel's own extravagant prose, even *if* (against a more moderate reading) Hegel is himself charged with championing such a conviction. Pragmatism was always intent on the sparest possible such loyalties.

There you have a glimpse of one of the principal visions by which we still guide ourselves two hundred years beyond its first formulation—a fortiori, the nerve of the argument by which pragmatism's evolving advantage (over analytic and continental philosophy) may be effectively advanced. It explains, in passing, for instance, the inordinate (however instructive) contemporary interest in John McDowell's slack recovery of the relevance of Hegel's conception of *Bildung* for late analytic philosophy: you may indeed find the object of that same interest matched (a little more suggestively at times, though still at a puzzling distance and in not much detail—perhaps by way of a less than perspicuous detour—inferentialism) in Robert Brandom's recent allusions to Hegel's relevance for contemporary philosophy.[5]

This same interest in recovering Hegel answers to our sense of the unfinished project of pragmatism's classic period—if you draw on Dewey's *Experience and Nature* or the obvious affinities between Peirce's and Dewey's versions of fallibilism. But Dewey, opposing Peirce's florid anticipation and eventual acceptance of parts of Hegel's Idealist idiom, characteristically economizes by way of a more Darwinized reading of pragmatic success. Emphasizing the common conditions of animal and human intelligence and survival (the evolutionary continuum: the clever rhetoric of his "problematic situation"),[6] Dewey's fallibilism acknowledges in one breath the difference between the human analogue of animal life and the "higher," more complex requirements of a valid science. In Dewey's hands, the phrasing assures us that we need not (and ought not) insist on any essential discontinuity between the resolution of our animal needs and the sui generis puzzles of scientific rigor. That is surely the point of the bridging function in Dewey's deliberately informal advocacy of what he names "warranted assertibility"—in place of (Peirce's infinitely pursued) truth.[7]

Peirce was much clearer than Dewey about the difference between the animal continuum of practical impasses and the uncertainties of science, between the doubts of existential life and the doubts of scientific conjecture; but Dewey was clearer about the improbability of ever reaching a unique convergence in open-ended inquiry. In different ways, each endorsed the infinity of our search for the uniformities of nature: Peirce elects the utopian option of a unique and progressive outcome; Dewey, the relaxed accommodation of whatever time may disclose. But neither is in error, since the endlessly unfinished purpose of inquiry is committed to a form of Hope, *not* any pretended grasp of the ultimate telos of history. Dewey is more literally pragmatic, since questions of truth or warranted assertibility are, for him, episodic rather than tied to conjectures about an infinite continuum; and Peirce is more ingenious and more penetrating, since he finds a telling regulative (pragmatic) use for the concept of infinite inquiry, despite the fact that infinite inquiry is, trivially, impossible to pursue in finite time. It is, in fact, in this way that Peirce makes such a telling use of the indissolubility of realism and Idealism, without treating metaphysics in idealist terms. I take this to have been wrongly diagnosed by Hilary Putnam.[8] The genuine force of Peirce's fallibilism shows itself to advantage best when compared with Cassirer's seemingly similar insistence on the "infinity" of scientific inquiry. Cassirer was better placed, historically, to make the case for the radical innovations of physics at the turn of the twentieth century, but Peirce escapes the regressive Kantianism that Cassirer ultimately yields to (for instance, in his contrast between science and history).

My own intuition is persuaded that Dewey's economy must still be tempered within the ampler terms of Peirce's early papers (1877–1878), especially "The Fixation of Belief" and "How to Make Our Ideas Clear," which already signal the importance of the continuity between the animal and the human (a theme that may well precede Peirce's eventual acceptance of the Darwinian thesis). I find the clue to Peirce's subtlety and sense of the complexities of science (*beyond* the would-be "logic" of the resolution of animal "doubt" at the human level) in the verbal slippage Peirce permits himself (in "How to Make Our Ideas Clear"), moving from expressions such as, "to know what we think, to be masters of our meaning" (relative to the human continuation of the animal), down to these pointed claims—which use the same wording but change the weight of the possessive pronouns:

I only desire to point out how impossible it is that we should have an idea in our minds which relates to anything but conceived sensible effects; and if we fancy that we have any other we deceive ourselves, and mistake a mere sensation accompanying the thought for a part of the thought itself. . . . Consider what effects, which might conceivably have practical bearings, we conceive the object of our conception to have. Then, our conception of these effects is the whole of our conception of the object.[9]

Here, Peirce makes provision for his initial "animal" reading of pragmatism, which (we cannot fail to grasp) is meant to mark only, or primarily, the initial animal condition on which the evolved conception of science (occupied with the puzzling search for truth and reality) begins to eclipse the explanatory resources of animal doubt itself (a fortiori, the Darwinian discovery). Thus, in "The Fixation of Belief," Peirce already provides the following contrast, which Dewey somewhat conflates in his own economy:

The irritation of doubt causes a struggle to attain a state of belief. . . . The irritation of doubt is the only immediate motive for the struggle to attain belief. . . . With the doubt, therefore, the struggle begins, and with the cessation of doubt it ends. Hence, the sole object of inquiry is the settlement of opinion. We may fancy that this is not enough for us, and what we seek, not merely an opinion, but a true opinion. But put this fancy to the test, and it proves groundless; for as soon as a firm belief is reached we are entirely satisfied, whether the belief be true or false.

and

The object of reasoning is to find out, from the consideration of what we already know, something else which we do not know. Consequently, reasoning is good if it be such as to give a true conclusion from true premises, and not otherwise.... It is certainly best for us that our beliefs should be such as may truly guide our actions so as to satisfy our desires; and this reflection will make us reject any belief which does not seem to have been so formed as to insure that result. But it will only do so by creating a doubt in the place of that belief.[10]

This is prettily turned but exceptionally spare: it shows the continuity and difference between the brute resolution of animal doubt and the transformed persistence of a very different kind of doubt within the concerns of scientific inquiry. It anticipates (and in effect refuses) Dewey's simpler economy; anticipates (and in effect disallows, also in advance) William James's well-known (1898) rendering of Peirce's conception of truth, twenty years after the publication of "How to Make Our Ideas Clear"—which misreads Peirce's intention even as it introduces his pragmatism to the world; collects the nerve of Kant's and Hegel's critique of "pre-Kantian" philosophy; lays the ground for Peirce's complex conception of fallibilism, which obliges us to come to terms with the continuum of finite and infinite inquiry (already broached in the "pragmatic maxim" of the second paper in the *Popular Science Monthly* series); and wisely avoids any confident analysis of the animal mind.

Nevertheless, it is true (we need to remind ourselves) that the spare empiricist cast of Peirce's earliest view of pragmatic tests of meaning (in the service of an effective commitment to truth) was never seriously overhauled in terms of the constructivist, intermediary, enabling, conceptual processes by which the realist question might be convincingly resolved. That, I suggest, is precisely what the recovery of Hegel might facilitate. It harbors more than a glimpse of the congenial ground on which the rapprochement of the whole of Western philosophy might be advanced—hence, in passing, more than a clue as to how to construe the right reading of realism.

All this entrenches—however obliquely—the incipient "Hegelian" cast of Peirce's earliest papers, as well as their proto-Darwinian inclination. But what, finally, they yield (in the later papers) is the constant sense that precision in our conjectures about the nature of the world and our encounter with whatever may be found in it is forever hostage to the informalities of practical life—continuous with the animal and the protoplasmic—which then insuperably qualify the presumed rigor and systematicity of our grasp of the meaning of meaning, truth, and reality. In fact, it would not be unreasonable to read Peirce's penchant for extravagant mythic renderings of his own philosophical searches as so many ways of entrenching his appreciation of the lesson—as with his agapasm, synechism, the evolution of the laws of nature, the treatment of inquiry itself as a continuum of living and overlapping infinitesimals, the unity of the finite and infinite. These are all part of Peirce's cosmology, what he sometimes calls "guesses" (abductions of Hope, I think we may say).[11] They are also very clever anticipations of a fresh reading of the pragmatist conception of science, which I shall come to shortly.

I take these first ventures on Peirce's part to signal, subliminally, what was to be the growing (never quite consummated) union of Hegelian and Darwinian themes among the pragmatists. (By "Darwinian themes," I trust it's clear that I mean to feature the sequel to Darwin's own contribution that appears in the work of the paleoanthropology of the human self, the philosophical anthropology of figures like Marjorie Grene and Helmuth Plessner, and the enabling neurophysiology and *Bildung* of the human infant.) In any event, the idea accords with the deep informality and absence of cognitive privilege of any kind in resolving the "doubts" of practical life and of the sciences that build upon them and inevitably exceed their function in the evolving complexities of advanced inquiry; it accords with the flux of the experienced world and the inescapably ad hoc, fragmentary sufficiency of what we concede to be valid, though forever open to invented challenge; it answers the question regarding the general resources of realism by featuring the survival of the human world even where our grasp of the world clearly departs from animal intelligence and Cartesian certitude; and it trusts its inveterate optimism (abductive Hope, in Peirce's conception—a higher sort of animal or psychological hope in Dewey's) to the reflexive, sui generis powers of the historied cultures of the human world itself. (The puzzles of infinite inquiry must themselves be entirely settled within the boundaries of finite inquiry.)

But most of what Peirce and Dewey provide in this regard falls noticeably short of the strongest possibilities of "Darwinizing Hegel" and "Hegelianizing Darwin": that is, falls short of what now seems possible (and promising), given the radical notion of the artifactual self, the unique role of language, the differences between biological and cultural evolution, the analysis of history, and the completely altered expectations of a human world shorn of universalism, essentialism, substantive necessity, apodicticity, and any and all privileged sources of cognitive confidence beyond the passing adequacy of self-corrective practical guesses within a largely unknown and inexhaustible world.

On my reading, this *is* the Hegel of the twentieth and twenty-first centuries—naturalized by the pragmatists, the best of the Marburg Kantians, the Marxists, the Nietzscheans, and the early Frankfurt Critical School. Possibly then, it may also be Hegel's best reading of Hegel. What beckons beyond all that is the attraction of the concept of the artifactual self and all that that may contribute toward enhancing pragmatism's new ascendency. Of course, we must bear in mind that the analysis of the self, of the enlanguaged and encultured human world, of the very idea of historied existence, *is* the most neglected—incomparably the most important—part of current and future philosophy: suppressed (thus far) by the salience of the most reductive tendencies of analytic philosophy during the very interval in which pragmatism suddenly revived.

It needs to be said that the inherent informality of human inquiry that pervades Peirce's earliest papers and is favored even more insistently in Dewey's treatment of science has now begun to attract a growing number of knowledgeable inquiries into the philosophical foundations of the physical sciences: notably, in the work of Otto Neurath, Richard Feynman, Ian Hacking, Nancy Cartwright, and others who see the fragmentary, somewhat opportunistic, informally overlapping, rather ad hoc, "interested" and pragmatic reliability of any of our truth-claims as a valid challenge to the very primacy of the idea of the changeless laws of nature and the canonical standing of the hypothetico-deductive model of explanation.

Let me cite, without comment then, Feynman's well-known preference for the "Babylonian" conception of science over the "Euclidean," which affords a very good impression of the upstart attraction of (what I am calling) the developing pragmatist conception of science. "In physics," Feynman says, "we need the Babylonian method and not the Euclidean or Greek method . . . [or at least not, until] physics is complete and we know all the laws. . . . [Otherwise,] if all [our] various theorems are interconnected by reasoning [for instance, by alternative axiomatizations that yield mathematically strict equivalences at critical points but are 'completely unequivalent ("psychologically") when you are trying to guess new laws'], there is no real way [and no need] to say 'These are the most fundamental axioms.'" The Babylonian method, then, proceeds along the following, seemingly blundering lines:

> I happen to know this, and I happen to know that, and maybe I know that; and I work everything out from there. Tomorrow I may forget that that is true, but remember that something else is true, so I can reconstruct it all again. I am never sure of where I am supposed to begin or where I am supposed to end. I just remember enough all the time so that as memory fades and some of the pieces fall out I can put the thing back together again every day.[12]

The argument favors commonsense successes that are relatively episodic and pretty well under local practical control; by contrast, theorizing tends to be global and takes conceptual liberties with what is relatively assured locally. I cannot imagine a general picture of science (favored as a form of rigor suited to the discipline given, as Aristotle says) that would be more congenial to a recuperated pragmatism.

Admittedly, the thesis I have in mind about the artifactuality of the self is a quarrelsome one, and possibly not entirely welcome, though it has its lesson. The end of the twentieth century witnessed the recycled failure (at a reduced level of ambition) of a great many of the most successful lines of inquiry of the first half of the century. The new wave of pragmatisms of our day, which are no longer merely parochial—perhaps then the whole of Western philosophy—depends upon that fact. We find ourselves obliged to reconsider what may have been lost or suppressed in analytic philosophy's massive avoidance (through most of the twentieth century) of any commerce with Hegel's thought, despite the plain fact that Hegel lays out the strongest, most ramified account of the possibility of a radical recovery of Kant's great innovation, which, if allowed, would entail the rejection of all of Kant's "pre-Kantian" assumptions. After Hegel, it no longer makes sense to think of Kant and Hegel separately, except in terms of the formation of one or another "Hegelianized" Kantianism.

The second round of philosophical failings (from, say, World War II to the end of the century) signifies a serious loss of confidence, much confusion, and above all a forced patience in the face of seeming stalemate and exhaustion, which, within the period of pragmatism's recovery, I associate most memorably—though equivocally—with Richard Rorty's terribly effective exposés and oddly relevant irrelevancies. Rorty was a philosophical talent of considerable daring who was obviously tempted by Hegel's courage but who was clinically unwilling to advance any sanguine improvements addressed to the fatigued (perhaps already superseded) options of recent philosophy (which Rorty tirelessly examined along pragmatist and Hegelian lines) and then debunked them all as impossible to validate. (Almost no philosophers of standing have followed Rorty in this.) In fact, Rorty construed his own dismissal of canonical philosophy as the true "postmodern" theme of pragmatism's own revival.[13] He meant this, at different moments, to be Hegelian, Heideggerian, Wittgensteinian, Sellarsian, Davidsonian, and Deweyian as well!

. . .

The shortest summary of the new turn I've been sketching—in effect, a prophecy of pragmatism's future: perhaps the future of the whole of Eurocentric philosophy—calls, as I've already remarked, for "Darwinizing Hegel" and "Hegelianizing Darwin." The manifesto was never explicitly embraced by the classic pragmatists, and its full implications are even now not entirely clear. (Its wording, however, *was* anticipated in one of Peirce's book reviews in the *Nation*, but we cannot be sure what Peirce would have had us understand by that.) What I mean to signal on the Darwinian side is that, once the earliest post-Darwinian speculations about *Homo sapiens* took form, pragmatism should have made the analysis of the concept of a person or self the absolutely decisive center of its own labor. If it had begun to think along these lines during the period in which classic pragmatism nearly expired (that is, in the 1940s and 1950s), it would by now have had the benefit of not fewer than sixty years in which to explore its essential and most elementary possibilities—all the while the energies of its principal rivals were deflected by insistent inquiries that have proved to be occasions for recycling the spent proposals of the first half of the twentieth century. Imagine!

Strange to say, this rather ordinary beginning—the analysis of the self—now promises to yield the most radical possible approach to the entire run of standard problems confronting any and all the current philosophical schools. Read along Darwinian lines, the least inquiry would have put in instant and deepest jeopardy a great many recalcitrant doctrines the pragmatists had hoped to topple by other means—and would have done so by a single stroke—even if not, let it be said, without risking the standing of their own perspective.

It would, I believe, have brought philosophy as close as we could possibly imagine to the presuppositionless objective of Hegel's original critique of Kant: the advantage of his minimal phenomenology. Pragmatism might have appeared then to have discovered the very nerve of one of the strongest possible versions of its evolving vision, in a way dialectically disclosed by the mounting exposé of analytic philosophy's own decline. In truth, the two outcomes are hardly more than the heads and tails of the same philosophical toss. No large claim of the relevant kind could expect to escape the challenge of its own revision and the changing forms of its legitimation. Of course, that is also the essential point of reading Hegel as the best of the enlightened "Kantians" of his own age—though probably not of ours, persuaded as we are by post-Darwinian reflections on the meaning of the unique history of *Homo sapiens*.

The Hegelian theme was always easier to flesh out than the Darwinian, but the Darwinian was easier to understand: the trouble has been (and still is) that the Darwinian theme (I include post-Darwinian developments) is, finally, more unsettling than the other. Nevertheless, it seems clear that the pragmatists are very well positioned to make good use of the unity of the two perspectives: there is almost nothing in recent Western philosophy that is seriously committed to the new possibility and there is nothing of comparable interest that could be drawn from the scatter of other parts of contemporary thought.

You have only to remind yourself that, already in mid- and late-eighteenth-century Europe, Kant and Hume were completely baffled by the inability of their own philosophies to generate a reasonable account of what it was to be a human subject or agent; and that, early in the nineteenth century, Hegel had already made it clear that there was no way to understand the human subject if separated from the specifically cultural and historied world in which the self is *gebildet*. I won't deny—the point is worth debating—that one may claim to find already in Hegel and Marx (Marx's *Grundrisse*, for instance) evidence of a deeper speculation about the inherently artifactual nature of the human agent. (I've been more than tempted by the same idea, but it needed a longer latency among the classic pragmatists—and, of course, ourselves.) It needs at least the notion of what I call "external" *Bildung*, that is, the effective evolutionary conditions (*not* primarily biochemical) that account for the originary presence (the artifactuality) of one or another stably enlanguaged and encultured society whose inherent paideutic powers may (then) be regularly enlisted (internally) in the intergenerational processes of (what I call) "internal" *Bildung*.[14] That is the decisive consideration that remains inaccessible to figures like Herder and Hegel (and Aristotle) and that have been ignored by contemporary figures like Gadamer (and ourselves) and certainly by much of late analytic philosophy (McDowell, for one, as I've already suggested). It needs a sense of the full transformation that post-Darwinian paleoanthropology makes possible.

Hegel's sense of *Bildung* remains committed to something like Aristotle's notion of moral grooming—"internal" *Bildung*, as I've said. But I find no evidence in Hegel that *Vernunft*, for instance, is (is rightly taken to be) a precipitate, an artifactual instantiation of the original (hybrid) evolution of an enlanguaged culture. All that Hegel vouchsafes is that *Vernunft* and *Geist* are, ultimately, one and the same ontologically. But is *Geist* (in the relevant sense) an artifact of an evolutionary continuum that begins with the prelinguistic proto-cultures of hominid primates (the precursors of *Homo sapiens* or the precursor phases of modern *Homo sapiens*), themselves still incapable of producing a true language? The question hardly arises before the advent of genetic theory at the turn of the twentieth century. It requires a fresh distinction between biological and cultural evolution: hence, a hybrid form of evolution by means of which the processes of external *Bildung* prove viable. Read this way, the whole of Western philosophy may be deemed to have been marking time—albeit with a growing anticipation (and some dread) that the relative fixities of its most admired doctrines will have to be abandoned or radically altered. (Consider, for instance, the inevitable eclipse of Aristotle's, Kant's, and Hume's moral doctrines.) This is indeed the nerve of the account I'm recommending. I suggest that something quite close to it has been on our lips at least since Dewey's and George Mead's floruit.

The essential key lies with the presumptive fact that true language is a datable achievement, an artifactual transform of the native communicative skills of the continuum of a run of primate species (both hominid and prehominid), which, even prelinguistically, accommodate (by entirely cultural means) the reliable transmission of stable forms of proto-cultural learning capable of yielding progressively developed (still sublinguistic) functions approximating more and more closely to true linguistic functions (reference and predication, say), possibly even among the monkeys.[15]

Grant all this and the decisive premise swims into view: the self or person (the human subject or agent) is a functional, hybrid transform of the biologically inherited cognitive talent of the primate members of *Homo sapiens*, the nominal agency that emerges, incipiently, *with* (*and as* the site of) the evolving mastery of one or another natural language, itself the individuated actualization of the gradually invented, collectively shared, species-centered ability to speak. Here, external *Bildung* makes internal *Bildung* possible, and internal *Bildung* makes the emergence of actual selves effective. Construed this way, the human self has no essential nature; it is primarily a history, the site of a causally generated run of functional powers uniquely marked by their reflexive ability to report and share interior experience and to act by choice in ways informed by reflecting on that experience, on the experience of other similarly formed selves, and the accumulating lore of an enabling society.

You cannot fail to glimpse the untapped power of this fresh conception. (I take it to be the promise of a new phase of pragmatism.) The human self is, effectively, a "natural artifact," meaning by that that the biology of *Homo sapiens sapiens* has evolved in ways that facilitate the unique form of the endlessly repeated "ontogenetic" mastering of the "phylogenetic" *cultural* competence of the species.[16] (The mixed phrasing may strike you as a little careless, but it is deliberately chosen, is now a routine metaphor, and is meant to be entirely benign.)

I draw a number of substantive lessons from this single theme, all pertinent of course to the prospective redirection of pragmatism's classic vision. The principal gain rests with pragmatism's dialectical advantage (its probable advantage) in competition with relevant analytic and continental inquiries. I will shortly offer a sustained example of how the argument is likely to go, when pursued in accord with certain scientific strategies of late analytic philosophy. But the whole of my brief is committed to the premise that, in claiming that the human self is a cultural artifact—a hybrid transform of the biological gifts of a notable species (our own)—I am claiming that the entire enculturing (human) world is, evolvingly, self-constructed (or self-constituting) insofar as its prelinguistic communicative powers gradually strengthen (that is, are societally remembered, developed, and reliably transmitted) in the direction of yielding a true language. In short, the emergence of the self *is*, effectively, nothing but the emerging communicative competence (and what it makes possible) as it becomes linguistically well-formed as speech.

In this sense, the self and its matched (enlanguaged) world are societally self-constructed realities (forms of being) as a result of the unique evolution (the intertwined cofunctioning of biological and cultural processes, overwhelmingly weighted in favor of the accelerating pace and mounting hegemony of enlanguaged transformation). So the self and the encultured world are, literally, social constructions—as are machinery, technologies, languages, institutions, traditions, artworks, and the like—not less real than mere physical things for that reason, but discernible as such only by those same hybrid agents (selves: ourselves) who are suitably transformed (enabled) to produce and discern what emerges in just such a world. You begin to see how, in accord with such a radical conception, the human world and the human way of grasping the natural world are essentially sui generis, in spite of the obvious biological continuity of the human and the animal. The admission infects the whole of science and philosophy.

I draw your attention, in passing, to the fairly obvious judgment that the artifactuality and historicity of the self, the cultural achievement of a true language by way of a combination of biological and cultural forces, the appearance of an entire world of culturally significant and significative phenomena (which I collect under a term of art, "Intentional," written with a capital "I"), are remarkable for their general absence (with important exceptions) in modern and contemporary Anglo-American philosophy. I press the judgment further in suggesting that these may well be the most promising themes of a redirected pragmatism (what I've brought under the motto "Darwinizing Hegel and Hegelianizing Darwin"); *and* that no such effort could prosper without conceding the detailed continuity of philosophy and the work of the human sciences and, as a result, a certain tolerance for the conceptual informality of arguments about how best to construe the logical, methodological, semantic, epistemological, ontological, and normative puzzles that bear on the definition of the world in which the unique achievement of human selves and human societies may be mapped.

I mean, quite simply, that analytic philosophy, drawn (often productively) by very strong scientistic intuitions, has largely failed to notice that the turn in late-twentieth-century philosophy leading to our own age will have to recover a better way of grasping the inseparability of the natural and human sciences, the primacy of language, and the conceptual novelty of a historied and encultured world. I am prepared to say flat out that the paradigmatic arguments so much favored by the analysts (as with Quine, early Carnap, Kripke, Donald Davidson, Edmund Gettier, and others—without prejudice to their actual force or importance) are simply unable to reconfigure their best skills in the context of the new orientation that (I say) philosophy's prospects now require. I don't think it's at all irrelevant to remind ourselves that the best specimens of analytic argument have themselves rested on a close adherence to an increasingly outmoded "picture" of the supporting discoveries of the natural sciences.

We may say here that the (broadly) cognitive powers of selves and the (broadly) cognizable features of the encultured world are "penetrated" in the same transformative way by the historically evolving language and culture of one or another enabling society. (In this sense, language, culture, history, and selves are publicly and objectively present in the world, *not* in any way confined to what is often said to be subjectively confined to the mind.) I'm speaking with some care here, because the formulation tendered will play an instructive role in examining the specimen quarrels I intend to introduce for the sake of isolating the most strategic (and disputed) features of the very space in which selves function. It's a stunning fact that even sensory perception is linguistically "penetrated" (indissolubly, continually transformed) through the whole of a self's career—hence, functions spontaneously ("naturally," second-naturedly) in its newly mastered *phenomenological* mode—as a decisive factor in any adequate post-Darwinian account of what to regard as objective experience, thought, and judgment vis-à-vis the "natural world," including the encultured world we construct or constitute and that, reciprocally, constructs us.

Nevertheless, we are not obliged to hold (as Kant holds) that we thereby "constitute" or construct the natural world we claim to know. Not at all: we dismiss any such disastrous option and move on. But it remains entirely open to us to admit that, in speaking of the "independent" world, under the insurmountable conditions of linguistic and cultural penetration—I don't mean a noumenal world of any kind—we find ourselves unable to define objectivity in naive-realist terms, except relative to our transient (conceptual) "pictures" of the world itself. We therefore escape representationalism and subjectivism in much the same way Hegel and the classic pragmatists do; hence, like them, we concede the continuing relevance of Kant's transcendental question and his own struggle to surmount representationalism: a fortiori, the impossibility of disjoining realism and the displaced residual Idealism of our constructed pictures of the world.[17] Thus far, at least, I see no important difference between (say) Peirce's and Cassirer's Hegelianized Kantianisms, except for differences in what they wish to salvage from Kant's vision and differences in how they judge the relevance of the Darwinian theme. But I have no objection to admitting that a viable realism must take a constructivist form or that Idealism (in the post-Kantian sense) can easily escape subjectivism. My most compelling clue—it takes a moment's reflection to grasp its force—rests with the remarkable fact that we actually *hear* (and grasp) speech directly, much as we hear sound.

This, then, is the conceptual route I recommend by which to construe pragmatism as a late Hegelian variant of a distinctly naturalistic cast: a variant that bids fair to complete its promise and philosophical power by radically Darwinizing its Hegelian themes. I say that pragmatism had already made an excellent start during its classic phase when it demonstrated (at least implicitly) how to resolve the realism question—by featuring the continuum of human and animal life and the dependence of science on the informal adequacy of the provisional habits of practical life itself. Proceeding thus, within a fluxive context that was seen to draw closer and closer to Hegel's vision, pragmatism joins the Hegelian and Darwinian themes by joining the aposteriorist reading of the transcendental question with the original continuum of the animal and the human.[18]

Nevertheless, in recovering the interlocking argument, we begin to see just how preliminary the pragmatists' actual efforts were in marking off the main lines of an acceptable theory of the human world. For example, to admit the artifactual constitution of the self—in the sense of dating its biologically enabling conditions: say, the placement of the larynx suitably for speech—we surely see that the objectivity of moral and cognitive norms cannot possibly be captured in any ordinary account of first- or second-order discovery: for those who regard selves as self-constituting artifacts, there can be no privileged essentialism suited to human practices (for instance, in the way of inherent facultative powers physically or biologically defined or legibly fixed, determinate, normatively binding universal interests). Although, to admit such limitations hardly deprives us of the ability to formulate "second-best" or reasonable (explicitly constructed, historically diverse, rationally constrained) norms of morality and science that enjoy a more modest (conditional) sort of objectivity.[19]

. . .

Certainly, to admit the artifactual nature of the self precludes any strictly cognitivist account of objective norms; but it need not preclude conditionally objective norms themselves, conjectural revisions of our sittlich practices, in either domain—for example, the achievement of effective predictability with regard to as yet unobserved particular phenomena, even on grounds ultimately deemed mistaken or evidentiarily problematic: Mendeleev's conjectures, say, or predictions about the unseen planet Neptune and the building of the atomic bomb.[20] It supports a notably robust novel intuition about objectivity accessible enough in concrete practice (an instance of Secondness, perhaps, in Peirce's sense) but difficult to legitimate in canonical terms (as Peirce himself discovers in speculating about fallibilism and the "logic" of abduction). Still, this same informality and seeming lack of precision has, fairly recently, been promisingly converted into a new scruple in the philosophy of science—as with Feynman and Cartwright—that draws on Peirce's original intuition (the famous one about the difference between a "cable" and a "chain" of reasoning)[21] that lends itself, along potentially radical lines, to the recuperation of the pragmatist cause.[22]

I come now to the specimen quarrels I've promised. For reasons of economy I draw them, first, from a very recent publication by John Searle, *Making the Social World* (2010), which, broadly speaking, affords a skillful attempt—diametrically opposed to my own approach and open to considerable dispute—to map what is philosophically required in any adequate analysis of the same enlanguaged human world that I've been sketching.

The confrontation with Searle's analysis is a penny digest of a larger contest I envision between a recuperated pragmatism and an extremely spare attenuation of the most persistent scientistic convictions of late-twentieth-century analytic philosophy. The larger contest is increasingly centered on the analysis of the human world viewed as uniquely constituted and as the integrated space of the uniquely human form of life: hence, centered on the analysis of language, enlanguaged culture, history, the emergence of societies of selves or persons, and the human world's dependence upon, difference from, and functional interaction with physical and biological nature.

Searle argues in a very different way from what is often said to be the "best" work of the classic analysts—because he has no hesitation in applying his analysis of language to the analysis of a human society. He offers at least a halfway measure in bridging the gap between analytic scientism and the very different impulses of pragmatism and continental philosophy. Nevertheless, he falls back to scientistic solutions as a result of his unusually spare treatment of the supposed conditions of societal life. He is never drawn to the paleontological history of the genus *Homo* or to the emergence of historied human life itself or to the artifactual nature of language: he's not tempted by post-Kantian or Hegelian themes at all—or, of course, by any Hegelianized Darwinism. All this confirms the depth of the extraordinary avoidance by analytic philosophers of the essential themes that mark the special promise of a recuperated pragmatism. I fix the lesson in the spirit of a small prophecy by way of generalizing over the distinctive narrowing of the "metaphilosophical intuitions" of the analysts. But I confess I'm well aware of how preliminary the argument must be. I offer it as no more than a promissory note.

It's a remarkable fact that the whole of the cultural world and the unique formation of the human self still remain the least explored specialty of contemporary Western philosophy, though it forms the natural setting for a fully fashioned pragmatism and for any Hegelian-inspired philosophy—as yet still largely inchoate and puzzlingly inert. The pragmatists have yet to grasp the full possibilities of their post-Hegelian/post-Darwinian turn, and the analysts have still to explain why their self-impoverishing confinement within a choice of conceptual resources loyal to the failed paradigms of scientism's own history should not now be marked down as demonstrably inadequate to the task at hand.

The turn to the analysis of the enlanguaged human world and the emergence of the self is bound to yield effective conditions for assessing the adequacy of the philosophies of the near future. There can't be much doubt that they will feature the primacy of the human agent's role in science and inquiry, as in life and practical commitment, over the would-be canonical preference for the methodology of the physical sciences. But the self, as distinct from the mind, is still not much more than a surd in a large part of modern philosophy. One has only to think of Kant and Hume.

I'm convinced that we cannot understand the human construction or constitution of the encultured world, including what I've characterized as the emergence of the artifactual self, without an explanation of how language may have arisen (or, in Kantian terms, how language is itself "possible"—transcendentally, perhaps, but not in any apriorist sense). This is the neglected philosophical problem I associate with the novel notion of external *Bildung*, applied to the work of post-Darwinian paleoanthropology.

It's enough for my present purpose, therefore, to offer strong bits of telling evidence, as in countering Searle's proposal, which is already uncharacteristic of prevailing analytic practice, in actually addressing the problem of analyzing the very nature of a human society and the social dimension of human agency and speech acts. It might also be enough to examine the self-impoverishing economies of philosophical argument, otherwise so much admired among the best specimens fashioned by figures such as Quine and Kripke, which are easily read in terms of narrowly circumscribed "metaphilosophical" intuitions themselves rarely open to review from the alien vantage of counterintuitions that insist on the need to understand the effective role of the enabling cultural world within the context of which alone (so it may be claimed) the cameo arguments of the analysts are rightly assessed. There's a risk of scatter there that I cannot expect to escape.

On my reading, you remember, external *Bildung* accounts for the originary appearance of true language as the emergent outcome of a continuous series of progressive transformations of the forms of prelinguistic hominid communicative powers through the processes of cultural evolution, themselves applied to the enabling capacities that emerge in the last phases of the biological evolution of *Homo sapiens sapiens* (as in the placement of its laryngeal system, essential for speech, which, it's been argued, may not have been sufficiently matched in the evolution of Neanderthal, now extinct and now no longer viewed as a subspecies of *Homo sapiens*). On my view, external *Bildung* makes internal *Bildung* possible—internal *Bildung* having already become the preferred model (in philosophical circles) of how to explain the significance of the social rearing of the newborn members of the species—as with theorists as diverse as Aristotle, Herder, Hegel, Gadamer, and John McDowell. The trick is that internal *Bildung* appears not to presuppose external *Bildung*, *if* we treat language, as Searle does, as "a natural, biological phenomenon." Searle says that language is "an extension of biologically basic, prelinguistic forms of intentionality, and thus meets our basic requirement of showing how the human reality is a natural outgrowth of more fundamental—physical, chemical, and biological—phenomena." He remarks that "language is often seen as the primary form of intentionality" and chides philosophers such as Donald Davidson and Michael Dummett for holding that "without language, there can be no thought at all"—a view he claims "is more than a philosophical error; it is bad biology."[23] But he nowhere explains how language can be rightly counted as an essentially biological phenomenon narrowly construed (genetic, biochemical, epigenetic, say), apart from the unhelpful fact that it obviously arises among living organisms.

Davidson's and Dummett's thesis is hardly more than Cartesian: they have nothing to say about the enabling continuum of prelinguistic and linguistic communication—a fortiori, nothing about the emergence of the functional powers we associate with selves or persons. Searle glimpses an advantage here. But, for all that, he postulates prelinguistic hominid powers of thought (what he calls "intentionality") entirely adequate to the deliberate invention of true language from a position as yet deprived of a mastery of linguistic concepts. The upshot is that there is no pragmatically articulated difference between Davidson and Searle: in Davidson, according to Searle's reading, thought does not arise at all among prelinguistic creatures; on Searle's view, language has almost nothing to add to the mental powers of prelinguistic humans, because of course their native biological gifts are already sufficient for the deliberate invention of language. A thoroughly vacuous Kantian exercise. They are, effectively, persons before they are able to speak. I take both doctrines to be seriously in error, though common enough in analytic accounts.

Searle has restricted the dispute to a quibble that he settles by obiter dictum. My own suggestion is that the functional competence we call speech is no less than the artifactual achievement of a prolonged prelinguistic (but distinctly cultural) evolution within the span of a larger biological evolution among the hominids, culminating in the last phases of *Homo sapiens sapiens*. My thought is that the mastery of language (and of what language makes possible) is the same process (what I call external *Bildung*) that we also know as the artifactual transformation of the hominid primate, *Homo sapiens*, known as the self (the "artifactual self"). Linguistic competence is, in effect, nothing but the development of uniquely new powers of thought and experience and agency (notably, the power to report and share in a public and reflexive way the internal experience of the individual members of a society that knows itself through speech). In effect, post-Darwinian paleoanthropology shows us how to naturalize the Hegelian revision of Kant's transcendental innovation, so that the seeming difference between pre-Kantian empiricism and Kantian constructivism is essentially overcome. It's overcome by the hybrid production of the concepts by which humans come to understand their world—they themselves being the hybrid (artifactual) transforms of the members of *Homo sapiens* emerging, functionally, with the developing mastery of evolving language.

Searle, I claim, effectively denies the decisive discontinuities that mark what is unique to the human form of life within the larger continuities of animal life itself. There's the sense in which I've selected Searle to serve as a sort of stalking horse: his own theory, I confess, I regard as utterly arbitrary and unsupported, a massive *petitio* in its own terms, but then also, for that very reason, an extraordinarily revealing proxy for the widespread tendency, particularly within the practice and range of influence of analytic philosophy, to favor one or another extreme form of biologistic reductionism that moves to deny or eliminate any fundamental conceptual difference—any difference, say, that might be deemed to be "ontologically" significant—in contrasting what is now usually intended by distinguishing between biological and cultural evolution.[24]

From this point of view, Searle's work is especially instructive, since Searle is one of a small number of contemporary analytic philosophers who have made the analysis of language and social institutions central to our understanding of what I associate with the emergence of the self and human society—culture and history, in effect—which Searle attempts, heroically, to eliminate at the explanatory level. That is to say: Searle is himself a partisan of a softer "reductionism," since he admits the central importance of language in his account. I would say he has pursued scientistic prospects in the human world about as far as might make sense; so that its final collapse (unresolved questions and intolerable paradoxes) leads us to see that the support of the various versions of scientism in the heyday of positivism, the unity of science program, behaviorism, extensionalism, the covering-law model of explanation, indifference to the import of history and historicity, reliance on empiricisms largely confined to the phenomenal (without yielding adequately to the phenomenological) and related conceptual turns are simply too impoverished for the work at hand. In short, language is an ontological dangler in Searle, as in Davidson and most of analytic philosophy. It's a dangler in much the same sense in which *Homo sapiens* is a dangler in evolutionary theory.

My claim is entirely straightforward: language and what language uniquely makes possible in the way of the evolving powers of the human mind are emergent, artifactual, hybrid precipitates of the joint processes of biological and cultural evolution; accordingly, the functional powers that thus emerge we quite naturally assign to what we call the self or person (as their site), at first nominally and then, in a gradually strengthened way, as the human infant's mastery of language and of its own linguistically qualified forms of functioning begins to confirm the palpably growing fluency and phenomenological presence of reflexive awareness, spontaneous speech, and deliberate agency. But to admit the self as artifactually emergent, uniquely (however contingently) among the members of *Homo sapiens*, in tandem with the culturally artifactual emergence of our linguistic powers, is, in effect, to deny any sufficiently close "similarity" between the "mind" of the prelinguistic hominids of our own species and our own mental or psychological powers as fully enlanguaged selves.

Hence, to concede *that* difference *is* to defeat Searle's account of the conjectured ability of our prelinguistic ancestors to have *invented* natural language, as by contract or voluntary agreement (though lacking, as Searle admits, the concepts and conceptual powers that language first makes possible). The lack of a true language makes the *invention* of language impossible; it also requires, of course, an explanation of how language could have arisen over time, through the continuum of the gradually strengthened conjoint functioning of biological and pre- or protolinguistic processes of cultural evolution. There's the key to the novel linkage between Hegelian and Darwinian themes that I judge to be especially congenial to the best prospects of contemporary pragmatism—and, through pragmatism, congenial to a genuine rapprochement among the principal Eurocentric movements.

I find what Searle says here to be not unreasonable *if* read with an eye to avoiding certain equivocations and privileged "facts"—but not otherwise. Thus, language, on my view, *is* indeed "an extension of biologically basic prelinguistic forms of communication," but the extension requires (in an increasingly massive way) the effective processes of specifically cultural evolution (forms of social invention, for instance, socially directed learning and instruction, reliable ways of transmitting protolinguistic and eventually mature linguistic skills from generation to generation, within the life of a stable society, but not genetically or biochemically produced, or produced in any similar way). Call the innovation semiotic, if you wish. The evolution of language takes a complex hybrid form, intertwining biologically and culturally distinct but hardly separate processes—since the "cultural" itself signifies a sui generis mode of transforming the "biological" in ways that yield an emergent world (the enlanguaged world), the distinctive properties of which cannot (as we now understand matters) be described or explained in terms of the familiar features of what Searle calls "physical, chemical, and biological phenomena."

He calls language "a natural outgrowth" of such phenomena. But I would rather emphasize that it's an "outgrowth" so original, unique to the species, so powerful in its import and effects, so entirely absent from the rest of the animal world (except incipiently, as among the bonobos, under conditions of human contact), that it would not be beneath debate to claim that the appearance of the self *is* a development that fully justifies our speaking of a fundamental "ontological" difference between selves and prelinguistic hominid primates—in precisely the sense in which the emergence of living creatures (though part of a chemical continuum with the inanimate world) is rightly taken to be ontologically different from the mode of being of inanimate things, though the minimally animate has now been effectively shown to be a form of chemical complexity.[25] I don't believe Searle would concede the point; but the verbal quibble introduces deeper, more substantive sorts of challenge that classic philosophy never featured.

I continue, therefore, with an extended examination of Searle's analysis of the human world; I find that it exposes in the most compelling way (however unintentionally) the false leads of the scientific options favored by the strongest efforts of analytic philosophy, and, at the same time, the seeming (the falsely seeming) dialectical disadvantage of pragmatism's conjoined Hegelian and Darwinian proclivities, which cannot be satisfactorily captured in Searle's treatment of our prelinguistic ancestors' "intentional" powers and which, by and large, pragmatism has pretty well neglected to strengthen or improve further.

Let me add here two further preliminary comments on Searle's remarks (as cited). For one thing, I've taken the liberty of replacing Searle's formulation—namely, that language is an extension of "prelinguistic *intentionality*"—with the more neutral phrasing, language is an extension of "prelinguistic *communication*" (with whatever may prove to be relevant in the way of ontological differences). The reason is simply that "intentionality" is a much-contested notion, used in a heterodox and problematic way by Searle himself, and (thus construed) used in a way that cannot be freed from any assessment of Searle's own way of viewing the "facts" about language. Also, when he chides Davidson and Dummett (whose views I'm not willing to defend), Searle means to emphasize that *his* prelinguistic hominids (including the early forms of *Homo sapiens*) are indeed capable of "thought" without the mastery of language. As Searle explains: "By 'hominid' I mean to include prelinguistic humans. We are imagining a race of early humans possessing the biological forms of intentionality, both individual and collective, but lacking language. We imagine that they are capable of cooperative behavior and that they have the full range of perception, memory, belief, desire, prior intentions, and intentions-in-action. What do they acquire when they acquire language?"[26]

We must bear in mind that Searle never tells us whether or how the "thought" (or "perception") of his prelinguistic hominids differs from that of enlanguaged humans. He does say that "the formal structures of intentional states and speech acts are surprisingly similar" (which begins to bridge the prelinguistic and the enlanguaged); he also says that "an animal that is consciously able to cope with the environment already has the category [though not the concept] of object, or thing, because it can discriminate the things that it encounters from each other. . . . It has the categories of space and time because it observes objects as located in space, and it experiences changes through time."[27] But here, surely, we must weigh Jakob von Uexküll's familiar warning against anthropomorphizing "animal" thought and perception: we cannot really understand the way in which "thought" and "perception" take form in animal life (except, of course, heuristically, from our own vantage); this may be just as true of the difference between the prelinguistic competence of *Homo sapiens* and ourselves as selves (which bears on Davidson's and Dummett's insistence).[28] But the relationship between human infants and linguistically apt adults is hardly the same as that between human persons and their animal pets.

Simply stated: languageless animals are not lesser selves; they're not selves at all. Searle is at his weakest here. "My dog," Searle claims, "can see a burglar, but he cannot see that there is a burglar there, because he lacks the appropriate concept. All the same, he does see that something is there."[29] I find a fatal equivocation here between the familiarly paired propositional and nonpropositional objects of perceptual reports.

I don't believe Searle ever clarifies the sense in which his dog sees a burglar, or the would-be fact that he sees that "something is there" or that whatever he sees entails the same "categories" (as opposed to the same "concepts") of "objects" that we employ: or, in fact, just how we distinguish between bare human "thought" and "perception" subtracted (so to say) from what we report, linguistically, *as* our thought and perception—or how we rightly distinguish between our thought and perception and the thought and perception of Searle's hominid primates (or, conceivably, of his dog). I take human thought and perception to be "penetrated" and (thus) "transformed" by the mastery of *language*—so that what we suppose "remains" of biologized thought and perception apart from the "addition" of language must be a *dependent* conjecture of our own transformed powers. Think of the failings of sense datum theory, or the implications of our learning to hear meaningful speech as spontaneously as we hear sound. To what extent, I ask, are thought and perception altered and qualified by encultured learning (prelinguistic as well as linguistic)? The question seems to be permanently anthropomorphized—hence, inventively altered; it's also completely ignored by Searle—hence, too easily conflated with what merely precedes it.

In accord with his answers to questions of this kind, Searle moves on to his theory of the creation of "human institutions": in effect, to the whole of what he calls the human "social world," the "enlanguaged world" (as I prefer to say), of a society of apt selves. (Actually, Searle makes no use at all of the concepts of "self" and "culture.") He simply offers the extraordinary claim that "all institutional facts, and therefore all status functions, are created by speech acts of a type that in 1975 I baptized as 'Declarations.'" The principle applies, for instance, to "making" a certain kind of printed paper a twenty-dollar bill that may rightly circulate as money (that is, applies to imposing such a "function" *on* the paper); but it also applies, as Searle says, "to the most fundamental institution of all: language," except that language does not require a separate speech act (a separate "Declaration") in order "to count" as language.[30]

I'm persuaded that Searle's theory is demonstrably deficient in an essential and fatal way, and that it *must* (as a consequence) yield in the direction I've been favoring. A true language cannot possibly be deliberately constructed from prelinguistic sources, though it obviously must have evolved, over considerable time, from just such sources. The rest of my account of Searle's views is meant to support this charge. (I may then inadvertently slight some of the best features of Searle's theory where they do not bear directly on my counterargument). I shall have to confine my remarks to the briefest sketch.

Let me, however, clinch as much as possible of the decisive finding that's just surfaced, while we have it in view. My claim is that the transition from prelinguistic hominid communication to true language, though surely continuous, involves a deep change in the human capacity for thought, perception, belief, and the like, so fundamental that it goes contrary to the known facts to speak (as Searle does) of his prelinguistic hominids possessing the "full range" of such capacities—despite their lacking language. *In* lacking language, they lack the "full range" of such capacities! The reason is that the very mastery of language entails the unique emergence of the self as the nominal agent of an entirely new set of mental powers.

Failure to accommodate this fact amounts to a fatal *petitio*—or a regress, which I dub "Rousseau's joke" (drawing on Jean-Jacques Rousseau's

Social Contract), though it's not at all clear that Rousseau himself *was* clear about the joke's being a joke: that is, drawing on the puzzle that worries about whether, in order to engage in a *contract* to begin to speak a language (for the first time) or to live by certain formulated political rules, we must already (on the argument's own terms) have been party to effectuating a *first* contract of precisely the same sort!

If you ask, now, what are the new powers that we acquire?, I should say that they include the power to report in a public way and thus to share our newly formed reflexive awareness of our inner mental states; the linguistically altered ("penetrated") modes of perception, feeling, and thought and the newly minted objects thereby introduced (as in the auditory accessibility of speech and music, that is, language-dependent objects); new forms of intentionality created and made accessible by language and language-dependent processes (the semiotic features of artworks and human actions, for instance); the capacity for second-order discriminations (applied, say, to concepts, relationships between language and the world); and so on. The world, then, is altered and enlarged by the acquisition of language and of what language makes possible. Searle senses the difficulty of extending his view of speech acts and Declarations to the origination of language itself: it's the burden of Rousseau's joke.

There are, I would say, at least two prominent artifactual realities of the human world that *cannot* possibly have been—"originarily"—created by speech acts, by Declarations, or by any similar process. I concede Searle's example of the creation of money as legal tender by a sort of pronouncement—a speech act, if you like, but even that's too glib. Even so, language and selves cannot be produced by any such pronouncement; that would be magic—or a kind of redundancy. They are surely unique precipitates of the autonomous processes of cultural evolution running continuously from the prelinguistic to the linguistic.

The complexity of these two achievements, not quite inventions but contrived, so different from one another but inseparably intertwined, cannot account for their own functional fluencies—a language that remains intact though continually changing over immense periods of time, clever selves that arise as transforms of the prelinguistic infant primates of the species with their own maturing mastery of language and the culture that that makes possible—*without* admitting the mysterious fabric of the enlanguaged culture selves share (as we say) that sustains them as they acquire a mastery of their own society's home language.

This "fabric" (as I call it) is a uniquely unified ensemble—an explicative construct, let me say, abstracted, heuristically hypostasized originally from our actual practices, interpreted and marked as a collective possession of viable societies, and then gradually experienced as a palpable presence by experienced selves—of a sort that cannot be analyzed solely or primarily in terms of the independently aggregated acts of the individual members of any society. (The acts of agentive selves may be said to incarnate in individual ways the collective potentialities of a society's distinctive ethos or *Geist*—what I've named the "fabric.") Searle's very different reading, confined essentially to the intentional *mental states* of individual agents already competent, *prelinguistically*, to produce (as by contract) a language and an encultured world in which certain pieces of paper can circulate as legal tender, produces only insuperable paradox. We say that we share a language, a culture, a tradition, the deepest institutions of our society. We share them aggregatively, cooperatively, because we are ourselves individual, individuatable selves; but we are also culturally formed and transformed, *ensemble*, by virtue of learning to share these complex things effectively. Hence, we share them *aggregatively*, because our own enlanguaged "second nature" incorporates what every society of selves shares *collectively*.

We, spontaneously formed by mastering language, acquire thereby the capacity to support and transmit the collective culture that we internalize (idiosyncratically). Hence, in mastering language, we learn, reflexively, to recognize ourselves as effective cultural agents, to discern the presence of the collective culture that accounts for our own transformation, and to grasp our own role in enabling the transformation of future cohorts of our own primate (infant) offspring. (I have no doubt that the cultural "fabric" must be more closely examined.)

We are imprinted (as we are transformed into selves) with the distinctive, publicly accessible aptitudes of our society, which we internalize and manifest as our own talents (in speaking, making love and war, transacting business). What I offer here, then, is not yet an argument, though it is the clue to an argument that Searle's way of proceeding cannot possibly match without producing instant paradox. I have supporting arguments to propose and will turn to them. But recall, please, that I'm primarily concerned to make an initial guess at pragmatism's best future. I could not proceed without sketching some of the grand puzzles of the new inquiry that catches up pragmatism's own interests and a sense of the way in which Hegelian and Darwinian themes may be joined.

We must probe a little further into the most important of Searle's distinctions. Begin with this: "An institution is a system of institutional facts"; and (as we've seen) an institutional fact is "created by speech acts" of the kind Searle calls Declarations. Searle adds the following extraordinary claim: "there are five, and only five, possible types of speech acts, five types of illocutionary acts." He names them straight out: Assertives, Directives, Commissives, Expressives, and Declarations. About the last of these, he says: "In a Declaration we make something the case by declaring it to be the case"; that is, we "make" institutional facts by Declaration.[31] But as far as I can see, Searle never actually affords a clear statement of the sufficient conditions on which a Declaration *is* an effective Declaration. The conditions surely include an understanding and supportive society.

Now, I take Searle's claims to be benign enough when rightly embedded in an adequate theory of the enabling powers they require to be effective—which, in Searle's hands, seems to begin and end with speech acts and intentionality. I'm convinced that that can't possibly be enough.

We need not take very seriously Searle's claims that there are only five distinct kinds of speech acts. I see no reason why we cannot admit Avowals, for instance, as a sixth kind of speech act: first-person avowals have distinctive features that bear directly on the acknowledged emergence of selves. Prelinguistic hominids *cannot* have any Searlean-like "intentional states" akin to avowals. Avowals already entail reflexive powers that presuppose linguistic mastery. Of course, the very idea of speech acts (which play a pivotal role in Searle's theory) implicates the presence of agents capable of realizing or embodying certain reflexive roles. Hence, there must be an insuperable difference between the "thoughts" of selves and the "thoughts" of prelinguistic hominids. But if that is so, then it becomes suddenly unclear just what Searle could possibly have meant in urging (as reported) that "the formal structures of intentional states and speech acts are surprisingly similar." They *can't* be similar *enough* to account for the transition from prelinguistic communication to the mastery of language: the putative similarity cannot possibly advance Searle's argument.

Here, though I'm happy to acknowledge the force of George Mead's account of the dialectic of the "I" and the "me" and his analysis of the role of the "generalized other," I confess I don't find Mead entirely clear about the relationship between the original ability to *assume* the role and the acquisition of language itself. On my view, the acquisition of a so-called natural language *is* the process by which the self is *first* formed and emerges: there is no prior play between the roles of the "I" and the "me"; *that* would be a step in Searle's direction. The roles themselves are artifacts of the self's formation.

It becomes clear, then, that Searle's final sort of speech act, Declarations, cannot quite belong to the same run of acts that the four other sorts of speech act do, because if we acknowledge the function of Declarations, we see that Searle's other kinds of speech act (Assertives, Directives, Commissives, and Expressives) must, in a certain sense, already co-opt the function of Declarations—though, normally, without requiring any explicit (Declarative) speech act: thus, Assertives must (on Searle's view) "create [such] social and institutional [realities]" as "statements, descriptions, assertions"; Directives must create "orders, commands, requests"; and so on.[32] There's a *reductio* there.

Can we, or must we, be able to make Declarations effective reflexively? Can a would-be Declaration make itself an actual Declaration? Can it make itself a linguistic utterance? Must it be able to do that? If yes, then Searle's system becomes hopelessly defective, a victim of Rousseau's joke; and if no, then the functional status of language itself (what Searle calls the conferred "status function" that "Status Function Declarations" confer, as "in creating and maintaining institutional facts": money, for instance) becomes a complete mystery.[33] There must be a further, as yet unmentioned, enabling condition that governs the very possibility of language—hence, governs speech acts and social institutions—that Searle has simply failed to supply. It can't itself be captured by a speech act, because that would generate the regress noted. Furthermore, if we admit Declarations as speech acts, we can admit them only if they are coordinately denied the right to apply to originating language itself, or to creating the institution of creating institutions (or speech acts). Hence, then, speech act theory *can't* be adequate to explaining the construction of Searle's "social world" (or my "enlanguaged world"); *and*, as a consequence, it's no longer clear how many kinds of speech acts there may be: after all, there will be an instant need for second-order speech acts at least (call them Explicatives) that specify the conditions under which alone these or those first-order institutions and speech acts effectively obtain! We are back to the dialectic of internal and external *Bildung*.

Searle is careful enough to acknowledge that "prelinguistic thoughts lack representations" (that is, the representational function of language or speech acts, by which, for instance, Declarations "enable us to create a reality by representing that reality as existing").[34] Fine. But then, Searle also says: "All human social institutions are brought into existence and continue in their existence by a single logico-linguistic operation that can be applied over and over again. [He means Declarations or what in the mere exercise of language preempts the need for explicit speech acts.] [L]anguage is constitutive of institutional reality, and consequently . . . all human institutions are essentially linguistic."[35]

Here, Searle says something stronger and weaker than his claims about Declarations. I agree with at least part of what he says, but I don't believe he's earned the right to claim that part of the argument: as we have just seen, language cannot be created by Declarations, since that would generate Rousseau's joke; that's precisely what, on my view, the empirical facts regarding external *Bildung* and the transcendental function of those same facts supply—the missing assumption: what I take Hegel to have glimpsed but not to have analyzed in a way perspicuously suited to our own idiom—hence, to what a recuperated pragmatism might supply.

. . .

Let me bring this part of the argument to a close with a final objection to Searle's general strategy. I've been suggesting that a sufficient theory of the human world must admit what I've called the "fabric" of the human world itself, some actual public world populated by culturally artifactual things—selves and their enlanguaged minds, artworks, actions, technologies, machines, sentences, histories, traditions, institutions, and the like, all hybrid transforms of whatever populates the physical and biological world, indissolubly emergent within the space of the latter but marked in innumerable ways by features that depend on the transformative power of language and the language-dependent nonlinguistic (or, perhaps better, nonverbal) cultural powers that language makes possible—"lingual" powers, as I name them (those, for instance, of the ballet, haute cuisine, and skiing, which, doubtless, have their prelinguistic counterparts as well).

Searle believes he can, in principle, generate the entire human world from the resources of what he calls "intentionality," which he ascribes to *both* his prelinguistic hominids (ourselves, deprived of language) and selves (ourselves, possessing language)—the latter (ourselves) being (on my view) radical transforms of the former. But what *is* intentionality in Searle's sense? I've signaled its importance for Searle without explanation, and I've delayed mentioning Searle's actual characterization. But Searle's entire argument depends on it: "'Intentionality,'" Searle says, "is a fancy philosopher's term for that capacity of the mind by which it is directed at, or about, objects and states of affairs in the world, typically independent of itself."[36]

Searle's notion is loosely associated with Franz Brentano's recovery of its medieval usage; adjusted by Searle, however, it appears to have abandoned part of its original scope, since it no longer features the interesting possibility that "intentional" objects (as of fear and belief) may include things that literally don't exist (ghosts, for instance, which, of course, require linguistic resources). Apart from that, Searle is quite emphatic in insisting that "all human intentionality exists only in individual human brains"—"There isn't any other place for intentionality to be except human brains"—a claim that raises an obvious puzzle about so-called We-intentionality (also called "collective intentionality"), which Searle reconciles with the constraint just mentioned. The matter is decisive, because Searle believes that "the capacity for collective intentionality" is indeed "the fundamental building block of all human social ontology and human society in general."[37] I find two important mistakes here: one, the notion that animal or prelinguistic hominid intentionality could account for the institution of language; the second, that intentionality in the enlanguaged sense (or mind) "exists only in individual human brains."

Searle is also mistaken about the scope of intentionality. Consider only that Michelangelo's *Pietà* is, in a thoroughly familiar sense, intentionally "about" the Pietà involving Mary and her expired son; yet the sculpture has no mind or mental states. Intentionality (in an enlanguaged world) ranges over a great deal more than mental states: it ranges over everything that is a cultural artifact to which we rightly attribute meaning or significance or signification (as expressive or representational or symbolic or *geistlich*: language, traditions, institutions, practices, products, and actions most particularly, all of which are actual and objective—not at all confined to what Searle means by the human mind or brain). I name this sort of intentionality, "Intentionality" (written with a capital "I"), according to which whatever is culturally significant or significative is inherently *Intentional*.[38] It's part of my counterclaim to Searle's account—congenial to my guess at pragmatism's future—that every viable theory of the enlanguaged cultural world of humans must admit its Intentional presence: otherwise, it will appear as a fiction or an artifact confined within the human mind, which would surely generate an intolerable paradox. But

Intentionality itself requires the functional presence of selves, *not* the presence of prelinguistic primates.

I take Searle's notion of collective intentionality to be the nerve of his entire theory. He says explicitly that "human beings, along with a lot of other social animals, have the capacity for collective intentionality." Searle is opposed to reducing "'We intend' statements . . . to 'I intend' statements": the reduction, he says, is not required by his theory, and "the proposed reductions fail."[39] Fine. Nevertheless, his theory requires that his hominid primates be capable of sharing beliefs and purposes in common, capable of becoming aware that they do, and, as a consequence of that, capable of cooperating and agreeing to cooperate in various shared undertakings—that is to say: choosing to cooperate on the basis of understanding that the project requires their adopting a common objective or intention. In short, Searle's primates possess the capacity for "collective intentionality" despite their lacking language—and in a way that permits them to create and master language itself. The latter capacity, Searle claims, makes it possible for them to acquire the capacity to make promises and pacts and to enter into conversation. So the problem is solved.

Well, yes and no. Certainly, no one wishes to deny that prelinguistic *Homo sapiens sapiens* did indeed create and master natural language. That's not the issue. The trouble is, Searle's solution merely iterates the known fact that prelinguistic humans somehow succeeded in creating language; or else it fails because it falls victim to Rousseau's joke. The best that I can make of Searle's argument, as an explanation of the "possibility" of language, is that it ignores the equivocation between the prelinguistic and the enlanguaged forms of "thought," "belief," "agreement," "cooperation," and the like. Once it admits the still-problematic nature of the claim that there must be a prelinguistic form of mental states that can stand as effective (intentional) equivalents of this or that pertinently enlanguaged variant, Searle's solution will appear to generate a *petitio*. Here is the knockdown evidence: Searle claims that "there is a ground-floor form of collective intentionality, one that exists prior to the exercise of language and which makes the use of language possible at all." (Think of engaging in a conversation or making a promise in a conversation.) Searle continues:

You do not need a promise in order to have collective intentionality: indeed, the very conversation in which the promise is made, and is accepted or rejected, is already a form of collective intentionality. The conversation presupposes a Background capacity to engage in conversation, and the Background capacity depends on having a more fundamental prelinguistic form of collective intentionality. . . . You have to have a prelinguistic form of collective intentionality on which the linguistic forms are built, and you have to have the collective intentionality of the conversation in order to make the commitment [to a promise or a conversation].[40]

In a way, what Searle says may be read, equivocally, as reasonably correct: all the ingredients noted must indeed be present, *somehow*, in the process of what I've called external *Bildung*. Nevertheless, insuperable defects remain in Searle's solution—obscured by his wording. I shall mention only two that are essential. First, as far as I can make out, Searle means to restrict what he calls "Background" (as opposed to what he calls "Network") as entirely *non*-intentional. ("Network," I should add, is thoroughly intentional.) Thus, Searle says: "Consciousness and intentionality are caused by and realized in neurobiology"; again, speaking of his intending to drive to his office, Searle says: "I take that ability for granted, and the ability does not consist in a set of intentional states"; and, again, he says: "We need [in our theory] a set of abilities, capacities, and so on for applying [our] intentional states. This set of abilities and capacities I will call the Background. The Background consists of all of those abilities, capacities, dispositions, ways of doing things, and general know-how that enable us to carry out our intentions and apply our intentional states generally."[41] But then, the transition from the prelinguistic to the linguistic fails to meet the threat of Rousseau's joke, because the explanation finally depends on *non*-intentional factors. There must be a bridging condition, and the condition must be intentional in some as yet unexplained (non–question-begging) way. (That is, it must be Intentional-with-a-capital-"I.")

The second failing rests with Searle's claim that "collective mental phenomena of the sort we get in organized societies are themselves dependent on and derived from the mental phenomena of individuals."[42] We've already heard that all forms of intentionality are confined in the brain (are, or implicate, mental states). But that generates the puzzle (which Searle regards as benign) that collective intentionality (though not reducible to individual intentionality) *is* indeed confined to some form of aggregated individual instances of intentionality (with suitably added beliefs); and *that*, as far as I can see, does produce a version of Rousseau's paradox (Rousseau's joke). There must be a version of intentionality that is *not* confined to the mental; that takes a discernibly public form even in prelinguistic communication; that emerges with the proto-cultural (prelinguistic) forms of learning apt for improving the effectiveness of our biological gifts *for* at least prelinguistic communication; *and* that contributes to the stable and reliable transmission of learned communicative skills (by culturally shared means) that, over time, could actually evolve, incipiently, along protolinguistic lines (for instance, in the gradual improvement of prelinguistic referential and predicative functions without yet producing any actual grammar—which may conceivably begin to take form even among the apes and monkeys).

The sequence is perfectly straightforward, but you cannot get to it by way of the assumption that the intentionality of prelinguistic and linguistic communication is entirely derived from some merely aggregated forms of the intentionality of psychological states. Think, rather, of language or tradition as the abstracted, highly structured, public space we share (and produce) by acquiring an agentive mastery of our language and cultural practices, that becomes objectively accessible (itself) to newborn members of our society who have had of course no part in its original formation or transformation but who may, in acquiring their own fluency, thereupon affect its evolving structure and causal processes in such a way, in turn, as to alter the way the offspring of later generations will have to achieve *their* mastery of the "same" language and culture.

If you allow the suggestion, you may as well venture a congruent speculation regarding prelinguistic communication—one, say, that might help to explicate the "Darwinian" theme so severely compressed in Dewey's notion of the transformation of an "indeterminate situation" into a "problematic situation" and in Peirce's extravagantly spare remarks about "protoplasmic" intelligence.[43] Peirce and Dewey offer very little else in this regard, but they are more responsive than Searle. Frankly, I think a better clue is afforded in Wittgenstein's careful reflections (centered on Augustine), in the opening pages of *Philosophical Investigations*, of a child's first start at learning a language.

I concede that Peirce, James, and Dewey are in a general way hospitable to the picture I'm presenting; nevertheless, it's hard to draw a robust confirmation from any of them. The most I'm prepared to venture is that, read along the lines already sketched, among the classic pragmatists, George Mead comes closest to providing a plausibly companionable statement. With Mead's account of the conditions for the emergence of the self and the primacy of the social world in hand, it's not unreasonable to construe the views of the others congenially. Because Mead's paper "Concerning Animal Perception"—among others of his papers—published as early as 1907, explicitly depends on Dewey's extremely important piece "The Reflex Arc Concept" (itself published in 1896), it helps in reading *Dewey's* piece perspicuously. It explains the complexity of the pragmatist account of perception and thought (chiefly Dewey's version, it's true), so that we see at once how much is missing in Searle's account—how improbable it would be to rely on Searle's sketch of how the resemblance between animal (and prelinguistic hominid) perception and thought and enlanguaged perception and thought might validate his own picture of the invention of language (and its attendant culture). Searle's notion of the bridging power of (prelinguistic) collective intentionality is hardly close at all to what we need. Mead's is closer but still not close enough.

Mead says in this regard, reflecting Dewey's ramified account of the interactive influence of eye and hand in perception and behavior—which greatly complicates the supposed transition: "it is hard to believe that a consciousness of a 'thing' can be segregated from [an animal's] instinctive activities. . . . [W]e need only to recall what has been brought out by Dewey and [G. F.] Stout that perception involves a continued control of such an organ as that of vision by such an organ as that of the hand, and vice versa. We look because we handle, and we are able to handle because we look."[44] Mead and Dewey anticipate in this way the deep significance of Uexküll's warning against anthropomorphizing animal life—which Uexküll himself never rightly grasped. But neither Mead nor Dewey ventures far enough along post-Darwinian lines.

Given his trim remark, we are able to seize the sense in which Dewey would make much the same point Mead makes—and through Dewey, the sense in which James and Peirce could not be far from the same instruction. Nevertheless, with the exception of Mead, the classic pragmatists move too quickly to the far side of internal *Bildung*. James and Peirce emphasize distinctly opposed, though not entirely irreconcilable, views about the self, that move in very different directions. Both have interesting things to say: Peirce, surprisingly, even more that is relevant to the social construction of the self than James, despite the greater detail of James's account of the self and the self's mode of thought—in *Principles of Psychology*.

James famously declares (in *Principles*) that "every thought tends to be part of a personal consciousness. . . . The only states of consciousness that we naturally deal with are found in personal consciousness, minds, selves, concrete particular I's and you's. Each of these minds keeps its own thought to itself. . . . Absolute insulation, irreducible pluralism, is the law."[45] Peirce takes an opposed view (as in a sense does Mead)—in fact, he actually confronts James's statement: "The recognition by one person of another's personality [in effect, the content of the second's mind] takes place by means to some extent identical with the means by which he is conscious of his own personality. . . . At the same time, the opposition between the two persons is perceived, so that the externality of the second is recognized" (6.160)[46].

Peirce is quite daring here, in a way that is particularly encouraging for a theory of the self's artifactuality. The linkage is strengthened by his view that the self is itself a sign (5.313). Peirce also holds that selves are "mere cells in a social organism" (1.647), which clearly anticipated Mead (and may indeed have influenced him) and, in any case, confirms a surprisingly apt convergence between Peirce and Dewey. (I take all this to catch up the most promising themes in Hegel and the post-Darwinian inquiries.) Even so, the larger record confirms the judgment that, on the whole, the classic pragmatists (even Mead, who is the most adventurous in this regard) were quite slack in pursuing the analysis of the human world in terms of the self's artifactuality—that is, in terms of Darwinizing Hegel and Hegelianizing Darwin. You see this very clearly in Mead's very promising forays (not always easy to fathom), as in "The Social Self" (1913) and other papers collected in *Mind, Self and Society* and *The Philosophy of the Act*.[47]

The fact is, the pragmatists tended to explore these matters in a phenomenological spirit, which may have dampened the speculative work that needed to be pursued. (Up to a hundred years have slipped by.) Perhaps the prophecy is no more than a reminder of an unfinished venture. The point is that it's still there for the taking. That is, if you allow a phenomenology—by subtractive guess—of the prelinguistic hominid world (the human infant, say) and of the sublinguistic animal world (whether among dogs or chimpanzees), which is at least heuristically conceivable,[48] then Mead may be questioned fairly closely on whether taking the role of the "generalized other" could actually obtain *prelinguistically* (so that the acquisition of language may be said to perfect, but need not be held responsible for actually generating, the self). I find the proposal—in effect, Searle's, or at least something close to Searle's, though never quite explicitly affirmed, as far as I know—more than improbable. Furthermore, to admit the verdict is to insist on the radical difference between, but also the inseparability of, biology and culture. There's the clue to pragmatism's future.

It's but a step from here to the larger lesson that the quarrel "shared" this way with Searle must be shared as well with all the principal movements of the Eurocentric world—say, among pragmatists, analysts, and continentals alike. There can be no doctrinal barriers or privilege at this level of reflection. Admittedly, as I've already remarked, Searle is not a typical "analyst." He addresses many of the standard issues of analytic philosophy, it's true; he's a nonreductive materialist, entirely willing to treat "consciousness" in physical terms. Nonetheless, he does not rely, in the manner of Quine, Davidson, or Kripke (or even Edmund Gettier)—to stay with the most frequently cited analytic exemplars—on the vaunted precision and power of miniaturized analytic arguments. He tends, as we've seen, to turn directly to what, not inaptly, have been called "second-order," "metaphilosophical" questions and "intuitions" that the most admired "first-order" analytic arguments (of the sorts just signaled) must be informed by: say, the challenge of adequately limning the entire sprawling sweep of the enlanguaged social world human beings have themselves produced (as Vico famously remarks)—for which reason humans must understand that world better than they understand nature (which, as Vico also says, is God's work and therefore more opaque than history and culture).[49]

Searle is a materialist in a sense akin to that in which Noam Chomsky is a materialist: not because he (or Chomsky) is a reductionist, but because, in treating consciousness, mind, intentionality, agency, and language in biological terms, that is, as biologically complex and thus materialist in whatever surprising forms such phenomena take, he simply "christens" the entire cultural world as materialist. He admits no need to explain how the emergent differences of the cultural world remain descriptively and explanatorily continuous with what is paradigmatically physical. (Think, here, of light and force as "material," but also of intentionality.)

Here, I've adopted a more parasitic strategy, shadowing the general thesis recently favored by Gary Gutting (in *What Philosophers Know*), in treating the "first-order" cameo arguments of the best-known analytic philosophers of the past fifty-plus years as being relatively autonomous and freestanding, as being effective *and* as affording compelling evidence of having actually made progress in contributing to philosophical knowledge. Gutting is candid enough to admit, however, that the best specimens almost never gain their stated objective. Hence, from Gutting's point of view, their contribution to philosophical knowledge proceeds largely by what we are able to extract from the failure of their usual first-order ventures—

along (say) the lines of "second-order" or "metaphilosophical" conjectures about how to understand and appraise philosophical arguments! The trouble is that analytic philosophy's best specimens hardly ever venture a sustained exchange on the merits of competing metaphilosophical options. Certainly, they almost never review the possible bearing of the innovations due to the all-but-inseparable interventions of Kant and Hegel or the possibilities of "Darwinizing Hegel and Hegelianizing Darwin" or other such options. But if they do not, then Gutting's own argument lacks an essential premise—a premise by which to explain how to recover sunlight from cucumbers: how the failed or doubtful arguments of the analysts' first-order sorts can be made to yield second-order, metaphilosophical discoveries apt to improve the general efforts of the academy.

So analytic philosophy's largest lesson remains stubbornly the same: the human world is at least as quarrelsome as nature, and Searle is effectively wedded to much the same metaphilosophical obiter dicta as the relevant cameo arguments of other analysts; for one thing, he treats his thesis as if it could have been cast compellingly in miniature form, which is not possible; for another, he is not willing to acknowledge that the choice of a "metaphilosophical" orientation is an entirely open-ended matter, regarding which dialectical arguments of a looser and more expansive sort must be admitted; and, for a third, he falls back to scientific strategies, without any sustained confrontation of the very differently motivated metaphilosophical intuitions that appear among pragmatists and continentals: for instance, the conviction that the human world depends on the artifactual emergence of language, which cannot itself be explained in minimal biological terms (biochemical terms, say), but must acknowledge the possibility of a decisive difference between biological and enlanguaged cultural processes. Perhaps we are all tempted to favor something close to Searle's economy. But it won't do: somewhere, the contest among the largest philosophical visions must confront one another.

Here, I've been suggesting, we must begin with the idea, most instructively explored in the "philosophical anthropologies" of figures like Helmuth Plessner and Arnold Gehlen, that centers on the unique and distinctly problematic sense in which humans are regarded as animals that may be straightforwardly compared, in biologically confined terms, with the animals more easily accessible to Darwin's mode of analysis (and to that of a less than successful anti-Darwinian like Uexküll). Human beings *are* animals, of course, but their evolution and development cannot be confined in biological terms. In fact, the very idea of "natural selection" is severely challenged by the artifactuality of the self—that is, by the proliferation of the human race (and the deep artifactual transformation of the entire earth).

My sense is that Searle ventures to speculate about the adequacy of a biological (and materialist) account of the psychological and the linguistic (or cultural) but finds no need to go beyond the straightforward plausibility of christening that entire world as "material." It may be for that reason that he favors the extreme economy featured in the best-known cameo arguments of analytic philosophy in his larger conjectures about the right analysis of the powers of language. The trouble is that the underlying materialism the analysts have preferred since at least the opening decades of the twentieth century has effectively failed—or shows little promise of having found new sources of potential success. Thus, it is no longer convincing to suppose that either Searle or the more usual champions of the analytic "method" of argument are entitled to forego a more sustained contest between their metaphilosophical "pictures" of the world and those offered by their principal rivals. Searle's inquiry counts as a sort of halfway house between a stubborn reductionism and a more adventurous account of the sui generis features of history and cultural process that would be needed even if we wished to reconcile any such inquiry with one or another form of nonreductive materialism.

In any event, it's here that we must search for new clues drawn from history or practical experience or the specialized work of the natural and human sciences that may inform the still-viable options of philosophy in the large. That *is*, in truth, the ulterior motivation of the manifesto behind my motto. For all its rigor and global presence, analytic philosophy has been more candidly parochial than either pragmatism or continental philosophy. The trouble is that it has bet on the wrong horses.

The analysts have of course largely agreed among themselves: they tend to insist that the ultimate explanation of the human world must finally be cast, as Searle himself says, in "physical, chemical, and biological" terms. But what if language is best construed as a hybrid artifact that has evolved by distinctly cultural means that, though such enabling factors depend on underlying biological processes and are able to emerge from certain prelinguistic processes, they themselves cannot be explained in biological terms alone or primarily, and, as they continue to develop, are accounted for almost entirely in terms of their uniquely evolved cultural powers? What if such an evolution begins to yield a constructed world, technologies, forms of agency, reflexive powers of mind that appear nowhere else in nature, that co-opt and transform the whole of physical nature so as to manifest significative, semiotic, informational features that are productively unique and intelligible only to enlanguaged creatures (selves or persons) like ourselves—and are characteristically, as in action and speech and art, materially embodied and not merely conventionally joined? Wouldn't that demand an answer at the metaphilosophical level?

The most famous cameo arguments of the analysts (as I'm calling them) tend to be committed to perfecting their would-be decisive logic in a spirit more or less indifferent to the larger debates they seem to invite but avoid engaging (those, especially, that I've just been sketching). Quine, for instance, in "Two Dogmas," seems convinced that we can discard "analyticity" and "necessity" just about everywhere that truth-claims arise—in the name (say) of some pragmatized or empiric advantage. Thus, famously, he affirms: "Any statement can be held true come what may if we make drastic enough adjustments elsewhere in the system. . . . Conversely, by the same token, no statement is immune to revision."[50] But does that apply to the laws of logic and does the sense of "system" in the phrase "elsewhere in the system" set substantive constraints on the flexibilities of "elsewhere"? (Quine has no interest in answering such questions.)

Objections to Quine's remarkable economy insist that we must spell out the relevant differences and uniformities of logical, arithmetic, geometric, essentialist, theoretical, semantic, and related distinctions before we can support Quine responsibly (as Hilary Putnam, for one, effectively suggests); or they complain that Quine's triumphant defeat of the analytic/synthetic distinction (on the strength of the indissoluble conceptual bond between "analyticity" and "synonymy," directed against Carnap), ignores Carnap's own "systematic" preconditions;[51] or they demonstrate the implausibility of overriding the role of "necessity" in so-called metaphysical contexts bearing on the use of proper names, empirically discoverable identities, the attribution of essential properties, and related forms of common usage (as Saul Kripke argues).[52]

Yet, in spite of such reasonable hesitations, Kripke's own famous revival of metaphysical "necessity" in his account of rigid designators and related usage never (in my opinion) demonstrates the ineluctable advantage of admitting strict necessity, in epistemically qualified contexts, when speaking of proper names as rigid rather than nonrigid designators (except in terms of a speaker's intentions); or, when speaking of the "necessary a posteriori" (as with statements like "Hesperus is Phosphorus" or "Gold is the element with atomic number 79"), we simply abbreviate our account of certain devilishly complex sentences that (otherwise) appear to be simple, or where imputations of necessity are entirely provisional and less than strict.

The issue is a muddy one. (I cannot do full justice to it here.) Kripke treats both "Hesperus is Phosphorus" and "Gold is the element with the atomic number 79" as "necessary a posteriori" statements. I would say Kripke never makes the case compellingly; moreover, I don't believe he ever shows the need to treat our specimen sentences in just that way. Consider, for instance, that in the preface to *Naming and Necessity* Kripke admits that "'Hesperus is Phosphorus' could sometimes be used to raise an empirical issue while 'Hesperus is Hesperus' could not." If this be admitted, then the sentence "Hesperus is Phosphorus" might be said to convey a complex statement to the effect that "Hesperus *is* Phosphorus" is empirically true *and* that if or since it is true, it is, by further reference to Leibniz's law or something similar, necessarily true. In that case, it may be a posteriori *and* necessarily true, while not actually being a necessary a posteriori statement!

Suppose, for example, someone learns, "empirically," that "the sum of the angles of any (Euclidean) triangle is equal to the sum of two right angles" and claims, correspondingly, that the proposition is a "necessary a posteriori truth." Surely he's mistaken: we might say he'd learned a necessary truth by empirical means. The Euclidean sentence conveys a geometric truth, whereas the Hesperus/Phosphorus case is, under the circumstances given, a discovery about the empirical world. Furthermore, the identity, if true, is necessarily true, without regard to what it actually affirms; so that empirical certainty need not figure in the reasoning required. (Note, please, that these considerations are very different from those that arise regarding the "essential" properties of material things.) Kripke has simply not provided an adequate "second-order" context of philosophical dispute in which to resolve the matter.

About the sentence involving the atomic number of gold: Kripke himself asks, "Given that gold does have the atomic number 79, could something be gold without having the atomic number 79?"[53] Well, suppose the current atomic theory were mistaken, though "nearly right" in a sense akin to that in which Mendeleev was "nearly right" in construing the table of known elements in terms of atomic weights instead of atomic numbers—say, because it might still turn out that more than one element might have the same atomic number. Here, the would-be essential or necessary truth, bearing on what Kripke calls "theoretical identifications," which he confesses to not knowing much about, clearly depends on the contingent history of chemistry. In a way, Kripke has himself raised the question as to whether "atomic number" may yet prove to be only part of the story. The question is a fair one wherever empirical substances are at stake; it would never arise in the closed system of Euclidean geometry. About rigid designators, I dare add (in the briefest way) that I have never been persuaded by Kripke's proposal that proper names are, in any sense (except perhaps at the moment of original "christening"), necessarily rigid designators. The proposal is both unworkable and superfluous.

In general, the best cameo arguments are usually defective or deflected from their intended target. Quine demonstrates the semantic entwinement of analyticity and synonymy in natural-language contexts; he does not rid us of commonplace analytic sentences that are not affected by his argument ("All bachelors are unmarried," say); he effectively ignores the systematic restrictions Carnap wishes to experiment with in an effort to secure the analytic/synthetic distinction; and he fails to provide a general argument in favor of "pragmatizing" all linguistically presented distinctions uniformly, regardless of their seemingly conceptually important differences. Kripke's arguments in favor of supporting the "metaphysical" import of the "necessary" characteristically draws on epistemically qualified convictions that may well be subject to substantive revision as a result of possible developments in one or another science or in usage subject to related forms of revision. And arguments like Gettier's against the "justified true belief" conception of knowledge seem to ignore the fact that nearly all accounts of knowledge, truth, and meaning are unlikely to function criterially at all, apart from the simple fact that his own counterinstances to JTB are illicit in epistemic contexts.

I find the pattern widely confirmed: for instance, in Donald Davidson's attempt to bypass the correspondence theory of truth in advocating the coherence theory (and then abandoning the latter and readmitting the former as reasonable, though without fully explaining the sense in which a formal semantics, Alfred Tarski's perhaps, can be said to capture the full sense of "true" in robust inquiries having practical or empirical import).[54]

There are almost no specimen arguments among the pragmatists and continentals that attempt to match what I've been calling the cameo arguments of the analysts. I assume this is due to the intuition that philosophy is all of a piece; that cameo arguments are never or very nearly never self-evidently decisive; that the seeming validity of severely restricted such arguments, lacking a greater sense of philosophical context than that afforded by the mere accumulation of earlier such exemplars (which themselves provoke revision or rebuttal), pretty well depends on what is very nearly an a priori ideology (one or another form of reductionism, for instance); and that the pragmatists and continentals (who are not opposed to ideological privilege themselves) are chastened by the fate of the analytic example and also, perhaps, by their recognition of the relatively seamless expanse of the Kantian/Hegelian heritage that begins the inquiries that I've called Eurocentric—those of "modern" modern philosophy. At any rate, it's in that spirit that I've championed the prophecy embedded in the motto "Darwinizing Hegel and Hegelianizing Darwin."

My surmise, read metonymically, is simply that Gutting's appeal to "intuition"—whether in favor of analytic practice among the cameo arguments he admires or, more generally, in accord with *any* conjectures regarding fruitful metaphilosophical speculation—touches (no more than touches) on a seriously neglected dimension of philosophical inquiry— which confirms that analytic precision cannot answer questions about its own philosophical force and relevance except in an open-ended exchange that sets no a priori limits on possible second-order objections. In short, the precision of Gutting's would-be autonomous specimens depends on the deep informality of metaphilosophical dispute itself.[55]

My conjecture is that, in some remarkably deep way, the most admired legacy of analytic philosophy has ignored the hybrid artifactuality and historicity of the life of human selves and human societies; and that, though they have (in their own way) also gone astray, neither pragmatism nor "continental" philosophy has abandoned the corrective themes that derive from the master turn of "modern" modern philosophy in the interval spanning Kant and Hegel and that they could actually lend themselves, now, to one or another venture that might prosper under the banner "Darwinizing Hegel and Hegelianizing Darwin." I suggest it could lead to a philosophical spring.

Notes

Chapter 1

"The Point of Hegel's Dissatisfaction with Kant," now considerably enlarged and revised, appeared originally in *Hegel and the Analytic Tradition*, ed. Angelica Nuzzo (New York: Continuum, 2010), pp. 12–39.

1. The slippage is clear enough in the first *Critique*. But it is even more obvious and makes a more problematic difference in Kant's *Foundations of the Metaphysics of Morals*: because, of course, the concept of duty introduces a constraint on moral theory that Kant cannot assure us does not affect in some quarrelsome way the conception of reason itself. Think, for example, of recent challenges to the viability of the very idea of a "law of nature" (invoked by Kant, of course, to provide a fixed norm of rationality) in the analysis of the natural sciences. I have in mind the pragmatically oriented views of Richard Feynman and Nancy Cartwright, and others, who regard the canonical thesis of a law of nature as some sort of idealization or distortion of the more modest (but empirically adequate) contingent, perhaps even passing generalizations drawn from our limited observations and experiments among the physical sciences. See, for example, Nancy Cartwright, *The Dappled World: A Study of the Boundaries of Science* (Cambridge: Cambridge University Press, 1999). All references to Kant's first *Critique*, I should add, are to Immanuel Kant, *Critique of Pure Reason*, ed. and trans. Paul Guyer and Allen W. Wood (Cambridge: Cambridge University Press, 1999).

2. I'm indebted here to a most instructive treatment of the complex relationships between Kant's and Hegel's undertakings, viewed in the context of contemporary disputes about the right way to read the issue, provided in Robert Stern, *Hegelian Metaphysics* (Oxford: Oxford University Press, 2009), introduction and Ch. 1. The line from Houlgate (cited by Stern, p. 19n46) is from Stephen Houlgate, *The Opening of Hegel's "Logic"* (West Lafayette, Ind.: Purdue University Press, 2006), p. 141. The remark is directed against the view offered in Robert B. Pippin, *Hegel's Idealism: The Satisfaction of Self-Consciousness* (Cambridge: Cambridge University Press, 1989). See also Robert B. Pippin, "Hegel and Category

Theory," *Review of Metaphysics* 43 (1990), p. 839 (for a clarifying remark, cited by Stern). Stern's sympathies are largely with Pippin (against Houlgate and similar-minded theorists); but Stern means to be (and is) scrupulously fair in airing both sides of the dispute.

3. See Georg Wilhelm Friedrich Hegel, *Lectures on the History of Philosophy*, vol. 3, trans. E. S. Haldane and Frances Simson (Lincoln: University of Nebraska Press, 1995), p. 427; see the rest of the passage on Kant in the context of section 3. Paul Guyer, a temperate champion of Kant, takes up a good many of Hegel's charges in the *Lectures*, the *Encyclopaedia Logic*, and other of Hegel's texts in "Thought and Being: Hegel's Critique of Kant's Theoretical Philosophy," in *The Cambridge Companion to Hegel*, ed. Frederick C. Beiser (Cambridge: Cambridge University Press, 1993), pp. 171–210. I don't think Hegel's essential complaint can be rightly met by recovering Kant's texts more accurately than in Hegel's treatment. The complaint, as I understand it, is that Kant's arguments against the cognitional dogmatism he himself defeats raise a cognate question regarding the validation of his own alternative, which he does not address in the way required (regarding objective knowledge). I return to this important charge in different parts of this book. See further Hegel, *Lectures on the History of Philosophy*, vol. 3, pp. 439–440.

My own reading of key materials in Hegel persuades me that it is of the first importance to emphasize the polar contrast between Kant and Hegel *philosophically*—that is, in terms of what I call Kant's "kinematic" and Hegel's "dynamic" strategies. I take Hegel's example to be promising for the present and future in a way that (if I am right) is not true of Kant unless Kant himself is Hegelianized (as indeed he has been)—in a way that confirms the point.

The entire thrust of the present book is to isolate the importance of that contrast in terms that hardly depend on the idiosyncratic apparatus of either thinker (that is, by linking historicity, its bearing on the very idea of a concept, the significance of dialectical reasoning, and the conditions of objective knowledge under the constraint of cultural formation as a form of living history). The issue, as I see matters, is to isolate what we must save from the "confrontation" between Kant and Hegel for the then-future development of philosophy (that is, in *their* time) and, even more suggestively, for the now-future possibilities of Eurocentric and global philosophy. What I offer is no more than a first step. See further Pippin, *Hegel's Idealism*, particularly Chs. 1–2; and Pirmin Stekeler-Weithofer, "The Question of System: How to Read the Development from Kant to Hegel," *Inquiry* 49 (2006), pp. 80–102.

4. This accords, for instance, with the work of Hans Reichenbach and the logical positivists, who attempted to defeat, on empirical grounds, the would-be necessary (transcendental) truths of Euclidean geometry in the light of relativity physics. See Alberto Coffa, *The Semantic Tradition from Kant to Carnap: To the Vienna Station* (Cambridge: Cambridge University Press, 1991). Indeed, it is not too much to claim that the success of Kant's transcendental turn (in the first *Critique*) depends directly on the defective example of Kant's apriorist reading of Euclid and Newton: the point is that the natural correction of Kant's argument is already "Hegelian"—hence, a lesson that analytic philosophy cannot afford to ignore.

Perhaps the most famous example of the fruitfulness of empirically erroneous theories involves Dmitri Mendeleev's pioneer invention of the periodic table of elements as a basis for anticipating chemical elements not yet discovered, the reasonably accurate prediction of the chemical and quantitative properties of as yet unknown elements on the basis of periodicity, and the ordering of the known elements in a promisingly "lawlike" way despite Mendeleev's opposition to featuring the role of the physical atom (as then understood) and the as yet undiscovered atomic structures yielding the concepts of atomic number and isotopy. For a very brief summary of Mendeleev's achievement, see Eric R. Scerri, *The Periodic Table: Its Story and Significance* (Oxford: Oxford University Press, 2007), Ch. 4.

5. For a sense of Kant's limitations without invoking Hegel, see John H. Zammito, *Kant, Herder, and the Birth of Anthropology* (Chicago: University of Chicago Press, 2002).

6. See Thomas S. Kuhn, *The Structure of Scientific Revolutions*, rev. ed. enlarged (Chicago: University of Chicago Press, 1970), section 10.

7. See Hegel, *Lectures on the History of Philosophy*, vol. 3, p. 427.

8. Ibid., p. 440.

9. See Kant's letter to Marcus Herz, February 21, 1772, in Immanuel Kant, *Correspondence*, ed. and trans. Arnulf Zweig (Cambridge: Cambridge University Press, 1999), pp. 132–138.

10. Compare Charles Sanders Peirce, "Some Consequences of Four Incapacities" (1868) and "The Fixation of Belief" (1877), in *The Essential Peirce*, vol. 1, eds. Nathan Houser and Christian Kloesel (Bloomington: Indiana University Press, 1992), pp. 28–55 and 109–123.

11. I can do no better than draw your attention to Robert Stern's explication, involving a close comparison between Hegel and Peirce, in "Hegel and Pragmatism," *Hegelian Metaphysics*, pp. 207–237. Stern runs through the principal variants of the argument that would make Hegel out to be a Cartesian on the matter of doubt and presuppositionlessness. A particularly straightforward specimen of the Cartesian (and Kantian) positions is provided in Stephen Houlgate, *An Introduction to Hegel: Freedom, Truth and History* (Oxford: Blackwell, 2005); and *The Opening of Hegel's "Logic"*. Stern leads us unerringly to a strong convergence between Hegel and the pragmatists: "not only is Hegel's concern with presuppositionlessness compatible with pragmatism; these concerns are ones shared by the pragmatists themselves" (*Hegelian Metaphysics*, p. 230). The argument is unusually well-crafted.

12. See G. W. F. Hegel, *Phenomenology of Spirit*, trans. A. V. Miller (Oxford: Oxford 1997), preface and introduction, particularly §78, which signals the close ties between Hegel and Peirce.

13. See C. I. Lewis, "A Pragmatic Conception of the A Priori," *Journal of Philosophy* 20 (1923), pp. 169–177. For a brief but up-to-date overview of the fortunes of Hegel in American philosophy, see Richard J. Bernstein, *The Pragmatic Turn* (Cambridge: Polity, 2010), Ch. 4.

14. For a sense of his conception of "absolute knowing," see Hegel, *Phenomenology of Spirit*, section DD, "Absolute Knowing."

15. For a discussion of the Kantian issues, see Michael Friedman, *Kant and the Exact Sciences* (Cambridge, Mass.: Harvard University Press, 1992), Ch. 3.

16. See ibid., pp. 91–92. Friedman cites the passage on Euclid at Bxi–xii (*Critique of Pure Reason*). Kant seems to have been forced to break with Leibniz and the Wolffians largely because of the insuperable incompatibility of Newtonian physics and a Leibnizian-inspired monadology. See for instance ibid., introduction. Nevertheless, Kant also criti-

cizes Newton along the lines that the physical sciences require a "metaphysics" within the bounds of experience. In fact, ironically, Kant argues against Newton's appeal to God's direct intervention in accounting for the order of the universe—Newton apparently took the space between the planets to be "empty" and so to preclude any usual causal account. But, here, precisely, Kant speculates that the order of the universe that we now concede may not have been always thus! He might (then) have seen that the concepts of time and space (his own) could have evolved, like the heavens themselves. Had he done so, he might have come closer to something akin to Hegel's charges against his own *Critique*. See Frederick C. Beiser, "Kant's Intellectual Development: 1746–1781," in *The Cambridge Companion to Kant*, ed. Paul Guyer (Cambridge: Cambridge University Press, 1992), pp. 26–61.

17. See Paul Guyer's brief but extremely helpful discussion of the matter in *Kant and the Claims of Knowledge* (Cambridge: Cambridge University Press, 1987), pp. 82–83. Still, Guyer provides no reason to think Kant ever succeeded in an "empirically realist" way—or ever could. Compare Guyer's afterword.

18. See Hegel, *Lectures on the History of Philosophy*, vol. 3, pp. 440–443.

19. This is a muddled and complex matter—to which I return in a separate inquiry—that involves Hegel's intended use of "dialectical logic" and his larger program of (objective) Idealism.

20. Guyer has made a careful effort to answer Hegel's detailed criticisms of Kant's *Critique*. But his essential purpose is to save (if he can) the coherence of Kant's actual work and Kant's conception of his own undertaking. His response to Hegel is, in this sense, entirely textual and internal. It's true that, in his *Kant and the Claims of Knowledge*, Guyer shows both Kant's running dissatisfaction with his own transcendental arguments and his attraction to transcendental strategies that depart quite radically from his more standard views about "transcendental proofs"—for instance, would-be proofs analogous in spirit (let us say) to the following example (cited by Guyer at p. 418): "In the transcendental analytic . . . we have derived the principle that everything which happens has a cause from the unique condition of the objective possibility of a concept of that which in general happens: that the determination of an occurrence in time, thus [the determination] that this (occurrence) belongs to experience, would be impossible unless it stood under such a dynamical rule" (A 788/B 816). But consider that what (rightly) may have seemed impossible to conceive at times may, with the evolving experience of new possibilities in the sciences (and elsewhere), become entirely intelligible. A convincing argument of this sort has been formulated by Hilary Putnam, "Objectivity without Objects," in *Ethics without Ontology* (Cambridge, Mass.: Harvard University Press, 2004), pp. 20–63. (I will make further use of this possibility later in this chapter.) But let me say that Putnam's argument (which Putnam suggests is close to notions in Hegel and the pragmatists) could be easily and effectively brought to bear against the whole of Kant's account of synthetic a priori truths—and so could threaten the entire project of the first *Critique*. It also clarifies in a modern form an essential and compelling ingredient in Hegel's opposition to Kant.

Guyer, as I say, does not pursue considerations of this sort, except where they appear to do an injustice to Kant's own argument. In *Kant and the Claims of Knowledge*, Guyer remarks: "In the work just completed, I have tried to discover in all their multiplicity and complexity, Kant's own arguments on the issues in theoretical philosophy which he perceived as most important and to critically assess these arguments on grounds that Kant himself would have recognized as compelling" (p. 417). Just so. Compare, in the same spirit, Guyer, "Thought and Being." By contrast, Putnam's argument and example show, quite persuasively (though not intentionally), just how natural it is to embrace Hegel's most compelling arguments within the general idiom and spirit of analytic philosophy. There's no question, for instance, that Putnam's attack on the supposed changelessness of "conceptual truths" confirms in a quiet and tactful way the larger sense in which empiricist and Hegelian resources come together in the post-Kantian "Kantian" reflections of the logical positivist movement on its own analytic resources. The same tendency appears, of course, in Ernst Cassirer's and Charles Peirce's Hegelianized Kantian reflections on the inescapability of conceding the infinitely postponed characterization of the objective world of the physical sciences under the conditions of its evolving history, which, then, is at once an instance of Hegelian *and* "analytic" thinking at its most powerful.

I've singled out Guyer's treatment of Kant precisely because Guyer's admirable skills tend to favor textualist accuracy—therefore I risk scanting a philosophical assessment of Kant's contribution, come what may. I have the highest regard for Kant's originality and ingenuity (and Guyer's scruple); nevertheless, concessions here cannot but defer the exposé of the serious defects in Kant's actual argument. I'm not recommending either Guyer's or Putnam's assessment of the Hegelian challenge to Kant's position. (There is no assuredly compelling account of that.)

21. See, particularly with regard to the dispute between Heidegger and Cassirer, Michael Friedman, *A Parting of the Ways: Carnap, Cassirer, and Heidegger* (Chicago: Open Court, 2000).

22. See Ernst Cassirer, *The Philosophy of Symbolic Forms*, 3 vols., trans. Ralph Manheim (New Haven, Conn.: Yale University Press, 1983–1987), especially vol. 3.

23. For an exemplary (and sympathetic) analysis of the line of thinking issuing from Rorty's reading of Sellars's "Empiricism and the Philosophy of Mind" and the flowering of McDowell's and Brandom's "recovery" of Hegel, see Paul Redding, *Analytic Philosophy and the Return of Hegelian Thought* (Cambridge: Cambridge University Press, 2010). See also Richard Rorty, introduction to Wilftrid Sellars, *Empiricism and the Philosophy of Mind*, with a study guide by Robert Brandom (Cambridge, Mass.: Harvard University Press, 1997). Sellars gave a version of this essay in a series of lectures at the University of London (1956). In 1954–1955, Strawson gave some lectures at Oxford University, on which he based *Individuals: An Essay in Descriptive Metaphysics* (London: Methuen, 1959); he subsequently used the material of the lectures in a seminar conducted at Duke University, in 1955–1956, before the appearance of *Individuals*. Effectively, Sellars and Strawson arrive at much the same finding (from different premises) regarding the dependence of the offending "Given" (a certain very limited version of the "given"), best illustrated by so-called sense-datum theory (again, a certain version of sense-datum theory). The fact is, this kind of theory was already at the point of being discarded when Sellars and Strawson published their respective arguments. It couldn't have had an inning among the Quineans or the classic pragmatists, of course. It's quite a stretch to attempt to recover Hegel for analytic philosophy per Sellars's critique of the Myth of the

Given, now more or less shelved for more than fifty years, never really focused on the recovery of Hegel. (Never mind the reference to "méditations hégeliennes"!)

Not only that, but, as far as I know, neither Sellars nor Rorty, nor McDowell nor Brandom, for that matter, acknowledges that Hegel—and may I now add Charles Peirce (as a phaneroscopist)—*had* indeed championed a perfectly viable (and useful) version of the phenomenologically "given" that, as "presuppositionless," very neatly solved the problem of how to secure a form of "empirical" realism without falling afoul of the "given" that Sellars and Strawson roundly defeat. Also, of course, neither Sellars nor Strawson could rightly be said to be Hegelian in orientation. The point is that whatever may be genuinely recovered of Hegel's philosophical contribution—in McDowell and Brandom—must rest on arguments no more than distantly connected with the slim linkage even Redding lends too much credence to. I will touch, later, very lightly, on other aspects of the analytic retrieval of Hegel.

24. See Wilfrid Sellars, "Philosophy and the Scientific Image of Man," in *Science, Perception and Reality* (London: Routledge and Kegan Paul, 1963), pp. 1–40.

25. See Rorty, introduction to Sellars, *Empiricism and the Philosophy of Mind*. See also John McDowell, *Mind and World* (Cambridge, Mass.: Harvard University Press, 1994, 1996); and Robert B. Brandom, *Making It Explicit: Reasoning, Representing, and Discursive Commitment* (Cambridge, Mass.: Harvard University Press, 1994); also, Wilfrid Sellars, "Language, Rules and Behavior" and "A Semantical Solution to the Mind-Body Problem," in *Pure Pragmatics and Possible Worlds: The Early Essays of Wilfrid Sellars*, ed. Jeffrey F. Sicha (Atascadero, Calif.: Ridgeview, 1980, 2005), pp. 117–136 and 186–214.

26. See Zammito, *Kant, Herder, and the Birth of Anthropology*.

27. For a sense of the enabling argument, cast in contemporary—in effect, in "analytic"—terms, see my *Historied Thought, Constructed World: A Conceptual Primer for the Turn of the Millennium* (Los Angeles: University of California Press, 1995).

28. Compare, for instance, Kant's letter to Marcus Herz, in Kant, *Correspondence*.

29. C. I. Lewis's essay "A Pragmatic Conception of the A Priori" may well be the single most perspicuous analytic rendering of the transformation of Kant's doctrine along lines congenial to the Hegelian view—in the pragmatist way.

30. The classic effort along these lines is, of course, developed in Cassirer, *The Philosophy of Symbolic Forms*.

31. B6–7.

32. P. F. Strawson, *The Bounds of Sense: An Essay on Kant's Critique of Pure Reason* (London: Methuen, 1966), p. 15.

33. Ibid., p. 23.

34. Ibid., p. 20.

35. This was, in fact, the view of the logical positivists, reviewing the status of Euclidean geometry in contemporary physics. See note 4, above.

36. See Guyer, "Thought and Being." Guyer tracks Hegel's analysis chiefly through the texts of *Faith and Knowledge* (trans. Walter Cerf and H. S. Harris [Albany: SUNY Press, 1977]) and *The Encyclopaedia Logic (with the Zusätze)*, trans. T. E. Geraets, W. A. Suchting, and H. S. Harris (Indianapolis, Ind.: Hackett, 1991).

37. See, for instance, J. N. Findlay's emphatic opinion in his foreword to Hegel's *Phenomenology*, p. xiv.

38. Hegel, *The Encyclopaedia Logic*, §10.

39. Kant's essential claim appears at *Critique of Pure Reason*, B130. The full argument is given in §§15–18. Recent eliminativist discussions of these issues are, of course, not inclined to favor any form of a priori necessity, though I find none of these extreme views persuasive—for reasons that hardly strengthen Kant's alternative. Let me mention, however, several such texts for the sake of the record: Daniel C. Dennett, *Consciousness Explained* (Boston: Little, Brown, 1990); Paul M. Churchland, *A Neurocomputational Perspective: The Nature of Mind and the Structure of Science* (Cambridge, Mass.: MIT Press, 1990); and Sellars, "Philosophy and the Scientific Image of Man." Texts of these sorts confirm in spades the "analytic" gain made possible by applying Hegel's critique of Kant as an "Idealist" guide to the cognate critique of analytic arguments of the Anglo-American sort just mentioned.

40. For a particularly candid account, see Guyer, *Kant and the Claims of Knowledge*, pp. 92–94, 212–214, 385–387.

41. See H. S. Harris, "Thirdness: A Response to the 'Secondness' of John Burbidge," *Owl of Minerva* 33 (2001–2002), pp. 41–43; and Stern, *Hegelian Metaphysics*, Ch. 9. The remarkable thing is that Harris invokes Peirce's category of Thirdness, in addition to Secondness, in responding to a challenge from John Burbidge that itself invokes Peirce's Secondness. See John W. Burbidge, "Secondness," *Owl of Minerva* 33 (2001–2002), pp. 27–39.

42. I explore the Sellarsian option briefly (in Brandom's spirit) in "Tensions regarding Epistemic Concepts," first presented in a symposium (with Harold L. Brown and Dimitri Ginev), American Philosophical Association (Eastern Division), December 2007; published in *Human Affairs* [Slovak Academy of Sciences] 19 (2009), pp. 169–181.

Sellars's account of "material inference" has been recently revived by Robert Brandom as at once a promising model for the redirection of pragmatism and for affording a logic close to Hegel's conception of dialectical reasoning. I'm afraid both conjectures are seriously mistaken. The Sellars Brandom invokes is committed to an extremely improbable attempt at a more or less formal canon of material inference, which Brandom himself attempts to flesh out in *Making It Explicit: Reasoning, Representation, and Discursive Commitment* (Cambridge, Mass.: Harvard University Press, 1994), pp. 102–104; and *Between Saying and Doing: Towards an Analytic Pragmatism* (Oxford: Oxford University Press, 2008). See also Wilfrid Sellars, "Inference and Meaning," in *Pure Pragmatics and Possible Worlds*, ed. Sicha, pp. 218–237, which provides one of the principal texts Brandom depends on but which offers almost nothing beyond a manifesto. Of course, one thing Hegel's "logic" is *not* is a relatively formal ("explicit") canon of inference. There's certainly some point to comparing Hegel's dialectic and Peirce's abduction, but only on the assumption that both are forms of rational intuition about how to guess at fruitful hypotheses and interpretations of scattered data that may yield an inferential thread. I would never deny that we do indeed have a strong sense of the validity of actual instances of "material inference" (that is, of inferences strongly qualified by the intertwined import of syntax and semantics in concrete contexts of actual interest and involvement); but I see no evidence at all that collections of inferences of this sort would ever yield anything approaching a canon strengthened by the inclusion of causal regularities or the like. Even causality tends to become fragmented in human practice—largely, I surmise, because the categories that we favor there are themselves selected for practical reasons and do not normally lead in the direction of covering laws or the like. Our sense of the reasonableness of such inferences depends largely on our immersion in the practices of our own society rather than on regularities that may be usefully abstracted from such practices and generalized so as to apply from one society to another. I frankly think the venture—shared in some measure by Sellars and Brandom—leads to a complete dead end.

43. The formula is explored in John W. Burbidge, *On Hegel's Logic: Fragments of a Commentary* (Atlantic Highlands, N.J.: Humanities Press, 1981), p. 195 (emphasis in the original). Even Karl Popper, who has contempt for Hegel, admits the plausibility and reasonableness of Hegel's thesis. But how could he not, since he is himself strongly influenced by Peirce, whose own sense of the triadic logic of evolving interpretation (and even abduction) is distinctly Hegelian. See Karl R. Popper, *The Open Society and Its Enemies*, vol. 2, rev. ed. (Princeton, N.J.: Princeton University Press, 1950), Ch. 12 (mentioned by Burbidge, in *On Hegel's Logic*).

I should add here, explicitly, that I favor treating Peirce as at least obliquely a "Hegelian," not easily shown to be actually following Hegel; though a convergence of sorts appears tantalizingly strengthened as Peirce's own work matures—influenced, it's said, plausibly enough (though not to a certainty), as a result of Peirce's prolonged exchange with Josiah Royce. Dewey, also, is distantly, though more obviously, a "Hegelian," but he's erased most of the textual clues.

44. See further my "The Greening of Hegel's Dialectical Logic," in *The Dimensions of Hegel's Dialectic*, ed. Nectarios G. Limnatis (London: Continuum, 2010), pp. 193–215.

45. J. N. Mohanty, "Hegel's Concepts of Necessity," in *Logic, Truth and the Modalities: From a Phenomenological Perspective* (Dordrecht: Kluwer, 1999), p. 216.

46. See, for a specimen, [Nāgārjuna,] *The Fundamental Wisdom of the Middle Way: Nāgārjuna's Mūlamadyamakakārikā*, trans. Jay L. Garfield (New York: Oxford University Press, 1995).

47. §24 (p. 56).

48. Hegel, *Lectures on the History of Philosophy*, vol. 3, p. 331.

49. Ibid., p. 427.

50. Ibid., p. 449.

51. Ibid., p. 439.

52. See *The Collected Papers of Charles Sanders Peirce*, 8 vols., eds. Charles Hartshorne, Paul Weiss, and Arthur W. Burks (Cambridge, Mass.: Harvard University Press, 1931–1935, 1958), 6.25.

53. I have introduced elsewhere the suggestion that we construe all cultural phenomena ("Intentional," in my idiom) as being artifactual, objective in their sui generis way, inherently interpretable, determinable but not determinate (in the way physical objects are said to be descriptively determinate), collectively shared in the way of societal life, not inherently mentalistic or psychologistic but not inhospitable to enlanguaged and encultured forms of the mental, and subject to historicized forces affecting the perceived meaning and significance of the experienced world. See my *Historied Thought, Constructed World*. I

take the "Intentional" (as a term of art) to approximate to all the predicative aspects of the *geistlich* in Hegel.

54. Putnam, *Ethics without Ontology*, p. 61.

55. Burbidge, *On Hegel's Logic*, pp. 195–196.

56. I can do no more than recommend, here, one or another specimen argument of a textually careful sort. I don't believe it makes sense to require a compelling proof of the truth of Hegel's Idealism, but, of course, we do want to know whether Hegel is talking nonsense. A particularly courageous attempt to track Hegel's progress along the lines I've summarized has recently surfaced in Klaus Düsing, "Ontology and Dialectic in Hegel's Thought," trans. Andres Colapinto, in *The Dimensions of Hegel's Dialectic*, ed. Limnatis, pp. 97–122. Düsing cites and comments, passingly, on a remark by Hegel (in his *Science of Logic*) on the ubiquity of contradiction: "The thinking of contradiction is the essential moment of the concept" (see Hegel, *Hegel's Science of Logic*, trans. A. V. Miller [New York: Humanities Press, 1969], p. 835).

57. See Redding, *Analytic Philosophy and the Return of Hegelian Thought*, p. 19. Redding has explored the entire issue in considerable detail: Ch. 7 repays a very careful reading.

58. *Hegel's Science of Logic*, trans. A. V. Miller (Atlantic Highlands, N.J.: Humanities Press International, 1990), p. 439; see also the rest of the section, pp. 440–443.

59. Ibid., p. 440. The rest of his discussion runs in a similar vein.

60. Sellars, "Language, Rules and Behavior," p. 139.

61. I should add a last thought that keeps recurring. Given the dominant economies of Eurocentric philosophy, I find it very reasonable to suggest that it makes less and less sense to read Kant and Hegel in a way that requires that we always treat them as the entirely separate authors of two distinct sets of texts. They have become, inseparably, differently abstracted "parts" of the same "philosophical voice" addressed to defining the larger *Geist* they belong to, focused on the matter of what to treat as the true relationship between "realism" and "Idealism" and between the "empirical" and the "transcendental." For what it's worth, I would say that much the same is true of Plato and Aristotle, for entirely different reasons, and that there are no other such emergents of comparable importance in the Western tradition.

Chapter 2

"Rethinking Peirce's Fallibilism," now considerably enlarged and revised, first appeared in *Transactions of the Charles S. Peirce Society* 43 (2007), pp. 229–249.

1. On the quarrel between Putnam and Rorty, see my *Reinventing Pragmatism: American Philosophy at the End of the Twentieth Century* (Ithaca, N.Y.: Cornell University Press, 2002).

2. I find myself very much taken by the thoroughness with which Paul W. Franks, in his recent *All or Nothing: Systematicity, Transcendental Arguments, and Skepticism in German Idealism* (Cambridge, Mass.: Harvard University Press, 2005), reexamines the philosophical relationship between Kant and the tradition of German Idealism. I take the evidence to establish that the "Idealists," as post-Kantians, did indeed attempt, as Franks remarks (p. 13), "to complete the revolution begun by Kant, which, they believe, requires

them to go beyond Kant himself," though they cannot possibly succeed in the monistic and systematic way they intend. Franks leaves the matter open for possible recovery, but he himself (I would say) signals its improbability. The argument of the Idealists (more or less constant through all its variations) is committed to the ancient, "least contemporary . . . idea that the threat of Agrippan skepticism underlies all the problems of philosophy, and that the solution may lie in some (perhaps heterodox) version of philosophical theology"—perhaps the Spinozistic "ontotheology" the German Idealists came to favor under the surprisingly influential argument (recommended by Franks) offered by Friedrich Heinrich Jacobi (pp. 392–393).

According to Franks, the German Idealists accept Jacobi's claim that "it is Benedict Spinoza—not Leibniz or the pre-critical Kant—who has shown what would be required for a genuine justification [of their principal epistemological claims] that escapes the Agrippan trilemma"; they are led to believe that "genuine justification can be achieved only within a system that meets two conditions: the *holistic condition* that every particular (object, fact, or judgment) be determined through its role within the whole and not through any intrinsic properties; and the *monistic condition* that the whole be grounded in an absolute principle that is immanent and not transcendent" (pp. 9–10).

The Agrippan trilemma charges that any justification leads "either to an arbitrary assumption, or to a vicious circle, or to an infinite regress" (p. 8). Franks's reading has it that the Idealists "never cease to inherit some version of Kantian dualism" (p. 9), that is, the dualism of the transcendental and the empirical, and that we, also, may be driven to some form of Spinozism—in effect, to some form of "Holistic Monism," which signifies that "finite things are intelligible only in virtue of their position within the whole, which is therefore prior to its parts"; in this sense, Jacobi argues, "the *omnitudo realitatis* is one and the same as the *ens realissimum*" (pp. 88–89).

What struck me most forcibly in reading Franks's account was that I saw at once that Peirce had, in his ingenious way, not only escaped the trilemma, but showed the way to retiring the entire episode involving the original German Idealists insofar as they may be adequately read according to Franks's sense of the essential role of Jacobi's argument against Kant. If that's reasonable, then it suddenly becomes clear how to construe the Hegelian contribution along "naturalistic" lines!

I would be willing to say that Peirce's fallibilism successfully *dismantles* the skeptical threat of the Agrippan trilemma rather than *constructs* a successful "German Idealist" alternative that escapes its threat head-on. This is the point of Peirce's doctrine of the indissolubility of realism and Idealism, of the regulative contribution of transcendental Hope, and of the complete openness of the finite/infinite continuum of thought and being brought to bear on the theory of truth and reality. I find both satisfying and convincing this way of reading Peirce—as returning the post-Kantian tradition to good sense—by inventing an ample form of pragmatism as a worthy successor to German Idealism. In that way, the Idealist themes fulfill their own promise by dissolving into Peirce's fluencies, which then, in turn, converge, in the remarkable way they do, with Cassirer's intermediate sort of Hegelianized Kantianism and with Dewey's more labile, Darwinized pragmatism. In effect, this comes closest to the esoteric meaning of Peirce's fallibilism.

3. I spell out my reading of Cassirer's failing and success, in a pertinent regard, in a longish paper, "Toward a Theory of Human History," *Journal of the Philosophy of History* 4 (2010), pp. 245–273.

4. The best-known recent victim of this confusion (misled by a reading of William James's representationalism) is surely Hilary Putnam's "Sense, Nonsense, and the Senses: An Inquiry into the Powers of the Human Mind," Dewey Lectures 1994, *Journal of Philosophy* 41 (1994), pp. 495–517.

5. Fisch's essays are collected in *Peirce, Semiotic, and Pragmatism: Essays by Max H. Fisch*, eds. Kenneth Laine Ketner and Christian J. W. Kloesel (Bloomington: Indiana University Press, 1986). The worry mentioned affects the argument of a number of Fisch's essays but is particularly telling in the context of two papers: "Peirce's Progress from Nominalism toward Realism" (1967) and "Hegel and Peirce" (1984), pp. 184–200 and 261–282. Fisch is noticeably influenced by Josiah Royce's insistent claim that Peirce's account of comparing specimen phenomena from different fields that could then be rightly interpreted in accord with his triadic schema of Firstness, Secondness, and Thirdness "is, historically speaking, a theory not derived from Hegel, by whom at the time he [Peirce] wrote these early logical papers, [he] had been in no notable way influenced." Royce goes on to say: "I reply, further, that Peirce's concept of interpretation defines an extremely general process, of which the Hegelian dialectical triadic process is a very special case. Hegel's elementary illustrations of his own processes are ethical and historical. Peirce's theory of comparison is quite as well illustrated by purely mathematical as by explicitly social instances." The passage appears in Josiah Royce, *The Problem of Christianity* (Washington, D.C.: Catholic University of America Press, 2001), Ch. 12 (p. 305); see also Ch. 11. I'm persuaded that Fisch's emphasis on the bearing of Peirce's "realism" on the predication question has been read (uncritically) as somehow supporting the "realism" Peirce addresses in the same space in which he advances his Idealism. Peirce's Idealism does not depend on his improved reading of Hegel, through his exchange with Royce. On the contrary, Peirce was probably persuaded to read Hegel more sympathetically because he saw the force of Hegel's refusal to disjoin realism and Idealism. Fisch fails to make the connection.

There is no straightforward argument from the realism of predicates to the realism of science (or to the laws of nature); on the contrary, the realism of predicates is itself meant to conform with the realism of natural laws. There's no question that Peirce was a "realist." The question, however, is, What does Peirce's realism signify? I would say: nothing that requires a disjunctive treatment of realism and Idealism. On the narrower Scotist issue, see John F. Boler, *Charles Peirce and Scholastic Realism: A Study of Peirce's Relation to John Duns Scotus* (Seattle: University of Washington Press, 1963).

6. See Strawson, *The Bounds of Sense*; and G. E. Moore, "The Refutation of Idealism," in *Philosophical Studies* (London: Routledge and Kegan Paul, 1958), pp. 1–30.

7. See, for instance, the careful argument advanced by C. J. Misak, *Truth and the End of Inquiry: A Peircean Account of Truth*, expanded ed. (Oxford: Clarendon, 2004); also, Susan Haack, *Evidence and Inquiry: Towards Reconstruction in Epistemology* (Oxford: Blackwell, 1993).

8. See Nathan Houser, "Peirce in the 21st Century," *Transactions of the Charles S. Peirce Society* 41 (2005), pp. 729–739. The paper was originally presented as his Presidential Ad-

dress, December 28, 2003, in Washington, D.C. Houser has extended his account in "Peirce's Contrite Fallibilism," in Rossella Fabbrichesi and Susanna Marietti (eds.), *Semiotics and Philosophy in Charles Sanders Peirce* (Newcastle upon Tyne: Cambridge Scholars, 2008), pp. 1–14 (originally presented in Milan, Italy, April 6, 2005, at a conference titled "*Semiotica e Filosofia* in Charles Sanders Peirce," sponsored by the Università degli Studi di Milano Departimento di Filosofia). The printed copy of "Peirce's Contrite Fallibilism," which the editors of *Transactions* provided, with an invitation to respond, was unpaginated and may well have been page proofs for an independent book. (The essay is marked "Chapter 1.")

See also Elizabeth Cooke's summary of the fallibilism issue. She approaches matters in a way congenial to my approach, but then (unaccountably) misinterprets my own account. She wrongly supposes that the claim that Peirce "fails" to validate *his* fallibilism (my claim, for instance, which she reviews in some detail) ultimately rests on the false need to recover a strong form of Cartesian foundationalism. Of course, that's not the point at all: the point is simply that Peirce's "success" cannot be reconciled with a disjunctive reading of realism and Idealism. Cooke is committed to that finding as firmly as I am. You have only to read what she selects (from Peirce himself) as her opening epigraph and the opening lines of her own text. See Elizabeth F. Cooke, *Peirce's Pragmatic Theory of Inquiry: Fallibilism and Indeterminacy* (London: Continuum, 2006), pp. xiii, 1; also pp. 109–127 and Ch. 7. What, in effect, Peirce demonstrates—the long reach of his fallibilism down to our own day—is that *his* fallibilized realism (the realism *we* are bound to accept, according to Peirce) cannot be the recovery of that other, canonical form of realism that rejects Peirce's own inflexible commitment to Idealism. (The rejection of this constraint I take to be the more than doubtful assumption on which Misak's argument rests.) I capitalize "Idealism," I should emphasize, for much the same reason as I do "Hope," wherever the "idealist" doctrine is *not* meant to be psychologistic or disjunctive but only to signal that realism is a certain embedded philosophical stance regarding objective truth and mind-independent reality: that is, the stance of a cognizing subject regarding the indissoluble, noncompositional conditions on which it adopts that stance. Peirce is affirming that we cannot escape a certain minimal lesson he draws from the interval spanning the work of Kant, Schelling, and Hegel. I take him to be right about that. It's the central lesson of his fallibilism.

9. The original paper of mine, the one Houser discusses, appears as "Peirce's Fallibilism," *Transactions of the Charles S. Peirce Society* 41 (1998), pp. 535–589.

10. References using this sort of numbering are made to the numbered entries in the eight-volume edition of the *Collected Papers of Charles Sanders Peirce*, eds. Charles Hartshorne, Paul Weiss, and Arthur C. Berks (Cambridge, Mass.: Harvard University Press, 1931–1958). I am aware that the editors of the *Collected Papers* have sometimes fiddled with the wording of some of Peirce's essays.

11. See Ernst Cassirer, *The Philosophy of Symbolic Forms*, vol. 3, trans. Ralph Manheim (New Haven, Conn.: Yale University Press, 1957).

12. See my *Pragmatism's Advantage: American and European Philosophy at the End of the Twentieth Century* (Stanford, Calif.: Stanford University Press, 2010).

13. See Royce, *The Problem of Christianity*, particularly part 2.

14. Cheryl Misak's reading of Peirce provides the clearest example.

15. Charles Sanders Peirce, "The Three Normative Sciences" (MS 312), in *The Essential Peirce*, vol. 2, ed. the Peirce Edition Project (Bloomington: Indiana University Press, 1998), p. 197.

16. For an excellent (and telling) example of how (phenomenologically) "Secondness" manifests itself in physics, see Ian Hacking, *Representing and Intervening: Introductory Topics in the Philosophy of Natural Science* (Cambridge: Cambridge University Press, 1983), regarding Millikan's 1908 attempt to measure the electrical charge on the electron (pp. 22–24). Hacking has a distinctly pragmatist bent.

17. A growing literature drawn in part from Peirce and figures like Otto Neurath regarding the use of multiple, overlapping lines of inquiry opposes the utopian prospects of a single closed system of science and converges rather well with Peirce's infinitist theme. I single out, particularly, Richard Feynman, *The Character of Physical Law* (Cambridge, Mass.: MIT Press, 1967); and Cartwright, *The Dappled World*. Effectively, the trend favors challenges to the confirmation of exceptionless laws and the confinement of reliable testing to relatively narrow, interest-driven regularities of a practical bent.

18. Charles Sanders Peirce, "Immortality in the Light of Synechism" (MS 886, 1893), in *The Essential Peirce*, vol. 2, p. 1.

19. Peirce, "The Three Normative Sciences," p. 196.

20. Ibid., pp. 196–197.

21. Charles Sanders Peirce, "What Pragmatism Is" (*Monist*, April 1905), in *The Essential Peirce*, vol. 2, pp. 342–343.

22. See Charles Sanders Peirce, "Sundry Logical Conceptions" (MS 428, 1903), in *The Essential Peirce*, vol. 2, pp. 267–272.

23. By a stretch of extreme imagination, I can see how this treatment of "phenomenology" might support the suggestion that William James's *Essays in Radical Empiricism* and *A Pluralistic Universe*—originally bound together, under Ralph Barton Perry's editorship, apparently in accord with James's instruction (New York: Longmans, Green, 1958)—helps to define the dependence and independence of James's "metaphysics" (or substitute for metaphysics) vis-à-vis Peirce's characteristic "monism." I think that's not an unhelpful guess, except that, in my opinion, James really had no need for the explicit schema of "pure experience" *anywhere* among his own specifically philosophical arguments. (He never actually applies the notion in any argument, as far as I can see.) That entire effort, introduced in the first two chapters of the *Essays*, finally looks like a spoof of the inflated metaphysics of figures like F. H. Bradley, whom James baits unmercifully. I don't think there can be any doubt that when James speaks of himself as an "empiricist," he's quite aware that he cannot be a phenomenalist—that he must mean to be a phenomenologist in a sense that interested Husserl (and, in a different way, Wittgenstein) and was sketchily systematized by Peirce. But then, the classic empiricists were, already, *not* "mere" empiricists in the restricted sense James displaces.

24. Charles Sanders Peirce, "The Basis of Pragmatism in Phaneroscopy" (MS 908, 1905), in *The Essential Peirce*, vol. 2, p. 362.

25. I find an important convergence here between Peirce's conjecture and the careful argument, developed in recent years, in Nancy Cartwright, *How the Laws of Physics Lie*

(Oxford: Clarendon, 1983). See also Peirce's comparison of a "chain" and a "cable" in "Some Consequences of Four Incapacities" (1868), in *The Essential Peirce*, vol. 1, which Cartwright takes as an epigraph in *The Dappled World*.

26. For a helpful review of Royce's thesis, see Douglas R. Anderson, "Who's a Pragmatist: Royce and Peirce at the Turn of the Century," *Transactions of the Charles S. Peirce Society* 41 (2005), pp. 467–481; see, also, Royce, *The Problem of Christianity*, part 2. Hilary Putnam formulates the more familiar notion of the "God's-Eye view" of realism in "Two Philosophical Perspectives," in *Reason, Truth and History* (Cambridge: Cambridge University Press, 1981). Peirce assigns his own version of the argument to what I'm calling an abductive Hope (one among many, never rightly confirmable) regarding finite inquiry itself. On my reading, most of those who have followed Max Fisch's reading of Peirce are also committed to what Putnam opposes as the God's-Eye view. I am inclined to think that it is the rejection of the God's-Eye view that explains the central importance of "the infinite long run" in Peirce's and (say) Cassirer's accounts of the sciences; and it is the failure to grasp Peirce's lesson correctly that has tempted recent pragmatists to suppose that they have captured the infinitist theme adequately in the consensually acceptable findings of finite inquiry. See, for instance, the cautious account of truth as the "aim of inquiry" in Christopher Hookway, "Fallibilism and the Aim of Inquiry," *Proceedings of the Aristotelian Society*, suppl. vol. 81 (2007). Hookway's argument suggests (to me) the profound difference between characterizing the pursuit of truth from the point of view of a single rational inquirer and from the point of view of the career of the sciences themselves: a mortal investigator cannot, as a pragmatist, aim at the imagined outcome of the long run; but science cannot be convincingly confined to whatever any individual might believe to be true at any given moment in the short run. See also the papers by Hookway and Misak, in *The Cambridge Companion to Peirce*, ed. Cheryl J. Misak (Cambridge: Cambridge University Press, 2004). Royce, I should note, expresses his own doubts about "Absolute" closure.

27. See, for instance, Otto Neurath, "The Unity of Science as a Task," in *Philosophical Papers 1913–46*, ed. and trans. Robert S. Cohen and Maria Neurath (Dordrecht: D. Reidel, 1983), pp. 115–120.

28. For a sense of Kant's excessive apriorism regarding the laws of nature, see Friedman, *Kant and the Exact Sciences*, Chs. 3–4.

29. See Margolis, *Pragmatism's Advantage*.

30. See Carl R. Hausman, *Charles S. Peirce's Evolutionary Philosophy* (Cambridge: Cambridge University Press, 1993), Ch. 4, pp. 168–193. Hausman does not challenge Peirce's "realism" here.

31. See Margolis, "Peirce's Fallibilism," pp. 537, 539.

32. See, for instance, John Dewey, *Logic: The Theory of Inquiry* (New York: Henry Holt, 1938). There is remarkably little in Dewey's writings of any fine-grained analysis of his view of the "laws of nature" to compare with Peirce's sprawling, but still incisive, account.

33. John Dewey, *The Later Works, Vol. 4: The Quest for Certainty* (Carbondale and Edwardsville: Southern Illinois University Press, 1984), p. 143.

34. Though his theory of science is very differently motivated from Dewey's, Bas van Fraassen's account of the (empirical) "adequacy" of any theoretical explanation of sensory

data ("saving the phenomena") suggests rather nicely the point of Dewey's replacement of "truth" by "warranted assertibility," See his *The Scientific Image* (Oxford: Clarendon, 1980).

35. For a recent addition to this literature, see William C. Wimsatt, *Re-Engineering Philosophy for Limited Beings: Piecewise Approximations to Reality* (Cambridge, Mass.: Harvard University Press, 2007).

36. For a classic formulation produced late in his career, see Edmund Husserl, "Author's Preface to the English Edition" (1931), *Ideas: General Introduction to Pure Phenomenology*, trans. W. R. Boyce Gibson (New York: Collier, 1962).

37. Hausman, *Charles S. Peirce's Evolutionary Philosophy*, pp. 140–147. The entire issue, which includes the reading offered by Christopher Hookway as well (which Hausman cites), remains inconclusive. Hausman cites a very careful formulation of the difference between realism and idealism offered in Christopher Hookway, "Pragmatism and 'Kantian Realism,'" *Peirceanna, Versus Quaderne di studi semiotici* 49 (1988), ed. M. A. Bonfantini and C. J. W. Kloesel, p. 105, which makes the opinions disjoint but not exclusionary. I take this to be in accord with the standard treatment of the matter (though very carefully framed). I concede that this is the sort of distinction Max Fisch requires (and Cheryl Misak favors, even more insistently). But that, I'm convinced, is just what Peirce finally opposes. Hookway, I believe, continues to favor separate defenses of Peirce's realism and idealism, but he seems to take the answer to Hausman's concern (about "the final opinion") to be distinctly neutral to the choice between realism and idealism. See Christopher Hookway, *Truth, Rationality, and Pragmatism: Themes from Peirce* (Oxford: Clarendon, 2000), Ch. 2 (particularly p. 77). Hookway may well be right about the possibility, but it goes against Peirce's intention.

38. Hausman, *Charles S. Peirce's Evolutionary Philosophy*, p. 159.

39. For an extended recent discussion of Peirce's phaneroscopy, see T. L. Short, *Peirce's Theory of Signs* (Cambridge: Cambridge University Press, 2007), Ch. 3.

40. I think its meaning—never more than stubbornly sketchy—is instructively aired in the essay "Humanism and Truth Once More," which appears in William James, *Essays in Radical Empiricism* (New York: Longmans, Green, 1912), but is omitted in the 1940 edition (both editions edited by Ralph Barton Perry, probably in accord with James's changeable wishes). The paper is little more than a blast against H. W. B. Joseph's harsh criticism of James's earlier treatment of truth. Nevertheless, James manages to begin to signal his own intention (which, quite correctly conceived, *cannot* be definitively captured). Here, he worries the terms "satisfaction" and "satisfactoriness" in terms of proposing what (today) we might call a "paradigm shift" rather than an attempt to capture the nerve of a settled concept. I think this follows the important clue, in the opening lines of "The Essence of Humanism," that appears in both editions (with the same pagination): "Humanism is a ferment that has 'come to stay'. It is not a single hypothesis or theorem, and it dwells on no new facts. It is rather a slow shifting in the philosophic perspective, making things appear as from a new centre of interest or point of sight" (p. 190). Correctly read, I think this justifies James's resistance to providing a stock answer. But then, of course, pragmatism as a new movement was deeply committed to *its* paradigm shift.

41. Notice of an argument against Peirce (no more than a notice) is given in Hilary Putnam, *The Collapse of the Fact/Value Dichotomy* (Cambridge, Mass.: Harvard University

Press, 2002), p. 123. Peirce's remarks about the meaning of "truth" and "reality" in science are designed, precisely, to acknowledge (and to make sense of) the paradox confronting pragmatism itself: it certainly is not intended to signify that there cannot be truths that, "in principle," are beyond human abilities to determine. I would say the opposite is intended: all general truths risk exceeding any reasonable requirements of finite verification. We are forced to compromise.

42. See Short, *Peirce's Theory of Signs*, pp. 56–59. I offer a suggestion on this important enlargement of the realism issue regarding Peirce's intent that's never more than partly in accord with Short's reading. I venture an opinion here with some trepidation, but it seems to me to be plausible and straightforward. In a way it sides, again only in part, with Hookway's instructive analysis of Peirce's "common-sensism." See Hookway, *Truth, Rationality, and Pragmatism*, Ch. 8. Both analyses center on the elaboration of Peirce's adjustments (some quite late) affecting certain key doctrines in his earliest papers—which seem to me to come to rest on a proper reading of "The Fixation of Belief" (1877).

43. Short, *Peirce's Theory of Signs*, p. 57.

44. Ibid., pp. 57–58.

45. Ibid., p. 200. Here, Short takes specific exception to Nelson Goodman's "idealist" thesis, in *Ways of Worldmaking* (Indianapolis, Ind.: Hackett, 1978), pp. 2–3. But Short is too quick in claiming that "idealism" (in effect, "Idealism," in the idiom I've introduced) cannot admit the first of the two theses just given above: that is, (1) Idealism need only hold that realism is a constructive posit within Idealism's logical space. One can be an Idealist, whether one affirms or denies (1), but only the first option is interesting in our time.

46. See, for instance, Short, *Peirce's Theory of Signs*, Ch. 7, particularly Short's citation of Peirce's 4.536; see also Chs. 11–12.

47. Ibid., p. 343. I find a hospitable approach to related questions in Hookway, *Truth, Rationality, and Pragmatism*, focused on Peirce's themes of what I call Hope. See, for instance, pp. 190–191 and Ch. 9. (Short is committed to a view rather like Putnam's here.)

48. Short, *Peirce's Theory of Signs*, p. 200. Short relies too heavily on Hilary Putnam, *Meaning and the Moral Sciences* (London: Routledge and Kegan Paul, 1978).

49. Short, *Peirce's Theory of Signs*, p. 82.

50. Ibid., p. 56.

51. Ibid., p. 57.

52. Ibid., p. 58.

53. See Peirce's discussion of the pragmatist treatment of probability (5.19–21).

54. Thus, Peirce says: "A proposition is a sign which separately indicates its object. A sign is only a sign *in actu* by virtue of its receiving an interpretation, that is, by virtue of its determining another sign of the same object" (5.569). There is no formal way to confirm that the "objects" of each such sign are the same or belong to a nested series that finds its own ideal limit in a determinate set of "Real things." (That is also the lesson of Hegel's notion of the "self-identity" of Absolute *Geist* read in accord with an ineliminable dependence on the fragmentary nature of phenomenological "data.") It may be helpful to add here that, of course, *any* thing that might function as a sign in Peirce's sense might also function, without contradiction, in some other way (that is, as not a sign). This need not disturb

Short's emendation, but it surely simplifies the matter of getting Peirce right, particularly with regard to the realist/Idealist bond.

55. See, for instance, 5.238 in the context of Peirce's mixed concessions to Hegel's phenomenological strategy (5.37–40). I take this to explain as well Karl-Otto Apel's confusion between Kantian transcendentalism and Peirce's transcendental Hope. Cooke is helpful here. See her *Peirce's Pragmatic Theory of Inquiry*, pp. 121–127; and Karl-Otto Apel, "Transcendental Semiotics and Hypothetical Metaphysics of Evolution: A Peircean or Quasi-Peircean Answer to a Recurrent Problem of Post-Kantian Philosophy," in *Peirce and Contemporary Thought: Philosophical Inquiries*, ed. Kenneth Laine Ketner (New York: Fordham University Press, 1995), p. 388 (cited by Cooke).

56. True to his abiding bias, Peirce insists that "Phenomenology, which does not depend upon any other positive science, nevertheless must, if it is to be properly grounded, be made to depend upon the Conditional or Hypothetical Science of *Pure mathematics*" (5.40)—the condition on which, finally, he says he distinguishes himself from Hegel.

57. Cassirer, *The Philosophy of Symbolic Forms*, vol. 3, pp. 20–21.

58. Ibid., pp. 475–476. See also Heinrich Hertz, *The Principles of Mechanics, Presented in a New Form*, trans. D. E. Jones and J. T. Walley (London: Macmillan, 1956), introduction.

Chapter 3

"Pragmatism's Future: A Touch of Prophecy," now considerably enlarged and revised, first appeared in *Contemporary Pragmatism* 7 (2010), pp. 189–218.

1. For an appraisal of samples of analytic philosophy in its "Quinean" phase, see my *Unraveling of Scientism: American Philosophy at the End of the Twentieth Century* (Ithaca: Cornell University Press, 2003). In loose connection with the themes of this chapter, I've also attempted a very differently conceived exploratory sketch of the kind of "cameo" arguments the analysts have favored and for which they have been so much admired—of the sort most famously advanced in Quine's "Two Dogmas of Empiricism," Saul Kripke's *Naming and Necessity*, and Edmund Gettier's "Is Justified True Belief Knowledge?" The essay itself, "Venturing beyond Analytic Philosophy's 'Best' Arguments to the Implied Inadequacies of Its Metaphilosophical Intuitions," was presented, in response to Gary Gutting's *What Philosophers Know: Case Studies in Recent Analytic Philosophy* (Cambridge: Cambridge University Press, 2009), at a symposium on Gutting's book at the Central Division of the American Philosophical Association, April 1, 2011. It's to appear in *Southern Journal of Philosophy*, sometime in 2012–2013.

Gutting had drawn attention, very neatly, to Aristotle's observation that, among finite arguments, we cannot expect to recover their ulterior premises from antecedent arguments; they must rest finally on "intuitions," statements taken as true without supporting argument. Gutting examines a variety of ways in which analytic arguments are insuperably informal (often problematic) with regard to how their would-be precision depends on second-order "metaphilosophical intuitions." On my reading, the most characteristic questions cannot but be misrepresented by the precision intended: for instance, in attempts to define truth and knowledge and meaning, "metaphilosophical" import cannot be confined to the analysts' most characteristic "intuitions" (say, reductionism, extensionalism, essentialism, metaphysical necessity, and the like). Furthermore, Aristotelian "intuition" has nothing in common with "intuition" in the context of Gutting's argument: in Aristotle, intuition is a distinct faculty (exercised, for instance, in directly discerning universals in the process of sensory reception); in the context of Gutting's argument, intuition ranges over any and every "metaphilosophical" guess at what might account for the success or near-success of the exemplary "first-order" analytic arguments Gutting surveys. This leads on to the theme of a Eurocentric rapprochement, which I favor. I return to this theme at the end of the present chapter.

2. For a slim summary of the fortunes of the St. Louis Hegelians, see Elizabeth Flower and Murray G. Murphey, *A History of Philosophy in America*, vol. 2 (New York: G. P. Putnam's Sons, 1977), Ch. 8. After completing this essay, I received a copy of an important addition to the literature confirming the Hegelian sources of Dewey's philosophy. I'd been anticipating its appearance, ever since James Good, one of its authors, was kind enough to provide me with a copy of the typescript of Dewey's 1897 lecture on Hegel, on the occasion of a chance encounter at one of the American Philosophical Association's Pacific Division meetings in San Francisco. There's been a great deal of resistance in the American academy to admitting the scope of the Hegelian influence in both Dewey and Peirce. The full import of the linkage has yet to be worked out. It was never worked out by the classic pragmatists themselves—and now cannot be ignored. The book in question, recently authored by John R. Shook and James A. Good, is titled *John Dewey's Philosophy of Spirit, with the 1897 Lecture on Hegel* (New York: Fordham University Press, 2010). What is needed is a fresh rereading of the St. Louis Hegelians in order to lay a proper ground at least for appraising Peirce's innovations before his extended encounter with Josiah Royce and a thorough analysis of the Peirce/Royce exchange. Dewey's Hegelian themes are better understood. See, further, James A. Good, *A Search for Unity in Diversity: The "Permanent Hegelian Deposit" in the Philosophy of John Dewey* (Lanham, Md.: Lexington Books, 2006).

3. Lewis, "A Pragmatic Conception of the *A Priori*"; and George H. Mead, *Mind, Self, and Society*, ed. Charles W. Morris (Chicago: University of Chicago Press, 1934).

4. See Kant, *Critique of Pure Reason*, §§16–17.

5. See McDowell, *Mind and World*; and Robert Brandom, *Tales of the Mighty Dead: Historical Essays in the Metaphysics of Intensionality* (Cambridge, Mass.: Harvard University Press, 2002).

6. See Dewey, *Logic*.

7. Ibid., Ch. 1.

8. See Putnam, *The Collapse of the Fact/Value Dichotomy*, pp. 123–124.

9. "How to Make Our Ideas Clear" (1878), in *The Essential Peirce*, vol. 1, p. 132.

10. "The Fixation of Belief" (1877), in *The Essential Peirce*, vol. 1, pp. 111, 114. (I have rearranged the order of the passages cited.)

11. See "A Guess at the Riddle" (1887–1888), in *The Essential Peirce*, vol. 1, pp. 245–279.

12. Feynman, *The Character of Physical Law*, pp. 47–49. See also Otto Neurath, "The Unity of Science as Task"; and Cartwright, *The Dappled World*.

13. For a brief overview of this aspect of Rorty's career, see my *Reinventing Pragmatism*. The late convergence between Davidson and Rorty on metaphysics, epistemology, and semantics is quite remarkable. No doubt the initial impetus regarding the treatment of par-

ticular issues goes in both directions, and no doubt the "conversion" of each to the other's views was never complete. But ultimately it does appear (to me) that Davidson may have been the most important (closet) convert to Rorty's "postmodernism" in the lists of analytic philosophy that can be named. I take this to be borne out in some degree by the appearance of Donald Davidson, "A Nice Derangement of Epitaphs," *Truth and Interpretation: Perspectives on the Philosophy of Donald Davidson*, ed. Ernest Lepore (Oxford: Blackwell, 1986); "A Coherence Theory of Truth and Knowledge" and "Afterthoughts," in *Subjective, Intersubjective, Objective* (New York: Oxford University Press, 2001); and Richard Rorty, "Twenty-five Years After," in *The Linguistic Turn*, ed. Richard Rorty (Chicago: University of Chicago Press, 1992). My sense is that both Rorty and Davidson were drawn to the need to restrict the speculative dimension of metaphilosophy, when viewed from the vantage of would-be analytic precision: Rorty converts philosophy to "conversation," which is not careful enough; and Davidson attempts to salvage what seems still viable in the disputes about the topics he favors. See, for example, Donald Davidson, *Truth and Predication* (Cambridge, Mass.: Harvard University Press, 2005). Apart from the skillful sifting of the flawed options that Davidson runs through, Davidson's recuperative product is disconcertingly meager, sparer by far than the doctrines he pursued in his early prime.

14. See Philip Kitcher, *Vaulting Ambition* (Cambridge, Mass.: MIT Press, 1985); and the candid concessions of a committed Darwinian, Richard Dawkins, in *The Selfish Gene*, rev. ed. (Oxford: Oxford University Press, 1989). I've sketched a preliminary account in support of the present thesis in "Constructing a Person: A Clue to the New Unity of the Arts and Sciences," *European Journal of Pragmatism and American Philosophy* 1 (2009), pp. 70–91.

15. For a relatively recent, well-informed speculation along related lines, see Steven Mithen, *The Prehistory of the Mind: A Search for the Origins of Art, Religion, and Science* (London: Phoenix, 1996); and *The Singing Neanderthals: The Origins of Music, Language, Mind, and Body* (Cambridge, Mass.: Harvard University Press, 2006). Mithen does not go as far as I would prefer. I find that those who speak chiefly of the prehistory of the *mind* tend (quite understandably) to enrich the concept of the biological (as Aristotle does), whereas those who speak of the origins of the *self* see very quickly the need for a firm distinction between the biological and the cultural. The decisive consideration seems to be the datable appearance of true language.

16. I borrow the phrase "natural artifact" from Marjorie Grene, "People and Other Animals," in *The Understanding of Nature: Essays in the Philosophy of Biology* (Dordrecht: D. Reidel, 1974), but I use it with a distinctly different emphasis. Grene shares the expression with Helmuth Plessner, which captures as well Adolf Portmann's helpful conjecture about the unique (and uniquely necessary) "social [that is, enculturing] gestation" of the human infant. Grene construes the artifactuality of persons chiefly in terms of the "naturalized" acquisition and extended use of cultural artifacts (including language); whereas I construe the original "emergence" of persons as itself an artifactual precipitate of the cultural evolution of language from prelinguistic sources. In this sense, both of us think of the self or person as hybrid and artifactual—but in distinctly different ways.

17. A good friend and a good philosopher, W. W., recently called my attention to the seemingly plain fact that constructivism *is* a form of subjectivism (or subjective idealism, as

it is in Kant). But I'm persuaded that both Hegel and Peirce successfully support a version of objective constructivism that (1) confirms the indissoluble union of realism and Idealism; (2) eschews representationalism (in the sense Kant acknowledges in his famous letter to Marcus Herz); and (3) still allows for representations or transcendental pictures, without entailing representationalism or the subjectivist construction of the actual world.

18. See Lewis, "The Pragmatic *A Priori*" and *Mind and the World Order* (New York: Scribners, 1929).

19. I have constructed a specimen morality of this second-best kind (constrained by prudential interests) in my *Moral Philosophy after 9/11* (University Park: Pennsylvania State University Press, 2004). See also my "A New Answer to the Question, What Is Moral Philosophy?," in *Pragmatist Epistemologies*, ed. Roberto Frega, (Lanham, Md.: Lexington Books, 2011), pp. 81–102. The parallel effort is more usual in contemporary philosophies of science. I take it, for instance, to be central to the account favored by Cartwright in *The Dappled World* and, more allusively, in Richard Feynman's account of the "Babylonian" model of science.

20. For Mendeleev, see Scerri, *The Periodic Table*.

21. See "Some Consequences of Four Incapacities" (1868), in *The Essential Peirce*, vol. 1.

22. See, for instance, the interesting argument offered by Wimsatt, *Re-Engineering Philosophy for Limited Beings*, pp. 46–52; also, Clark Glymour on "bootstrapping," in *Theory and Evidence* (Princeton, N.J.: Princeton University Press, 1980), cited by Wimsatt.

23. John R. Searle, *Making the Social World: The Structure of Human Civilization* (Oxford: Oxford University Press, 2010), p. 61. For a very spare sense of the remarkably widespread interest in models of the human world akin to (but not necessarily compatible with) Searle's own theory, see Georg Meggle (ed.), *Social Facts and Collective Intentionality* (Frankfurt A.M.: Dr. Hänsel-Hohenhausen, 2002). For all the variety of approaches that center on what is now called "collective intentionality"—which is really a form of aggregated individual intentional states—I find it very improbable that any of these alternatives can escape what I identify below as "Rousseau's joke." Perhaps the most prominent theorists of this entire company, apart from Searle himself, include Margaret Gilbert and Raimo Tuomela.

24. Compare, for example, E. O. Wilson, *On Human Nature* (Cambridge, Mass.: Harvard University Press, 1978), and Richard Dawkins, *The Selfish Gene*.

25. See E. Sue Savage-Rumbaugh, Jeannine Murphy, Rose A. Sevcik, Karen E. Brakke, Shelly L. Williams, and Duane M. Rumbaugh, *Language Comprehension in Ape and Child* (Monographs of the Society of Research in Child Development), Serial No. 233, vol. 58, nos. 3–4, 1993, C. 7 and appendix. On the emergence of the animate world, see the remarkable speculation offered by A. G. Cairns-Smith, *Genetic Takeover and the Mineral Origins of Life* (Cambridge: Cambridge University Press, 1982).

26. Searle, *Making the Social World*, p. 65.

27. Ibid., p. 67.

28. See Jakob von Uexküll. *Theoretical Biology*, trans. D. L. MacKinnon (New York: Harcourt, Brace, 1926); also note 47 below.

29. Searle, *Making the Social World*, p. 70.

30. Ibid., pp. 10–11. On "status functions," see p. 7.

31. Ibid., pp. 10–11, 69.
32. Ibid., p.69.
33. Ibid., p.19.
34. Ibid., p. 68.
35. Ibid., pp. 62–63.
36. Ibid., p. 25

37. Ibid., pp. 25, 43–44. See also, on "collective intentionality," p. 58, in the light of what Searle says about "prelinguistic intentionality" (cited below). For a number of alternative ways of construing the "mind" (for which Searle's term "intentionality" plays proxy), see Alva Noë, *Action in Perception* (Cambridge, Mass.: MIT Press, 2004), and *Out of Our Heads: Why You Are Not Your Brain, and Other Lessons from the Biology of Consciousness* (New York: Hill and Wang, 2009); also Shaun Gallagher, *How the Body Shapes the Mind* (Oxford: Clarendon, 2005). Neither Noë nor Gallagher, it needs to be remarked, ventures a theory of the self or person or attempts to integrate his account of the mind with the emergence of language and the self.

38. See my *Cultural Space of the Arts and the Infelicities of Reductionism* (New York: Columbia University Press, 2010), for a sustained account of Intentionality applied to the arts.

39. Searle, *Making the Social World*, pp. 43, 46. It's quite extraordinary how tentative our best interpretations of nonhuman primate cognition are, particularly with regard to the recognition and use of "categories" and an understanding of causality and intentionality. See, for instance, the summary in Michael Tomasello and Josep Call, *Primate Cognition* (New York: Oxford University Press, 1997), part 3. In a detailed text of more than four hundred pages, Tomasello and Call finally arrive at the following extremely cautious conclusion:

> *Although all primates understand the behavior of conspecifics as "animate" and "directed" and the behavior of physical objects as contingent on antecedent events, no nonhuman primate understands the behavior of conspecifics intentionally or the behavior of objects causally in humanlike ways.* This is because the understanding of intentionality and causality requires an understanding of the dynamic relationships among two or more entities by means of an intermediary (intention or cause) that organizes a web of possible antecedent-consequent sequences into a meaningful set. Nonhuman primates only understand one-to-one antecedent-consequent sequences, although because of the complex spatial and social fields in which they operate, predictions of the behavior of animate beings and objects based on these understandings may be quite complex. (p. 400)

Quite frankly, this seems to me to be utterly inadequate to explaining the complex behavior of elephant herds and baboon troupes. About the capacities of human primates, they add:

> The evolution of human [primate] cognition is a complex story, and there is currently too little evidence for theories to be put forth with much conviction. Nevertheless, we believe that current evidence is most consistent with the view that the uniquely human adaptation for social cognition and culture was a relatively recent one. . . . *It is likely that the initial social-cognitive adaptation for culture, for identifying with other persons and thus*

sharing intentional relations to the world with them, was a late-occurring one in human evolution, perhaps not constituting the unique cognitive skills of Homo sapiens sapiens. (pp. 427–429)

I note the questionable intrusion of the term "person." There is no account of the term's extension in *Primate Cognition*. These findings apply to primates in the wild; primates raised in a human setting often show further cognitive development. Searle is familiar with Tomasello's work but seems to be a good deal more sanguine than Tomasello is. I'm not convinced by either Searle or Tomasello, I should say.

40. Searle, *Making the Social World*, p. 50.//
41. Ibid., pp. 25, 31; compare pp. 3–4.
42. Ibid., p.4.
43. See Dewey, *Logic*, p. 104; and *Collected Papers of Charles Sanders Peirce*, 5.563, 5.583.
44. George Herbert Mead, "Concerning Animal Perception," in *Selected Writings*, ed. Andrew J. Reck (Indianapolis, Ind.: Bobbs-Merrill, 1964), p. 79.
45. William James, *The Principles of Psychology* (Cambridge, Mass.: Harvard University Press, 1983), pp. 220–221. I'm afraid James loses nearly all of the intuitive fluency of *Principles* in the late speculations of his *Essays in Radical Empiricism* (1912) and *A Pluralistic Universe* (1909) (edited, under James's instructions, by Ralph Barton Perry, 1942), published, with omissions, as a single volume (New York: Longmans, Green, 1958). His attempt to link his "psychology" and his "metaphysics" seems to me to be notably unsuccessful. For instance, the concept of "pure experience" seems to have no sustained function in James's text—certainly none that is not profoundly difficult to endorse. Dewey and Mead are more successful—and more instructive.
46. I've benefited here and in the rest of my remarks about Peirce's theory from a reading of Vincent Michael Colapietro, "Peirce's Account of the Self: A Developmental Perspective," in *Peirce's Approach to the Self: A Semiotic Perspective on Human Subjectivity* (Albany: SUNY Press, 1989), pp. 61–97.
47. Mead, *Mind, Self and Society*, and *The Philosophy of the Act*, ed. Charles W. Morris, John M. Brewster, Albert M. Dunham, and David L. Miller (Chicago: University of Chicago Press, 1938). I must mention, also, the influential account provided by Peter L. Berger and Thomas Luckmann, *The Social Construction of Reality: A Treatise in the Sociology of Knowledge* (New York: Anchor Books, 1966). My sense is that Berger and Luckmann have indeed been influenced by Mead, though it seems somewhat distantly on the matter of Mead's use of the notion of the generative play of the "I" and the "me": *they* emphasize a descriptive use of the roles, given the existence of selves, whereas Mead applies the thesis to the originary generation of the self itself (I'd say in a way that was probably incoherent or yielded a *petitio*). That is, neither Berger nor Mead satisfactorily addresses the problem of "external *Bildung*" as distinct from the important but insufficiently autonomous problem of "internal *Bildung*" (*paideia* or "second nature"). In any case, they are bolder and more direct than Mead regarding the social construction of the self. They are quite good on the distinction between the biological and cultural dimensions of the self. (They are also not careful enough, given their own emphasis, on the difference between the "construction" of the human or cultural world and the "construction of reality" tout court—which bedevils the sociology of knowledge.)

What is interesting about their account is that they have a clear sense of the strong convergence (on essentials) between Helmuth Plessner, *Die Stufen des Organischen und der Mensch: Einleitung in die philosophische Anthropologie* (Berlin: Walter de Gruyter, 1928, 3rd ed. 1975) (translated as *The Levels of Organic Being and of Man: Introduction to a Philosophical Anthropology*, by Scott Davis, unpublished); Arnold Gehlen, *Man: His Nature and Place in the World*, trans. Clare McMillan and Karl Pillemer (New York: Columbia University Press, 1988); and Mead, *Mind, Self, and Society*. In this regard, they grasp the primacy of the social over the individual in the formation of selves; the "incompleteness" of the human, biologically; the lack of an *Umwelt* (in Uexküll's sense) at the level of the human animal; the cultural as a sui generis capacity apt for transforming the environing world as a suitable setting for human life itself; the decisive role of natural language; the relative autonomy of the stages of cultural formation from any corresponding bodily evolution (against Max Scheler's influential claims); humanity's "eccentricity" (in Plessner's sense); the artifactuality of the self; limitations regarding "natural selection"; and the unique forms of interaction among human individuals and their social world. That is, they've collected some of the essential puzzles of philosophical anthropology, but we cannot rest with their solutions.

Searle's earlier book, *The Construction of Social Reality* (New York: Free Press, 1995), which *Making the Social World* more or less recasts (with some adjustments), both enshrines the paradox that besets Berger and Luckmann's "sociology of knowledge" (*Wissensozialogie*: Scheler's original term), though it obviously means to avoid it, and makes its solution all but impossible. Searle believes quite literally that an aggregate of relatively autonomous languageless primates effectively (agree to) "make" or "construct" the social world (in more or less the same sense of that term as appears in Berger and Luckmann's title). It is now nearly a hundred years since the first flourishing of the German, post-Darwinian "philosophical anthropology" that includes at least Uexküll, Scheler, Plessner, Gehlen, and Adolf Portmann—which finds already a convergence with certain cognate elements in pragmatism, in the work of Mead and John Dewey, Berger and Luckmann, and (from sources closer to the biology that informs the philosophical anthropologists) Marjorie Grene. The strongest formulation among the former authors seems to be Gehlen's. My sense, however, is that we are only at the beginning of a highly promising new inquiry.

48. See, for example, the intriguing "anti-Darwinian" speculations of Jakob von Uexküll, in *A Foray into the World of Animals and Humans* (published together with *A Theory of Meaning*), trans. Joseph D. O'Neil (Minneapolis: University of Minnesota Press, 2010), especially the sections titled "Progress" and "Summary and Conclusion" in *A Theory of Meaning*. It needs to be said that the "Afterword: Bubbles and Webs: A Background Stroll through the Readings of Uexküll" by Geoffrey Winthrop-Young provides a necessary warning. Nevertheless, Uexküll may be the most ingenious discussant of how to imagine the biology of the sensibilities of animals within their *Umwelten*. Since he resists treating the human apart from the animal, I find it particularly instructive to contrast Uexküll's model with George Mead's attempt to understand the biology of the human being's "phenomenology" of perceptual experience, feeling, and agency. There can hardly be any doubt that we've made very little progress here.

49. For the sense of the expression, "metaphilosophical intuition," see note 1, above. I've adopted the sense of Gary Gutting's idiom here, though, as will be clear, somewhat against his own conjecture. Gutting's *What Philosopher's Know* is the most sanguine recent review of the "best" arguments of analytic philosophy of "the last fifty years." Gutting explicitly takes himself to be an "analytic philosopher." He favors what I've called the cameo or miniaturized arguments of figures like Quine, Kripke, and Gettier, and he finds in their work exemplary contributions to "philosophical knowledge." His claim, however, is *not* that their arguments are decisive. Not at all. Here, for instance, is the gist of Gutting's undertaking:

> In searching for philosophical knowledge, I begin with three achievements for which some of the strongest cognitive claims have been made by many philosophers. W. V. O. Quine's "refutation" of the analytic-synthetic distinction, Saul Kripke's rehabilitation of necessity in metaphysics and the philosophy of language, and Edmund Gettier's counterexamples against the standard definition of knowledge. How often have we heard (or told others) that Quine refuted the analytic-synthetic distinction, that Kripke proved that there are necessary *a posteriori* truths, and that Gettier showed that knowledge cannot be defined as justified true belief? But, although I entirely agree that Quine, Kripke, and Gettier have achieved something of philosophical importance, a careful reading of their exemplary texts does not reveal any decisive arguments for the conclusions they are said to have established. . . . Nonetheless, I maintain, that these exemplary pieces of philosophy have generated important philosophical knowledge. (p. 3)

Gutting claims that his specimens "contribute to a body of 'second-order' knowledge about the prospects of general philosophical pictures"—that is, regarding the prospects of "broad views such as empiricism, materialism, and theism . . . for fruitful development"—by what he calls "persuasive elaboration," which demonstrates a picture's "ability to generate a series of increasingly more detailed and adequate theories"; and, also, "a substantial body of first-order philosophical knowledge—knowledge not about philosophical pictures but about the subject-matter (language, necessity, knowledge, etc.) treated by those pictures" (p. 4). My own sense is that this might be true if (and only if) Gutting (or others) could articulate a suitable "picture" of the best forms of dialectical exchange among the largest competing programs of Western philosophy. For example, I personally believe that reductive materialism is dead in the water but that the evidence for this can hardly be drawn from materials internal to analytic reductionism itself: it comes largely from external appraisals of what analytic philosophy may be said to accomplish on this score, viewed in good part from inimical approaches to the pretensions of analytic philosophy's best specimens. Otherwise, as far as I can see, the "knowledge" that Gutting collects risks being the accumulation of the recorded failures and misfiring of his best specimen statements. I think there cannot be a clear disjunctive approach to the largest philosophical issues confined to any strongly programmatic movement like analytic scientism or extensionalism or reductionism. It's in this spirit that I think we must seek a rapprochement among the principal movements of the philosophical tradition.

50. Quine, "Two Dogmas of Empiricism," in *From a Logical Point of View* (Cambridge, Mass.: Harvard University Press, 1953, 1980), p. 43.

51. Carnap is very explicit on the matter. In a note dated February 3, 1952, the year following the appearance of Quine's "Two Dogmas" paper in *Philosophical Review* 60 (1951), now labeled "Quine on Analyticity", he says the following: "It must be emphasized that the concept of analyticity has an exact definition only in the case of a language system, namely a system of semantical rules, not in the case of an ordinary language, because in the latter the words have no clearly defined meaning. Quine advocates the thesis that the difficulty lies in the concept of analyticity itself, not in the ambiguity of the words of ordinary language" (in *Dear Carnap, Dear Van: The Quine-Carnap Correspondence and Related Work*, ed. Richard Creath [Berkeley: University of California Press, 1990], p. 427).

52. See Saul A. Kripke, *Naming and Necessity* (Cambridge, Mass.: Harvard University Press, 1980). See also Hilary Putnam, "Rethinking Mathematical Necessity," in *Words and Life*, ed. James Conant (Cambridge, Mass.: Harvard University Press, 1994); Quine's 1934 "Lectures on Carnap" at Harvard University and Carnap's "Quine on Analyticity," in *Dear Carnap, Dear Van*.

53. Kripke, *Naming and Necessity*, p. 3.

54. See Davidson, "A Coherence Theory of Truth and Knowledge" and "Afterthoughts"; and *Truth and Predication*.

55. I have no doubt that there are topics that lend themselves to the cameo strategy—chiefly semantic or linguistic, I imagine—but certainly not the largest questions of epistemology and metaphysics (and the like) that must be shared with the advocates of every viable school of thought.

Index

abduction (Peirce), 70, 71, 87–88, 106, 108. *See also* Hope; realism
analytic philosophy: cameo (miniaturized) arguments, 113, 149, 150, 152; exemplary figures, 126–27; and recovery of Hegel, 115–16; reputable specimens, 113

"Babylonian" conception of science (Feynman), 120–21
Bildung: "external" and "internal," 123, 124, 125, 130, 131, 132, 145, 147; and linguistic competence, 132, 133–34
Brandom, Robert, 24–25, 34, 49, 116
Burbidge, John, 35, 47

Carnap, Rudolf, 112, 154
Cassirer, Ernst: and Hertz, 53, 107; on "idea of limit," 105–106, 107–108; and Peirce, as "Hegelianized Kantians," 51–52, 53, 57, 108
Chomsky, Noam, 149
"conceptual truths" (Putnam), 45–47, 160–61n20
constructivism(-ist), 8, 30, 38–39, 77: in Kant and Hegel, 39, 42, 43, 59–60, 66, 77; Peirce's realism, 60; and pragmatism, 44, 55, 66; two senses of, 38–39

continental philosophy, near-irrelevance of, 112–13, 114

Darwin, Charles (post-Darwinian), 10, 31–32
"Darwinizing Hegel and Hegelianizing Darwin," 19–120, 122–23, 126, 128, 148, 150, 155
Davidson, Donald, 131–32, 154
Dewey, John: compared with Peirce, 67–71, 79–82, 83; as fallibilist, 55–56, 58, 67, 68–71, 80–82, 83–84, 85; "hope" in, 58; "indeterminate"/"problematic" situation, 146; and Mead, 146–47. *See also* fallibilism; Peirce, Charles Sanders

Euclid, 14, 29
Eurocentric philosophy, 51–52, 76, 155
fallibilism: Cassirer's alternative to Peirce's, 53; Dewey's economies regarding, 81; Dewey's version of, 80–82; Eurocentric sources of, 52–53; Hegelian cast of Peirce's, 52–53; as lynchpin of Peirce's philosophy, 56–57, 70; paradox in Peirce's, 92; Peirce and Dewey compared, 83–85, 116–18; Peirce's, within classic pragmatism, 53, 87; three themes

183

184　Index

in Peirce's, 79–80. *See also* Hope; inquiry; Peirce, Charles Sanders

Feynman, Richard, 120–21
Fisch, Max, 54, 56, 62, 67, 75, 86
flux, in Peirce and Dewey, 68, 69, 70

Gehlen, Arnold, 150
German Idealism, 20, 54, 165–66n2
Gettier, Edmund, 154, 155
Grene, Marjorie, 119
Gutting, Gary, 113, 149, 149–50, 155, 180n47

Hacking, Ian, 75
Hausman, Carl, 85–86, 88
Hegel, G. W. F.: "absolute knowing" (*Phenomenology*), 18, 20, 21, 30; analytic recovery of, 115–16; beyond, 44–45; continuing and opposing Kant's project, 9–10, 11–12, 14, 24, 26, 27–28, 30, 31, 37–38, 29, 42–43, 123; "contradiction," 42, 43, 47–49; critique of Kant's subjectivism, 39–41; dialectical logic, 31, 34–36, 41, 47; *Erscheinungen* (*Phenomenology*), 20, 21, 30, 33, 40; "external" critique of Kant, 22, 27–28, 31, 33, 35–36; *Geist*, 12–13, 21, 43, 44, 60; Idealism/realism of, 20, 21, 31, 42–43; "Law of Contradiction," 47–49; "necessity," 34–36, 41–42, 43, 44, 47; and non-contradiction, 48–49; and Peirce and pragmatism, 10, 12, 15, 18, 20, 21, 30, 31, 33–34, 36; "presuppositionlessness" (*Phenomenology*), 15, 20; rejection of representationalism, 20, 30
Hertz, Heinrich, 53
historicity, 26–27, 29–30, 31, 51
Hookway, Christopher, 86
Hope, as abductive guess, 71–73, 74–75, 84. *See also* Peirce, Charles Sanders
Houlgate, Stephen, on Pippin on Hegel, 7
Houser, Nathan, 56–57, 60–62, 71–72, 75, 76, 77, 78, 83, 92–93

Husserl, Edmund, 27, 66, 84

idealism, subjective, 20, 91
Idealism, 55. *See also* realism/Idealism
infinitist inquiry, as abductive Hope, 73, 77, 85, 89, 96–97, 109, 118. *See also* abduction; Peirce, Charles Sanders
inquiry: animal and human doubt, 118; finite/infinite continuum of, 53, 116–17; Peirce and Cassirer compared, 117; Peirce and Dewey compared, 118
Intentionality (as term of art), 143

James, William, 83, 86, 89, 89, 90, 92, 93, 94, 95, 106, 118, 147–48

Kant, Immanuel: essential paradox in, 9–11, 19; on the "externality" of objects, 33; Lewis on, 18–19; and Newton, 12–13, 19, 29–32; realism/Idealism in, 8, 19–20; representationalism in, 15, 19; and the transcendental question, 8, 15–17, 21, 22–24, 28–29, 39; transcendental/empirical reciprocity in, 22; *Vorstellungen* (first *Critique*), 15, 20, 30
knowledge, "possibility" of, 10–11, 15, 21–22
Kripke, Saul A., 112, 152–54
Kuhn, T. S. (Kuhnian), 75, 76, 77
language: and artifactual self, 172; artifactuality of, 29–30; and *Bildung*, 123–25, 131–32; continuous with prelinguistic communication, 137; and human agency, 124–26; and "lingual" powers, 142; as ontological dangler, 133; Searle on, as biological, 131–33, 134; Wittgenstein on, 141. *See also* Searle, John

language and self. See *Bildung*; self
laws, problematic realism of, 68, 69, 74, 157n1
Lewis, C. I., 18–19, 115

Index

"material inference" (Sellars), 34
McDowell, John, 24, 25, 115
Mead, George Herbert, 115, 140–41, 145–46, 147, 148
Mendeleev, Dmitri, 24, 158–59n4
mind-independent, not "noumenal," 59–60
Misak, Cheryl, 56, 67
Mohanty, J. N., 35
Moore, G. E., 55
"Myth of the Given" (Sellars), 24–25, 26

naturalism, 18
"necessary," Kripke on, 152–54
"necessity" (Hegelian), 34–36, 39–41, 42, 43, 45–47
Newton, Isaac, 12–13, 19, 23, 29–32, 33
nominalism, 76
"noumenal," contrasted with "mind-independent," 59–60

"objective"/"subjective," as inseparable, 11, 15, 19, 70

"paradigm" and "prototype," 22–23, 30, 38
Peirce, Charles Sanders: "abductive logic," 34; and Cassirer, as "Hegelianized Kantians," 51–52, 58, 67, 69–71, 73–74, 75, 106, 109, 127; cosmology, 119; Dewey compared with, 55–56, 58, 67, 69–71, 74–75, 79–82, 83, 96, 116–18, 119; direct realist reading of, 21; double thesis on realism, 56; on doubt and its cessation, 117–18; fallibilism and synechism in, 56–57, 63–64, 74; fallibilist paradox (*reductio*) in, 92, 96; falls short on "Darwinian" themes, 119–20; Firstness, Secondness, and Thirdness ("firsts," "seconds," and "thirds"), 33, 60, 65, 66, 67–68, 77, 84–85, 87, 88, 89, 92, 106; "Hegelian" themes in, 10, 13, 14, 18, 21, 33–34, 53–54, 58–59, 61, 65, 67–68, 69–70, 71, 73–74, 75, 86; Hope, 21, 57–58, 60, 61, 64, 65–66, 109, 119; as Idealist, 54–55, 58, 69; on infinitesimals, 103, 105, 106; and nominalism, 54, 76; phaneroscopy (phanerons) or phenomenology (phenomena), 65–66, 67, 68, 70, 91, 106; "pragmatic maxim," 117–18; presents himself as realist, 61, 67, 71, 90; realism/Idealism of, 54–56, 57, 58–59, 60, 69, 70; on selves, 148; theory of truth, 90, 92–93, 94–97; union of Hegelian and Darwinian themes in, 117, 118–20. *See also* constructivism; fallibilism; Hope; pragmatism; realism
"philosophical anthropologists," 150–51
philosophy: as distinct science, 64–65; future of, 122, 123, 124–25, 126; modern, central paradox of, 7–9; postwar exhaustion of, 121
philosophy of science, new pragmatist initiatives in, 74, 120–21, 129
Plessner, Helmuth, 119, 150
pragmatism: advantages of, 125–26; conceptual economies of, 26–27; "Darwinian" themes in, 119; "Eurocentric," 45, 47; focused in Dewey's and Peirce's fallibilisms, 116–17, 118; gratuitous recovery of, 51, 111–12, 114; Hegelian themes in, 115; both Kantian and Hegelian, 115–16; and naturalizing Hegel, 53, 128. *See also* Peirce, Charles Sanders
"prototype" and "paradigm," 22, 23, 24, 26
Putnam, Hilary, 45–47, 116–17, 152

Quine, W. V., 102, 111, 112, 152, 154

realism: as abductive guess, 78, 92; analytic, 20, 21, 56, 59, 67, 87; constructivist forms of, 8, 42, 43–44; inseparability of, and Idealism, 8, 30, 31, 61; Kant's account of, 11, 15, 19–20; Peirce's, as constructivist, 60; scholastic, 76–78

realism/Idealism, 8, 20, 21, 30, 31, 51, 53–54, 116–17
reality (in Peirce) inseparable from Thirdness, 60, 86–87
representationalism, 15, 19, 20, 30, 60
Rorty, Richard, 24, 25, 76, 121–22
"Rousseau's joke," 137–38, 145
Royce, Josiah, 18, 72
Russell, Bertrand, 86, 89

Searle, John: analysis of human world, 134–36; "Background," "Network," 145; and "collective intentionality," 144–45; and Davidson, 131–32; and "Declarations," 137, 140, 141–42; and "hominid primates," 135–36; and human institutions, 137; on intentionality, 143–44; on language, 131, 132–34; and "prelinguistic intentionality," 135–36, 142–43, 144; on speech acts, 140, 141
Secondness (Peirce), 33–34, 37, 84–85
self (subject, agent): as artifactual, hybrid transform, 38, 51–52, 124–27, 128, 138–39; and cultural world penetrated by language, 127; and the "fabric" of enlanguaged culture, 138–39, 140; Hegel on, 124; historicity of, 126; Hume and Kant, inadequate theories of, 123; and mastery of language, 130–31, 132–34, 137; paleontology of *Homo* and, 129–31; Peirce on, 148; social construction of, 126–27; theory of, by way of *Bildung*, 124. *See also* Bildung; Searle, John
Sellars, Wilfrid, 24–26, 34
Short, T. L.: on Peirce's realism, 98–100; on Peirce's semiotics, 100–102
signs (Peirce), theory of. *See* Peirce, Charles Sanders; Short, T. L.
Strawson, P.F., 24, 29, 40, 55
"subjective"/"objective," as indissoluble, 11, 15, 19, 20, 39
synechism, 56–57, 63–64, 74, 76

Tarski, Alfred, 154
Thirdness, 60
truth: Dewey on, and "warranted assertibility," 94; James on, 94–95; Peirce on, 90, 92–93, 94–97; Putnam on Peirce's theory of, 96

Uexküll, Jakob von, 136, 147, 150

Vico, Giambattista, 149